AF147500

Communications
in Computer and Information Science

2264

Series Editors

Gang Li, *School of Information Technology, Deakin University, Burwood, VIC, Australia*
Joaquim Filipe, *Polytechnic Institute of Setúbal, Setúbal, Portugal*
Zhiwei Xu, *Chinese Academy of Sciences, Beijing, China*

Rationale

The CCIS series is devoted to the publication of proceedings of computer science conferences. Its aim is to efficiently disseminate original research results in informatics in printed and electronic form. While the focus is on publication of peer-reviewed full papers presenting mature work, inclusion of reviewed short papers reporting on work in progress is welcome, too. Besides globally relevant meetings with internationally representative program committees guaranteeing a strict peer-reviewing and paper selection process, conferences run by societies or of high regional or national relevance are also considered for publication.

Topics

The topical scope of CCIS spans the entire spectrum of informatics ranging from foundational topics in the theory of computing to information and communications science and technology and a broad variety of interdisciplinary application fields.

Information for Volume Editors and Authors

Publication in CCIS is free of charge. No royalties are paid, however, we offer registered conference participants temporary free access to the online version of the conference proceedings on SpringerLink (http://link.springer.com) by means of an http referrer from the conference website and/or a number of complimentary printed copies, as specified in the official acceptance email of the event.

CCIS proceedings can be published in time for distribution at conferences or as post-proceedings, and delivered in the form of printed books and/or electronically as USBs and/or e-content licenses for accessing proceedings at SpringerLink. Furthermore, CCIS proceedings are included in the CCIS electronic book series hosted in the SpringerLink digital library at http://link.springer.com/bookseries/7899. Conferences publishing in CCIS are allowed to use Online Conference Service (OCS) for managing the whole proceedings lifecycle (from submission and reviewing to preparing for publication) free of charge.

Publication process

The language of publication is exclusively English. Authors publishing in CCIS have to sign the Springer CCIS copyright transfer form, however, they are free to use their material published in CCIS for substantially changed, more elaborate subsequent publications elsewhere. For the preparation of the camera-ready papers/files, authors have to strictly adhere to the Springer CCIS Authors' Instructions and are strongly encouraged to use the CCIS LaTeX style files or templates.

Abstracting/Indexing

CCIS is abstracted/indexed in DBLP, Google Scholar, EI-Compendex, Mathematical Reviews, SCImago, Scopus. CCIS volumes are also submitted for the inclusion in ISI Proceedings.

How to start

To start the evaluation of your proposal for inclusion in the CCIS series, please send an e-mail to ccis@springer.com.

Debiao He · Jiajing Wu · Chen Wang ·
Huawei Huang

Editors

Blockchain, Metaverse and Trustworthy Systems

6th International Conference, BlockSys 2024
Hangzhou, China, July 12–14, 2024
Revised Selected Papers, Part I

Editors
Debiao He (iD)
Wuhan University
Wuhan, China

Chen Wang (iD)
Zhejiang Sci-Tech University
Hangzhou, China

Jiajing Wu (iD)
Sun Yat-sen University
Guangzhou, China

Huawei Huang (iD)
Sun Yat-sen University
Guangzhou, China

ISSN 1865-0929   ISSN 1865-0937 (electronic)
Communications in Computer and Information Science
ISBN 978-981-96-1410-3   ISBN 978-981-96-1411-0 (eBook)
https://doi.org/10.1007/978-981-96-1411-0

This Springer imprint is published by the registered company Springer Nature Singapore Pte Ltd.
The registered company address is: 152 Beach Road, #21-01/04 Gateway East, Singapore 189721, Singapore

If disposing of this product, please recycle the paper.

Preface

Blockchain and metaverse have become hot research topics in academia and industry. Blockchain and metaverse technologies are transforming industries by enabling anonymous, trustful, virtual and remote transactions in decentralized and trustless environments. As a result, blockchain, metaverse and other technologies for developing trustworthy systems can be used to reduce system risks, mitigate financial fraud and cut down operational cost. Blockchain, metaverse and trustworthy systems can be applied to many fields, such as financial services, social management and supply chain management.

This volume contains the papers from the proceedings of the 2024 International Conference on Blockchain, Metaverse and Trustworthy Systems (BlockSys 2024). This conference was the sixth in its series with an emphasis on state-of-the-art advances in blockchain, metaverse and trustworthy systems. The main conference accepted 34 papers, all of which have undergone a rigorous peer review process – each paper was reviewed by 2–3 experts. The accepted papers together with our outstanding keynote and invited speeches led to a vibrant technical program. We are looking forward to future events in this conference series.

The conference would not have been successful without help from so many people. We would like to thank the Organizing Committee for their hard work in putting together the conference. First, we would like to express our sincere gratitude to the General Chairs, Liehuang Zhu, Joseph Liu and Jian Shen, for their support and promotion of this event. We would also like to thank the program chairs, Debiao He, Jiajing Wu, Chen Wang and Huawei Huang, who supervised the review process of the technical papers and compiled a high-quality technical program. We also extend our deep gratitude to the program committee members whose diligent work in reviewing the papers led to the high quality of the accepted papers. We greatly appreciate the excellent support and hard work of the Publicity Chairs: Yi Sun, Wei Wang, Huijie Yang and Weibin Wu; Publication Chairs: Weizhi Meng, Tianqi Zhou, Vijayakumar Pandi and Wenqing Chen; Organizing Chairs: Jinjun Chen, Haowen Tan, Yanlin Wang, Jun Shao and Yizhi Ren; Advisory Board: Huaimin Wang, Jiannong Cao, Kuan-Ching Li and Michael R. Lyu; and Steering Committee: Hong-Ning Dai, Xiapu Luo, Yan Zhang and Zibin Zheng. Most importantly, we would like to thank the authors for submitting their papers to BlockSys 2024.

We believe that the BlockSys conference provides a good forum for both academic researchers and industrial practitioners to discuss all technical advances in blockchain, metaverse and trustworthy systems. We also expect that future BlockSys conferences will be as successful as indicated by the contributions presented in this volume.

July 2024

Debiao He
Jiajing Wu
Chen Wang
Huawei Huang

Organization

General Chairs

Liehuang Zhu	Beijing Institute of Technology, China
Joseph Liu	Monash University, Australia
Jian Shen	Zhejiang Sci-Tech University, China

Program Chairs

Debiao He	Wuhan University, China
Jiajing Wu	Sun Yat-sen University, China
Chen Wang	Zhejiang Sci-Tech University, China
Huawei Huang	Sun Yat-sen University, China

Organizing Chairs

Jinjun Chen	Swinburne University of Technology, Australia
Haowen Tan	Zhejiang Sci-Tech University, China
Yanlin Wang	Sun Yat-sen University, China
Jun Shao	Zhejiang Gongshang University, China
Yizhi Ren	Hangzhou Dianzi University, China

Publication Chairs

Weizhi Meng	Technical University of Denmark, Denmark
Tianqi Zhou	Zhejiang Sci-Tech University, China
Vijayakumar Pandi	Anna University, India
Wenqing Chen	Sun Yat-sen University, China

Publicity Chairs

Yi Sun	Chinese Academy of Sciences, China
Wei Wang	Beijing Jiaotong University, China

Huijie Yang   Zhejiang Sci-Tech University, China
Weibin Wu   Sun Yat-sen University, China

Industrial Chairs

Yong Yan   State Grid, China
Guang Yang   China Southern Power Grid Digital Platform
                                    Technology Company, China
Weiwei Qiu   Hyperchain Technology, China

Advisory Board

Huaimin Wang   National University of Defense Technology,
                                    China
Jiannong Cao   Hong Kong Polytechnic University, China
Kuan-Ching Li   Providence University, China
Michael R. Lyu   Chinese University of Hong Kong, China

Steering Committee

Hong-Ning Dai   Hong Kong Baptist University, China
Xiapu Luo   Hong Kong Polytechnic University, China
Yan Zhang   University of Oslo, Norway
Zibin Zheng   Sun Yat-sen University, China

Web Chair

Wenying Zheng   Zhejiang Sci-Tech University, China

Contents – Part I

Blockchain Performance Optimization

Contents – Part II

Blockchain and Data Mining

Intrusion Anomaly Detection
with Multi-transformer

Mengshuai Ma[1,2], Bin Wen[1,2(✉)], Wenlong Liu[1,2], Wanrong Du[1,2],
and Xiaoxun Wei[1,2]

[1] Key Laboratory of Data Science and Smart Education, Ministry of Education,
Hainan Normal University, Haikou 571158, China
`binwen@hainnu.edu.cn`
[2] School of Information Science and Technology, Hainan Normal University,
Haikou 571158, China

Abstract. With the rapid growth of network scale, more network
attacks have emerged, the types of network attacks have become more
diverse, and the harm they cause to users has become increasingly serious, which has challenged network intrusion detection and protection
methods. In order to further improve the quality of network intrusion
detection, the study proposes the Multi-Transformer method, which is
based on the switchable attention mechanism. It is a detection model
with higher security and greater applicability and is applied to the field
of network intrusion detection. The study improves the traditional Transformer model and uses self-attention(single head), multi-head attention,
and convolution attention in the attention module. At the same time, in
order to improve the interpretability of the model, LIME (Local interpretable Model-Agnostic Explanations) was introduced, using Multiple
public datasets for testing. The results show that the detection effect
of the Multi-Transformer model is better than other machine learning
methods. The proposed method is more secure and applicable, and has
better anti-noise ability, which has more practical significance in complex
and changeable network environments.

Keyword: Intrusion detection, Transformer, Attention mechanism,
Interpretability, Deep learning.

1 Introduction

Network intrusion detection [1] is a crucial aspect of cybersecurity, involving
various techniques and methods to monitor network systems to detect, prevent, identify, and respond to inappropriate network activities and attacks. Network Intrusion Detection Systems (NIDS) are typically categorized into two
types: signature-based detection systems and anomaly-based detection systems.
Signature-based systems identify attacks by matching them with known attack
patterns, while anomaly-based systems depend on analyzing abnormal patterns
of network behavior to discover potential threats.

D. He et al. (Eds.): BlockSys 2024, CCIS 2264, pp. 3–16, 2025.
https://doi.org/10.1007/978-981-96-1411-0_1

Currently, in the field of intrusion detection, the most used are machine learning [7] and deep learning [4]. Yu et al. [14] proposed a Bidirectional Long Short-Term Memory (BiLSTM) intrusion detection model with attention mechanisms. Mirsky et al. [8] used an autoencoder AE to reassemble network traffic for each segment, gradually improving its detection performance but disrupting the relationships between original features. Tan et al. [12] introduced a real-time intrusion detection method based on attention mechanisms. Li and Zhao [6] proposed the ECOD algorithm, an outlier detection algorithm based on empirical cumulative distribution. Ruff et al. [11] proposed a new anomaly detection algorithm, DeepSVDD, trained with the goal of anomaly detection. Bontemps et al. [2] introduced an RNN-based autoencoder model, RNN-AE, in which an LSTM RNN is trained with normal time series data before performing real-time predictions at each timestep. Jorge et al. [3] proposed a new anomaly-based Network Intrusion Detection System (NIDS) using the Transformer method, achieving better results on public datasets in terms of F-score and AUC metrics than previous methods.

The current methods of network intrusion detection face issues with low accuracy in anomaly recognition, poor security, and limited applicability. To address these problems, this paper introduces the Multi-Transformer method, which adds a switchable attention mechanism on top of the traditional Transformer. By changing the type of attention parameters, it switches between different attention mechanisms, extracting more complex and abstract features from network traffic data. This enables it to effectively capture long-distance dependencies in network traffic, allowing data separated by large intervals to influence the model's decision-making. Introducing noise interference improves the model's resistance to interference and applicability in multiple scenarios.

2   Multi-transformer Approach

2.1   Transformer Model

The Transformer model [5] is a deep learning architecture primarily used for processing sequential data, such as text. It was first introduced in 2017 by researchers at Google and quickly became a revolutionary technology in the field of natural language processing. The core feature of the Transformer model is its "attention mechanism," which allows the model to consider all elements of the input sequence simultaneously, thereby more effectively learning complex patterns in the data. This mechanism eliminates the sequential processing limitations of traditional Recurrent Neural Networks (RNN) and Long Short-Term Memory networks (LSTM), significantly increasing processing speed and efficiency. The Transformer has been used in various tasks, such as machine translation, text summarization, and question-answering systems, and serves as the foundation for many advanced language models, like BERT and the GPT series.

Self-attention Mechanism. The self-attention mechanism captures the relevant information between different input and output positions using the scaled dot-product attention, as shown in Fig. 1(a).

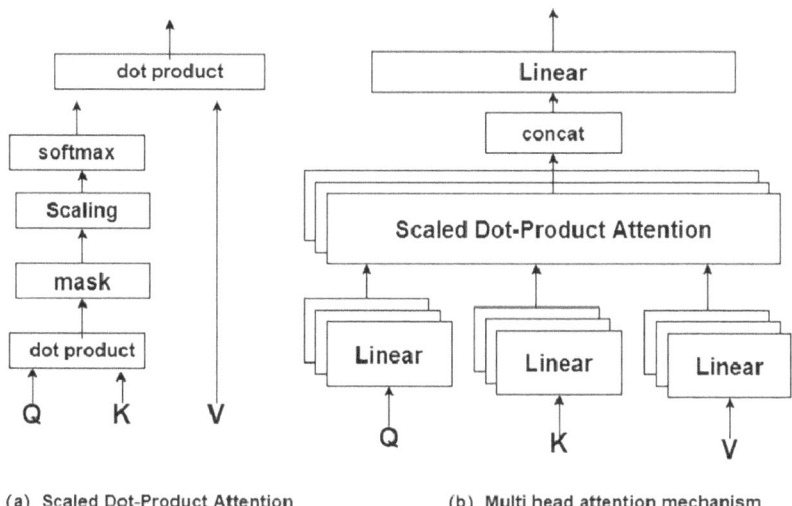

(a) Scaled Dot-Product Attention   (b) Multi head attention mechanism

Fig. 1. Structure of self attention mechanism

This module consists of three parts: Query Q, Key K, and Value V, Where $Q \in R^{d_k}$, $K \in R^{d_k}$, and $V \in R^{d_v}$. Each query calculates the scaled dot-product with all keys to obtain their similarities, then uses the softmax function to get the weights associated with the values, and finally, the weights and values are combined through dot-product to obtain the attention values. The Attention(Q,K,V) is as shown in Eq. (1):

$$Attention(Q, K, V) = softmax\left(\frac{QK^T}{\sqrt{d_k}}\right)V \qquad (1)$$

Specifically, the attention head operates on the input sequence $x = (x_1, x_2, \cdots, x_n)$, where $x_i \in R^{d_x}$, to produce the output sequence $y = (y_1, y_2, \cdots, y_n)$, where $y_i \in R^{d_y}$. The similarity e_{ij} is obtained through scaled dot-product attention, expressed as follows in Eq. (2):

$$e_{ij} = \frac{(x_i W^Q)(x_j W^K)^T}{\sqrt{d_k}} \qquad (2)$$

Then, the softmax function is used to calculate the weight coefficients λ_{ij}, represented by Eq. (3):

$$\lambda_{ij} = \frac{\exp(e_{ij})}{\sum_{k=1}^{n} \exp(e_{ik})} \qquad (3)$$

The output value is the weighted sum of the linear transformations of the input elements, represented by Eq. (4):

$$y_i = \sum_{j=1}^{n} \lambda_{ij}(x_j W^V) \tag{4}$$

Among them, W^Q, W^K, W^V are matrix parameters that satisfy W^Q, W^K, and $W^V \in R^{d_x \times d_y}$.

Encode. The encoder consists of N identical encoding blocks, each containing two sub-layers: a fully connected feed-forward network layer and a multi-head attention layer. The structure of the encoder is shown in the encoder part of Fig. 2. The multi-head attention essentially concatenates multiple self-attention blocks, transforming the original high-dimensional space into multiple low-dimensional spaces. After computation, the results are concatenated again to form outputs of the same dimension, which not only enriches the feature information but also reduces the computational load. The structure of the multi-head attention is shown in Fig. 1(b). Given all queries Q, keys K, and values V, where $Q \in R^{d_k}$, $K \in R^{d_k}$, and $V \in R^{d_v}$. First, the output value of each attention head, $head_i$, is calculated using the $Attention(Q, K, V)$ mechanism, as shown in Equation (5):

$$head_i = Attention(Q, K, V) \tag{5}$$

Then, the outputs of the different attention heads calculated are concatenated to obtain the MultiHead(Q, K, V) , as shown in Eq. (6):

$$MultiHead(Q, K, V) = Concat(head_1, head_2, \cdots, head_h)W^O \tag{6}$$

where h is the number of heads, $W_i^Q \in R^{d_{model} \times d_k}$, $W_i^K \in R^{d_{model} \times d_k}$, $W_i^V \in R^{d_{model} \times d_v}$, and $W^O \in R^{hd_v \times d_{model}}$, with d_{model} being the dimension of the model.

The fully connected feed-forward network consists of a ReLU activation function and two linear transformations. In the Transformer model, all the fully connected networks are identical. The computation process is as shown in Eq. (7):

$$FFN(x) = \max(0, xW_1 + b_1)W_2 + b_2 \tag{7}$$

Decode. The decoder is composed of N identical decoding blocks, with a structure similar to that of the encoding blocks. The structure of the decoder is shown in the decoder part of Fig. 2.

However, there are some differences from the encoding blocks. First, there is a masked multi-head attention layer in the decoding block, where a mask tensor is applied to the multi-head attention layer to mask future information during

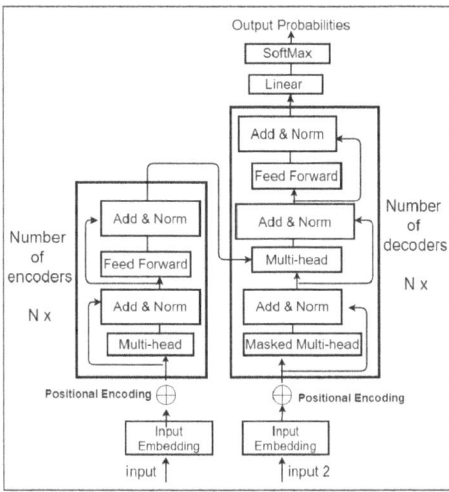

Fig. 2. Transformer structure

decoding. Secondly, the key and value inputs of the multi-head attention layer come from the encoder's output, while the query comes from the output of the decoding block.

2.2   Construction of the Multi-transformer Model

LIME Model. LIME (locally interpretable model diagnostic interpretation) is a technique used to interpret machine learning model predictions. The core idea of this technology is to create an interpretable model near the prediction of the model, which is trustworthy for local data, even if the global model may be highly nonlinear and complex. LIME can be applied to any machine learning model, providing a powerful tool to help people understand the decision-making process of complex models. The principle is that although a model may be inexplicable on a global scale, its behavior may become simpler and more linear in the local neighborhood of the input data. Therefore, the goal of LIME is to fit a simple model (such as linear regression or decision tree) within this local neighborhood, which can approximate the behavior of the original complex model.

The main advantages of LIME (Local interpretable Model-Agnostic Explanations) technology are its model agnosticity, improved transparency, and flexibility. As a universal explanatory framework, LIME can be applied to any machine learning model, whether it is a simple linear model or a complex deep learning model, to interpret its prediction results. This model's agnosticity greatly expands the applicability of LIME, making it a very powerful tool to improve the interpretability and transparency of machine learning models.

LIME approximates the behavior of complex models near specific instances by creating simple models, helping users understand how the model makes specific predictions. This local interpretation method provides transparency for the decision-making process of the model, enabling non expert users to understand the working principle and decision-making basis of the model, thereby increasing user trust in the model's predictions.

Attention Mechanism Switching. In this paper, innovative improvements have been made to the traditional Transformer model. Particularly, in the aspect of the attention mechanism, we introduced an independent module to support the flexible switching of attention mechanisms. This innovation includes three different types of attention mechanisms: self-attention (single-head), multi-head attention, and convolutional attention. This design significantly enhances the model's performance and generalization ability.

Through this switchable attention mechanism, the model can choose the most suitable type of attention according to different application scenarios and data characteristics. The three mechanisms, namely self-attention (single-head), multi-head attention, and convolutional attention, exhibit their advantages when dealing with different types of data and tasks, enhancing the model's capability to handle complex tasks. The self-attention mechanism is particularly adept at capturing long-distance dependencies. For text or time-series data, important correlations may exist between elements far apart in the sequence.

Self-attention, by computing the correlation between all pairs of elements in the sequence, can effectively capture these long-distance dependencies, thereby better understanding the overall sequence structure. The multi-head attention mechanism, by decomposing the attention into multiple "heads," can capture information from different perspectives or subspaces simultaneously. This mechanism allows the model to understand data more comprehensively, especially when dealing with data that has complex structures or multidimensional features. For instance, in processing natural language, different attention "heads" can focus on various aspects of a sentence, such as grammatical structure, semantic content, or contextual relationships. The convolutional attention mechanism, leveraging the characteristics of convolutional neural networks, is particularly suited for capturing local features. When processing images or data with distinct local structural features, convolutional attention can effectively extract and utilize these local pieces of information. This is particularly important for tasks such as image recognition and object detection.

The combination of these three attention mechanisms provides a powerful tool, enabling the model to handle various tasks more flexibly and effectively. The model can choose the most appropriate attention mechanism based on the specific requirements of the task and the characteristics of the data, thus ensuring accuracy and robustness of the processing results while maintaining efficiency. This is of significant importance for enhancing the model's applicability in various complex and changing environments.

3   Experimental Design

This section will detail the relevant settings of the network intrusion detection experiment. First, an overview of the characteristics and content of the two network intrusion detection datasets used in this study is provided. Secondly, the experimental environment settings and evaluation criteria used are clarified. Finally, detailed descriptions of experiment-related operations are provided, including details such as the model's parameter configuration. Figure 3 presents the overall technical roadmap for this experiment.

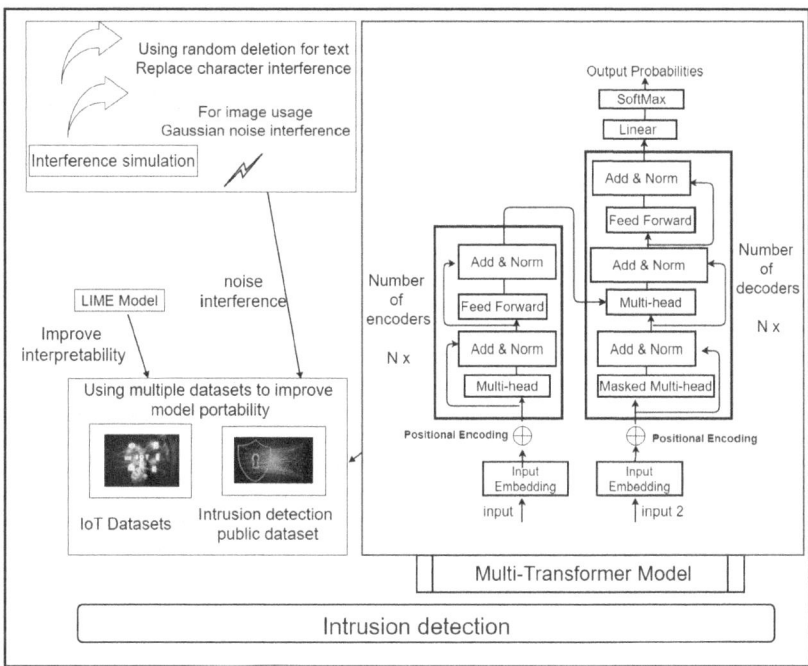

Fig. 3. Technical roadmap for Multi-Transformer detection approach

3.1   Experimental Environment and Evaluation Metrics

The experimental environment consists of an Intel(R) Core(TM) i7-12700F, 32GB RAM, Windows 10 operating system, and an NVIDIA GeForce RTX 4090 GPU. The Python version used is 3.8.5. The deep learning framework is Pytorch, version 2.0.0. The experiment evaluates the overall performance of the model using Recall, Precision, F1-score, and the AUC-ROC curve. The first three metrics are calculated based on True Positives (TP), True Negatives (TN), False Positives (FP), and False Negatives (FN). The AUC-ROC curve is a performance measurement method for classification problems under various threshold settings. ROC is a probability curve, and AUC represents the degree of separability. The area under the ROC curve is the value of AUC, which ranges from 0 to 1. The higher the AUC, the better the model performs. The calculation method is as shown in Eq. (8).

$$Precision = \frac{TP}{TP+FP}; Recall = \frac{TP}{TP+FN}; F1-Score = 2 \times \frac{Recall \times Precision}{Recall + Precision} \tag{8}$$

3.2 Experimental Procedure

This section introduces the model parameters and other details of the experimental setup. The Multi-Transformer model used in this section has 6 layers for both the encoder and decoder, and employs a softmax [13] classification function for the classifier. When using multi-head attention, the number of attention heads is set to 8, and when using convolutional attention, the convolutional kernel size is set to 3. The ELU activation function is used as the non-linear activation function. To prevent overfitting, the dropout method is applied to the attention coefficients with a rate of 0.1. The model framework used is Pytorch, with the Adam optimizer updating the neural network's weights during the training process to minimize the loss function. The number of neurons in the feedforward network layer is set to 512. The learning rate for the WUSTL_IIOT_2021 dataset is 0.0001, while the learning rate for the UNSW-NB15 dataset is set to 0.006. Due to the large size of the datasets, they are divided into training, validation, and testing sets at ratios of 80%, 10%, and 10%, respectively. In the experiments, Mean Squared Error (MSE) [10] is used as the loss function. The entire training process lasted for 25 epochs, with each batch containing 128 samples.

4 Results Evaluation and Analysis

This section compares the detection performance of the proposed Multi-Transformer network intrusion detection method with the Transformer algorithm and other machine learning and deep learning methods to explore their performance on different models. Additionally, the experiment subjects the Multi-Transformer model to noise interference to verify the performance of the method presented in this paper. Along with presenting the experimental data, an in-depth analysis and discussion of these data are also provided.

4.1 Network Intrusion Detection Performance Results

The experiment utilizes the aforementioned evaluation metrics to measure the detection performance of the Multi-Transformer intrusion anomaly detection method. To verify the improvement effects of the Multi-Transformer method proposed in this article, several machine learning and deep learning methods were selected for comparison, including the Outlier Detection Method based on Empirical Cumulative Distribution Function (ECOD), Deep One-Class Classification for Anomaly Detection (DeepSVDD), and the traditional Transformer

Table 1. Performance comparison of DoS data on different approaches.

Dataset	Method	F1-score	AUC
WUSTL-IIOT (DoS data)	ECOD	0.9251	0.9637
	DeepSVDD	0.9046	0.9346
	RNN-AE	0.8104	0.9309
	Transformer	0.9431	0.9744
	Multi-Transformer	**0.9565**	**0.9859**

model. Table 1 displays the performance of different detection methods on the DoS data part of the WUSTL-IIOT_2021 dataset.

This study focuses on evaluating the model's effectiveness in anomaly detection, thus primarily adopting a binary classification [9] approach. Additionally, to comprehensively assess the model's performance, we also tested its performance on another four types of data within the WUSTL_IIOT_2021 dataset.

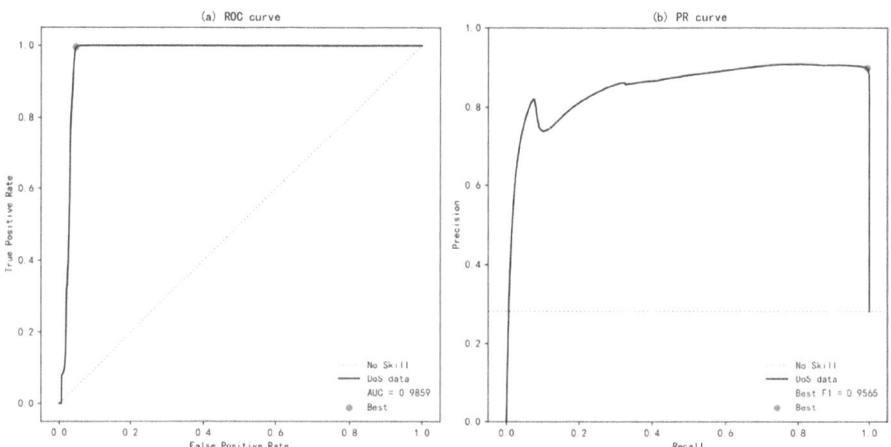

Fig. 4. ROC curve and PR plot of DoS data.

Firstly, in this study, we conducted comprehensive testing on the WUSTL_IIOT dataset, focusing on several main types of network attacks: DoS (Denial of Service), Recon (Reconnaissance Attack), Comm (Communication Attack), and Backdoor data. In the experiments, we used AUC (Area Under the Curve) and F1-score, two key performance indicators, to evaluate the effectiveness of the Multi-Transformer method. The results show that, whether in terms of the AUC metric or F1-score value, the Multi-Transformer method significantly outperforms other mainstream methods currently available. The AUC and F1-score for DoS data reached 0.9859 and 0.9565 respectively, the F1-score for Recon reached 0.8321, especially for Comm and Backdoor data parts, the

F1-score reached 0.9633, which is a noticeable improvement compared to other methods.

Additionally, we conducted partial validation on the UNSW-NB15 dataset. Taking DoS data as an example, its AUC value and F1-score were 0.9983 and 0.9952, respectively. Figure 5(a) shows its ROC curve, and Fig. 5(b) shows its PR curve.

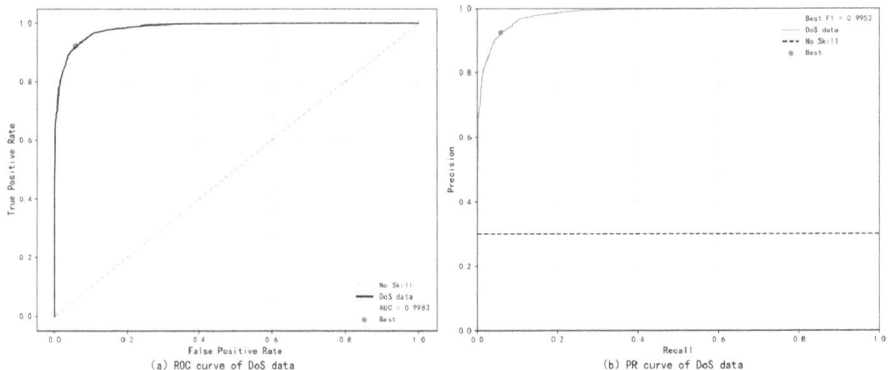

Fig. 5. ROC curve and PR plot of DoS data on UNSW-NB15.

Table 2 shows the model performance comparison of our method with various machine learning and graph neural network models on the UNSW-NB15 dataset. It can be observed that our method's AUC and F1-score are superior to other machine learning models and graph neural networks.

Table 2. Performance comparison of DoS data on different approaches.

Dataset	Method	F1-score	AUC
UNSW-NB15	DT	0.9938	0.9954
	LR	0.9942	0.9959
	E-ResGATv2	0.9949	0.9971
	Transformer	0.9694	0.9931
	Multi-Transformer	**0.9952**	**0.9983**

Next, the article will explore whether the model can still maintain good detection performance when facing noise interference.

4.2   Noise Interference Experiment

To explore the performance of various detection methods when subjected to noise interference [15], this paper adds random feature values to the training sets of the two datasets to achieve the purpose of noise interference. The specific approach is to randomly select values from the maximum or minimum values in each column of data, and the scale of noise added to the training set is controlled by the parameter p. The larger the proportion of p, the larger the scale of noise added to the training set. These detection methods are subjected to noise with different noise ratios p, and the impact of noise interference is judged by the change in AUC values. Figure 6 shows the curve of AUC values of different detection methods on the UNSW-NB15 dataset as the noise ratio p changes.

As shown in Fig. 6, as the noise interference increases, compared to other methods, the initial AUC values of the method proposed in this paper, Multi-Transformer, are higher than those of other methods and remain stable, indicating that it can maintain a stable state when trained with feature value noise interference. In contrast, the traditional Transformer method shows a gradually declining trend. Graph neural network methods like E-ResGATv2 and DT are very unstable when faced with noise interference, with an overall downward trend; while the LR algorithm plummets when p is 0.2, then maintains a lower AUC value unchanged, indicating that the LR algorithm loses its detection performance after suffering noise interference. Overall, the detection effect of the method proposed in this paper on the UNSW-NB15 is significantly better than that of other detection methods.

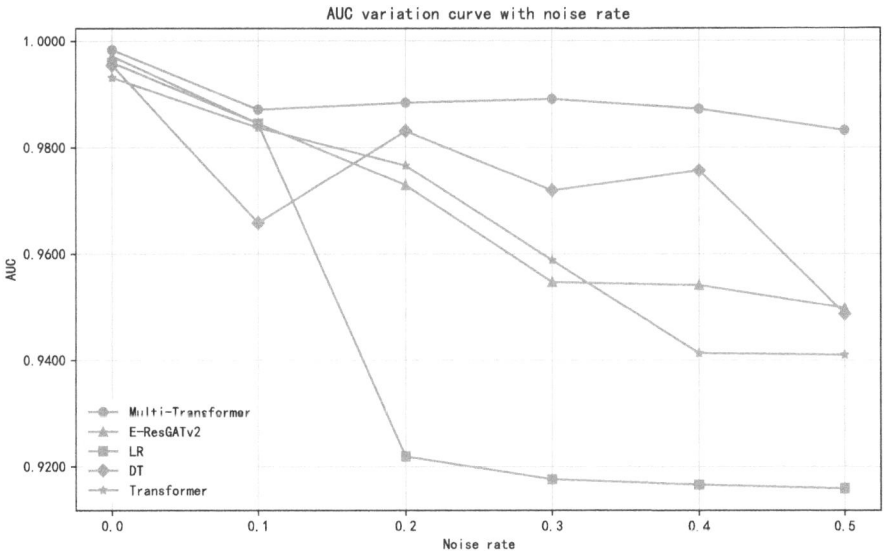

Fig. 6. The variation curve of AUC with noise ratio p for different detection approaches.

Considering the performance of our method after being subjected to noise interference on both datasets and comparing it with other methods, it can be observed that Multi-Transformer exhibits more stable detection performance.

This is particularly significant in complex network environments, where stability and robustness are crucial for effective intrusion detection.

4.3   Different Attention Mechanisms Comparison Experiment

The study introduces an innovative switchable attention mechanism on top of the classic Transformer architecture, which integrates self-attention, multi-head attention, and convolutional attention. In-depth experimental analysis was conducted on the WUSTL-IIOT dataset, and Fig. 7 clearly illustrates the AUC performance for DoS, Recon, and Comm data types under different attention mechanisms.

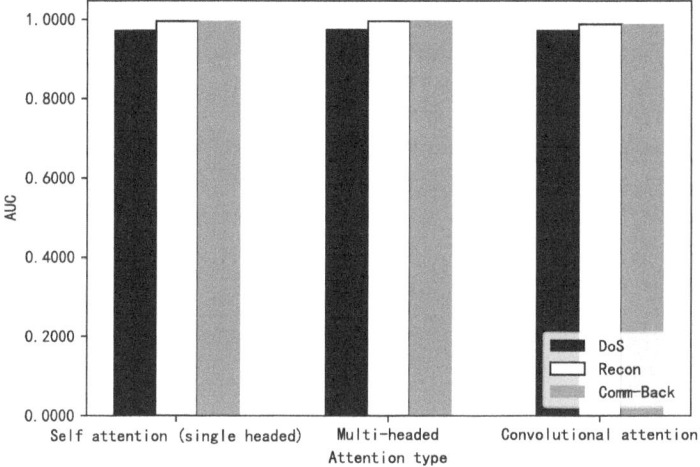

Fig. 7. AUC of DoS, Recon, Comm Back data under different attention mechanisms.

The results indicate that under the application of self-attention (single-head) and multi-head attention, Recon and Comm data types exhibit outstanding performance, while the DoS data type also demonstrates efficient detection capabilities. Considering that the dataset primarily consists of sequential text data, self-attention and multi-head attention perform exceptionally well in handling such data types, while convolutional attention, though slightly inferior, still maintains considerable detection effectiveness. This finding suggests that by selecting appropriate attention mechanisms for different application scenarios, this approach can significantly enhance the model's generalization ability and detection performance, thereby demonstrating greater flexibility and efficiency in responding to emergent events.

5   Conclusion

This study proposes an advanced method for network intrusion anomaly detection called Multi-Transformer, and comprehensively compares its performance with traditional machine learning methods and graph neural network techniques on two public datasets. The experimental results consistently show that Multi-Transformer significantly outperforms other machine learning and graph neural network methods in terms of AUC and F1-score performance indicators on both datasets. Furthermore, through in-depth comparison with the traditional Transformer method, the significant advantages of Multi-Transformer in detection efficiency and resistance to noise interference are further validated. These findings strongly indicate that our improved method is more suitable for the complex requirements of network intrusion detection.

This series of experiments delve into the widespread application potential and development prospects of Multi-Transformer in the field of intrusion detection, particularly demonstrating its significant robustness against noise interference. This achievement further confirms the significant advantages of Multi-Transformer in the field of network security. In future research, based on the current research findings, we plan to expand our exploration scope by considering the use of diverse datasets such as image data to verify the applicability and effectiveness of Multi-Transformer in various application scenarios.

Acknowledgement. This work was supported by National Natural Science Foundation of China (No.62362029) and Hainan Provincial Natural Science Foundation of China (No.623RC485), and by a grant from Postgraduates' Innovative Research Projects of Hainan Province.

References

1. Alamleh, A., et al.: Multi-attribute decision-making for intrusion detection systems: a systematic review. Int. J. Inf. Technol. Decis. Making **22**(01), 589–636 (2023)
2. Bontemps, L., Cao, V.L., McDermott, J., Le-Khac, N.-A.: Collective Anomaly Detection Based on Long Short-Term Memory Recurrent Neural Networks. In: Dang, T.K., Wagner, R., Küng, J., Thoai, N., Takizawa, M., Neuhold, E. (eds.) FDSE 2016. LNCS, vol. 10018, pp. 141–152. Springer, Cham (2016)
3. Casajús-Setién, J., Bielza, C., Larrañaga, P.: Anomaly-based intrusion detection in IIoT networks using transformer models. In: 2023 IEEE International Conference on Cyber Security and Resilience (CSR), pp. 72–77. IEEE (2023)
4. Lansky, J., et al.: Deep learning-based intrusion detection systems: a systematic review. IEEE Access **9**, 101574–101599 (2021)
5. Li, J., Du, J., Zhu, Y., Guo, Y.: Survey of transformer-based object detection algorithms. Comput. Eng. Appl. **59**(10), 48–64 (2023)
6. Li, Z., Zhao, Y., Hu, X., Botta, N., Ionescu, C., Chen, G.H.: ECOD: unsupervised outlier detection using empirical cumulative distribution functions. IEEE Trans. Knowl. Data Eng. **35**(12), 12181–12193 (2022)
7. Maseer, Z.K., Yusof, R., Bahaman, N., Mostafa, S.A., Foozy, C.F.M.: Benchmarking of machine learning for anomaly based intrusion detection systems in the CICIDS2017 dataset. IEEE Access **9**, 22351–22370 (2021)
8. Mirsky, Y., Doitshman, T., Elovici, Y., Shabtai, A.: Kitsune: an ensemble of autoencoders for online network intrusion detection. arXiv preprint arXiv:1802.09089 (2018)

 9. Pal, A., Selvakumar, M., Sankarasubbu, M.: Multi-label text classification using attention-based graph neural network. arXiv preprint arXiv:2003.11644 (2020)
10. Ren, J., Zhang, M., Yu, C., Liu, Z.: Balanced MSE for imbalanced visual regression. In: Proceedings of the IEEE/CVF Conference on Computer Vision and Pattern Recognition, pp. 7926–7935 (2022)
11. Ruff, L., et al.: Deep one-class classification. In: International Conference on Machine Learning, pp. 4393–4402. PMLR (2018)
12. Tan, M., Iacovazzi, A., Cheung, N.M.M., Elovici, Y.: A neural attention model for real-time network intrusion detection. In: 2019 IEEE 44th Conference on Local Computer Networks (LCN), pp. 291–299. IEEE (2019)
13. Wang, M., Lu, S., Zhu, D., Lin, J., Wang, Z.: A high-speed and low-complexity architecture for SoftMax function in deep learning. In: 2018 IEEE Asia Pacific Conference on Circuits and Systems (APCCAS), pp. 223–226. IEEE (2018)
14. Yu, Y., Liu, G., Yan, H., Li, H., Guan, H.: Attention-based bi-LSTM model for anomalous http traffic detection. In: 2018 15th International Conference on Service Systems and Service Management (ICSSSM), pp. 1–6. IEEE (2018)
15. Zeng, Y., Zhang, J., Zhong, Y., Deng, L., Wang, M.: STNet: a time-frequency analysis-based intrusion detection network for distributed optical fiber acoustic sensing systems. Sensors **24**(5), 1570 (2024)

A Federated Learning Method Based on Linear Probing and Fine-Tuning

Yang Li[1,2(✉)], Haoyu Chen[1,2], Jianming Zhu[1,2], and Youwei Wang[1,2]

[1] School of Information, Central University of Finance and Economics, Beijing 100081, China
liyang@cufe.edu.cn
[2] Engineering Research Center of State Financial Security, Ministry of Education, Central University of Finance and Economics, Beijing 102206, China

Abstract. Federated Learning is an emerging machine learning technology proposed by Google in 2016, which allows for collaborative training across multiple devices without the need to collect participants' data. This approach helps protect user privacy. Using pre-trained models as the initialization for federated learning algorithms has become common in recent work. However, many efficient methods for fine-tuning pre-trained models under centralized learning setting seem to have not been applied in these works. We notice that the two-stage fine-tuning (FT) method, linear probing then fine-tuning (LP-FT), performs well in centralized transfer learning, so this paper expands it to federated learning problems. This paper proposes a new federated learning method called FedLP + FT. The method adopts a two-stage strategy: in the first stage, the linear head of the model is trained using linear probing; in the second stage, fine-tuning update the entire model following the traditional federated learning approach. The experimental results show that the FedLP + FT has potential to reduce communication and compute costs while achieving better model performance.

Keywords: Pre-trained Model · Linear Probing · Fine-tuning · Transfer Learning · Federated Learning

1 Introduction

Over the past few years, technologies related to machine learning have seen rapid advancements, leading to a substantial rise in the requirements for data volume, communication overhead, and data processing capabilities. For instance [1], many e-commerce platforms gather user data to train recommendation algorithms, aiming to enhance the customer experience. However, some users are reluctant to share their data due to privacy concerns, which poses a challenge for achieving high model accuracy in machine learning applications without sufficient training data.

To address these issues, Google proposed federated learning technology [2]. The core idea of federated learning is decentralized training, which eliminates the need to collect and store all data on a single server by performing model training on dispersed local devices. Only the training results are sent to a unified central server for aggregation and updating, thereby reducing the risk of data leakage. Currently, federated learning is considered to have significant application prospects in fields such as finance, smart retail, and healthcare.

Many classic federated learning methods primarily train a model from scratch, which means the parameters of model is initialized randomly. These existing approaches are confronted by several challenges, including high communication costs and low accuracy caused by non independent and identically distributed client data [3]. In contemporary research, there has been a trend to apply model pre-training to federated learning to enhance parameter initialization. Some have shown that the model initialized with pre-trained parameters can reduce communication costs, improve accuracy and mitigate the problem of non-IID in federated learning [4]. Among these works, there is a fundamental question: how to efficiently fine-tune pre-trained models in federated learning.

Inspired by the fine-tuning method in transfer learning, this paper proposes a new federated learning algorithm FedLP + FT, which use a simple two-stage strategy: in the first stage, train only the classification layer and freeze the local feature extractor from pre-trained model, which is similar to linear probing; in the second stage, fine-tune the entire model. Such two-stage approaches have been shown to enhance performance in centralized learning setting [5]. Our main contributions are as follows:

First, this paper shows that in federated learning setting, training the classification layer of pre-trained model can be efficient. In some cases, simple linear probing can even achieve accuracy very close to the fine-tuning.

Second, the linear probing optimizes only the classification layer, which means there are less parameters that need to be communicated to the global server in the first training stage. Although the entire model is still trained in the second stage, the linear probing helps reduce the high communication costs. We will demonstrate that our algorithm can achieve high accuracy while reducing communication costs.

Finally, this paper uses pre-trained models based on local data instead of publicly available pre-trained models. Before the start of federated learning, each client had already trained a local model on its local dataset. This approach is useful in situations where pre-trained models are not directly available (Fig. 1).

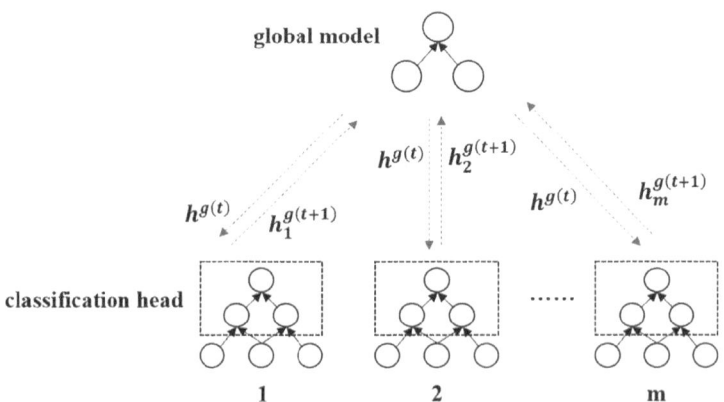

Fig. 1. Federated Learning with Linear Probing.

2 Related Work

2.1 Federated Learning

FedAvg is the simplest and most well-known version of federated learning, which was proposed by McMahan [2]. In each communication round of FedAvg, clients optimizes local models on their private data and send the parameters to central server, then the central server aggregates parameters, updates the global model and sends it back to the clients. A commonly cited problem is that FedAvg shows poor performance when dealing with non-iid or heterogeneous data, so many works attempt to improve it. For the purpose of tackling heterogeneity in federated networks, FedProx [6] added a proximal term to the local subproblem to restrict the influence of variable local updates. SCAFFOLD [7] used control variates to correct for the 'client drift' caused by heterogeneous data. Lin et al. [8] substituted weight averaging with model distillation. Despite the literature in the field of transfer learning, most studies still train a model from scratch. So this paper focuses on the impact of initialization on federated learning.

2.2 Transfer Learning

The method of learning from pretrained models has achieved tremendous success in natural language processing and computer vision [9, 10]. Research on transfer learning indicates that pre-training can reduce the convergence time of centralized models and improve their generalization ability [7]. Therefore, in recent research, using pre-trained models instead of random models for initialization has been considered an effective approach. Nguyen [4] shows that initialization with pretrained models not only reduces the training time but also mitigates the problem of non-iid data in federated learning. Chen [11] demonstrated that fine-tuned Transformer perform well in federated learning, and that the lightweight fine-tuning method enables quick convergence and reduces communication costs. Considering situations where pre-trained models are not directly available, Chen [10] explored pre-training with clients' data in a decentralized manner, and found that it can also improve FL notably. Kumar [5] compared two popular methods for fine-tuning pre-trained models: full fine-tuning (updating all the model parameters), and linear probing (updating the only last linear layer), and proposed a two-step strategy of linear probing then full fine-tuning (LP-FT). The experiments showed that this strategy improved the model's performance on out-of-distribution data. Inspired by Kumar, Legate [12] proposed FedNCM + FT, using a two-stage approach of obtaining the classifier through NCM (the nearest class mean method) and then fine-tuning the model. Compared to a single strategy, it gained advantages in communication cost and the ability to handle heterogeneous data.

Paper [4] used publicly available pre-trained models, but in situations of data scarcity, publicly available pre-trained models are often difficult to obtain. In contrast, the setting of using client-side local data for pre-training in paper [10] may be more widely applicable. The client-side pretraining in paper [10] employed a self-supervised learning method proposed by Lubana [13], mainly targeting scenarios where labelled data is difficult to obtain. This method outperforms existing federated self-supervised learning methods, but supervised learning is still a more common setting in federated learning.

The effectiveness of pretraining client-side data in a supervised manner remains to be explored. Paper [12] compared FedNCM + FT with only LP, only FT and other methods, except the LP-FT method suggested in paper [5]. According to the conclusion of paper [5], LP-FT performs better than only LP and only FT on both in-distribution and out-of-distribution data.

2.3 Linear Probing

In transfer learning, there are two popular methods for adjusting pre-trained models: updating all model parameters or freezing the lower-layer parameters and updating only the classification head. The former is known as fine-tuning, while the latter is known as linear probing. Research on centralized training has shown that when there is not much difference between the data distribution in the pre-training task and the downstream task, fine-tuning performs better than linear probing [5].

However, paper [5] has also shown that when there is a significant difference between the data distribution in pre-training and the downstream task, the performance of linear probing will outperform fine-tuning. The difference in data distribution between pre-training data and downstream task data in centralized training is similar to the difference in data distribution among clients in federated learning. Accordingly this paper tries to extend linear probing in centralized learning setting to the federated learning.

3 Problem Formulation

In FedAvg [2] (the most classical federated learning algorithm), the objective function is:

$$\min_{w} \frac{1}{n} \sum_{i=1}^{n} f(q_i) \tag{1}$$

Here f is loss function, n is the number of clients and $q_i \in \mathcal{Q}$ represents the model of the i-th client. In supervised training setting, the i-th client has a dataset with samples $\{(x_i, y_i)\}$. We assume the data in the i-th client is from a specific distribution D_i, which means $(x_i, y_i) \sim D_i$. The model $q_i : R^d \to \mathcal{Y}$ maps the input $x_i \in R^d$ to the predicted labels $q_i(x_i) \in \mathcal{Y}$. The purpose is to make $q_i(x_i)$ resemble the true label y_i.

In the standard federated learning setting, q_i is the randomly initialized model, and the client completely overwrites the local model with the global model sent by the server in each training round. However, when using a pre-trained model for initialization, completely overwriting the local model may not be beneficial, because the pre-trained model can already extract features based on the local data distribution effectively, whereas the aggregated model may not. Liang's [18] method has inspired us: he chose to train a global classification head and many local representation. We also find that this method can be combined with linear probing in centralized learning setting.

We consider the model q_i consisting of two parts: a specific feature extractor q_{ϕ_i} : $R^d \rightarrow R^k$, which is a function parameterized by $\phi_i \in \Phi$ that transforms the input with d dimensions to a representation with lower dimensions k; and a global classification head $q_h : R^k \rightarrow \mathcal{Y}$, which is a function parameterized by $h \in \mathcal{H}$ that transforms the k-dimensional representation to the label. During the first stage of FedLP + FT, we freeze the feature extractor and train only the classification head. So we can rewrite the objective function:

$$\min_{h \in \mathcal{H}} \frac{1}{n} \sum_{i=1}^{n} f(h, \phi_i) \tag{2}$$

This means in FedLP, all clients collaborate to train a global classification head, while each client maintains a fixed feature extractor from the pre-trained model.

4 Our Approach FedLP

4.1 Algorithm Description

FedLP + FT combines linear probing from centralized learning with federated learning through a two-stage strategy. We assume that for different clients, the classifier mapping from low-dimensional data representations to labels is similar. The fine-tuning in the second stage further optimizes the combination of the classification head and feature extractor obtained in the first stage, ensuring that the global model is generalized instead of overfitting to the data on a certain client. In the first stage FedLP, the pre-trained model is trained on local data. Therefore, the feature extractor from the pre-trained model can better extractor representations from local data compared to the model sent by the server. The second stage fine-tuning is no different from conventional federated algorithm like FedAvg essentially, so we primarily focus on FedLP.

Similar to the conventional federated learning setup, FedLP comprises a central server and multiple participating clients. Before the start of federated learning, each client completes pre-training on local dataset using stochastic gradient descent to obtain a local pre-trained model, rather than using a global initialized model uniformly distributed to all clients. Although the upfront pre-training requires time and computation costs, it enhances the convergence speed during the federated learning process.

The core idea of FedLP lies in integrating the linear probing method from large model fine-tuning into federated optimization, reducing computational costs while retaining the feature extraction capability of pre-trained models on local data. In classical federated learning approaches, after each round of updates, the local feature extractor is completely covered by the aggregated model. However, the feature extractor of the aggregated model performs poorly on clients with significant data distribution shifts, leading to local model biases and further performance degradation of the aggregated model. By preserving the local feature extractor, we mitigate local model biases, thereby enhancing the algorithm's robustness to heterogeneous data (Table 1).

At iteration t of global training, the server sends $h^{g(t)}$ to each client. The h^g denotes that these are parameters of the global classification head, to distinguish them from h^l, the parameters of local classification head from pre-trained model. Then the client update

Table 1. Algorithm of Federated Learning with Linear Probing

Algorithm 1 Federated Learning with Linear Probing

Parameters: number of participating clients m, number of local updates k, learning rate η

Server executes:

1: initialize the global classification head parameter h^g; initialize the local pre-trained model h_i^l and ϕ_i for the i-th client

2: for each round t = 1,2,... do

3:     $S_t \leftarrow$ (random set of m clients)

4:     for each client $i \in S_t$ in parallel do:

5:         $h_i^{g(t+1)} \leftarrow$ ClientUpdate(i, $h^{g(t)}, \phi_i$)

6:         $h^{g(t+1)} \leftarrow \dfrac{1}{m} \sum\limits_{i=1}^{m} h_i^{g(t+1)}$

ClientUpdate(i, h_i^g, ϕ_i):

7:     client m set $h_i^{g(t+1)} \leftarrow h_i^{g(t)}$

8:     for s = 1 to k do

9:         $h_i^{g(t+1)} \leftarrow h_i^{g(t+1)} - \eta \nabla f(h_i^{g(t+1)}, \phi_i)$

10:    return global classification head $h_i^{g(t+1)}$ to server

---

$h^{g(t)}$ to $h^{g(t+1)}$ using gradient-based methods. After a fixed number of local updates, the client sends $h^{g(t+1)}$ back to the server, where all models are aggregates by averaging.

The central concept of FedLP involves integrating the linear probing method from large model fine-tuning into federated optimization. This integration aims to reduce computational costs while maintaining the feature extraction capabilities of pre-trained models on local data. In traditional federated learning approaches, following each round of updates, the local feature extractor becomes fully encapsulated by the aggregated model. However, the feature extractor of the aggregated model tends to underperform on clients experiencing significant data distribution shifts. This phenomenon results in local model biases and further deterioration in the performance of the aggregated model. By preserving the local feature extractor, we can alleviate local model biases, thereby enhancing the algorithm's resilience to heterogeneous data.

4.2 Theoretical Analysis

This paper trys to demonstrate through an intuitive approach that training the classification head using linear probing is better than directly fine-tuning the entire model in federated learning. Refer to [5], assuming the feature extractor parameters of the pre-trained model initialized by the client k are w_0, and the parameters obtained after several rounds of local training are denoted as w^k, with the optimal feature extractor parameters denoted as w^*. Let f denote the function that maps samples to feature vectors based on the feature extractor parameters. According to the triangle inequality, we can derive the following equation:

$$E_{X_k}[||f(w_k; X_k) - f(w^*; X_k)||]$$
$$\leq E_{X_k}[||f(w_0; X_k) - f(w^*; X_k)||] + E_{X_k}[||f(w_k; X_k) - f(w_0; X_k)||] \tag{3}$$

Paper [15] argues that the second term on the right-hand side of the equation has an upper bound, and this upper bound depends on the quality of the classification head. For some constant c > 0, we have:

$$E_{X_k}[||f(w_k; X_k) - f(w_0; X_k)||]$$
$$\leq c \cdot E_{(X_k, Y_k)}[||e_{Y_k} - F(w_0, v; X_k)||] \tag{4}$$

where e is the standard basis. This equation indicates that when choosing a better classification head v, the upper bound of $E_{X_k}[||f(w_k; X_k) - f(w_0; X_k)||]$ will be smaller, thereby reducing the distance to the optimal. Therefore, using the classification head obtained by FedLP may lead to faster convergence compared to randomly initialized classification heads.

5 Simulation Results

We use a simple CNN as the training network. It is composed of the following module: a convolutional layer of 16 units, a maximum pooling layer of 2×2, a convolutional layer of 32 units, a maximum pooling layer of 2×2, and a fully connected linear classification head. Each convolution layer uses the convolution kernel of with a stride of 1 and a padding of 2.

The MNIST dataset, consisting of 60,000 training images and 10,000 test images, is initially transformed into a non-IID format by partitioning the training dataset into multiple fragments. Each fragment contains images with the same labels, and two such fragments are assigned to each client for training. Clients are limited to learning only the results associated with two labels, without access to training samples of other data, thus enabling a more realistic emulation of federated learning datasets.

Following this, the model is subjected to testing on a conventional dataset containing grayscale images. Prior to training, normalization is applied to each image pixel in both the training and test datasets by subtracting the mean and dividing by the sample variance. This normalization process is implemented to accelerate the model's convergence rate.

Table 2. Experimental results

Algorithm	Round	Acc
LP	234	0.88
FT	102	0.98
FedNCM + FT	70	0.9721
FedLP + FT	65	0.9887

LP, FT and FedNCM + FT [12] are used to compare with our method. The experimental results are shown in Table 2, comparing the communication round (Round) and accuracy (Acc). The sampling rate of clients is 0.25 for both. In our algorithm, the training model of federated learning uses convolutional neural network. FedLP + FT outperforms the other three methods in terms of both communication rounds and accuracy.

6 Conclusion

This paper proposes a new federated learning method called FedLP + FT. This method adopts a two-stage strategy: in the first stage training the classification head using linear probing, and in the second stage model fine-tuning is performed. We designed different experiments to compare the accuracy, total communication on the Non-IID MNIST dataset. The experimental results show that the FedLP + FT proposed in this paper has higher accuracy and lower communication than other methods.

Acknowledgments. This research is funded by the 2022 Central University of Finance and Economics Education and Teaching Reform Fund (No. 2022ZXJG35), Emerging Interdisciplinary Project of CUFE, the National Natural Science Foundation of China (No. 62372493).

References

1. Zhou, C., Sun, Y., Wang, D., et al.: A review of federated learning research. J. Cybersecurity Inf. Secur. **7**(05), 77-92.XU J, F., GLICKSBERG B S, S., SU C, T.: Federated Learning for Healthcare Informatics. J Healthcare Inform Res **5**, 1–19 (2021).
2. McMahan, B., Moore, E., Ramage, D., et al.: Communication-efficient learning of deep networks from decentralized data. In: Artificial intelligence and statistics, pp. 1273–1282. PMLR (2017)
3. Li, T., Sahu, A.K., Talwalkar, A., et al.: Federated learning: challenges, methods, and future directions. IEEE Signal Process. Mag. **37**(3), 50–60 (2020)
4. Nguyen, J., Wang, J., Malik, K., et al.: Where to begin? On the impact of pre-training and initialization in federated learning. arXiv preprint arXiv:2206.15387 (2022)
5. Kumar, A., Raghunathan, A., Jones, R., et al.: Fine-tuning can distort pretrained features and underperform out-of-distribution. arXiv preprint arXiv:2202.10054 (2022)
6. Li, T., Sahu, A.K., Zaheer, M., et al.: Federated optimization in heterogeneous networks. Proc. Mach. Learn. Syst. **2**, 429–450 (2020)
7. Karimireddy, S.P., Kale, S., Mohri, M., et al.: Scaffold: stochastic controlled averaging for federated learning. In: International Conference on Machine Learning, pp. 5132–5143. PMLR (2020)
8. Lin, T., Kong, L., Stich, S.U., et al.: Ensemble distillation for robust model fusion in federated learning. Adv. Neural. Inf. Process. Syst. **33**, 2351–2363 (2020)
9. Radford, A., Wu, J., Child, R., et al.: Language models are unsupervised multitask learners. OpenAI blog **1**(8), 9 (2019)
10. Chen, H.Y., Tu, C.H., Li, Z., et al.: On the importance and applicability of pre-training for federated learning. arXiv preprint arXiv:2206.11488 (2022)
11. Chen, J., Xu, W., Guo, S., et al.: Fedtune: a deep dive into efficient federated fine-tuning with pre-trained transformers. arXiv preprint arXiv:2211.08025 (2022)

12. Legate, G., Bernier, N., Page-Caccia, L., et al.: Guiding the last layer in federated learning with pre-trained models. Adv. Neural Inf. Process. Syst. 2024, 36.Chen, J., Xu W., Guo, S., et al.: Fedtune: a deep dive into efficient federated fine-tuning with pre-trained transformers. arXiv preprint arXiv:2211.08025 (2022)
13. Lubana, E.S., Tang, C.I., Kawsar, F., et al.: Orchestra: unsupervised federated learning via globally consistent clustering. arXiv preprint arXiv:2205.11506 (2022)
14. Kornblith, S., Shlens, J., Le, Q.V.: Do better imagenet models transfer better?. In: Proceedings of the IEEE/CVF Conference on Computer Vision and Pattern Recognition, pp. 2661–2671 (2019)
15. Ren, Y., Guo, S., Bae, W., et al.: How to prepare your task head for finetuning. arXiv preprint arXiv:2302.05779 (2023)
16. Huang, X., Li, P., Li, X.: Stochastic controlled averaging for federated learning with communication compression. arXiv preprint arXiv:2308.08165 (2023)
17. Wang, J., Liu, Q., Liang, H., et al.: Tackling the objective inconsistency problem in heterogeneous federated optimization. Adv. Neural. Inf. Process. Syst. 33, 7611–7623 (2020)
18. Liang, P.P., Liu, T., Ziyin, L., et al.: Think locally, act globally: federated learning with local and global representations. arXiv preprint arXiv:2001.01523 (2020)

Facilitating Feature and Topology Lightweighting: An Ethereum Transaction Graph Compression Method for Malicious Account Detection

Jiajun Zhou[1,2], Xuanze Chen[1,2], Shengbo Gong[1,2], Chenkai Hu[3], Chengxiang Jin[1,2], Shanqing Yu[1,2], and Qi Xuan[1,2](✉)

[1] Institute of Cyberspace Security, Zhejiang University of Technology, Hangzhou 310023, China
xuanqi@zjut.edu.cn
[2] Binjiang Institute of Artificial Intelligence, ZJUT, Hangzhou 310056, China
[3] Polytechnic Institute Zhejiang University, Hangzhou310015, China

Abstract. Ethereum has become one of the primary global platforms for cryptocurrency, playing an important role in promoting the diversification of the financial ecosystem. However, the relative lag in regulation has led to a proliferation of malicious activities in Ethereum, posing a serious threat to fund security. Existing regulatory methods usually detect malicious accounts through feature engineering or large-scale transaction graph mining. However, due to the immense scale of transaction data and malicious attacks, these methods suffer from inefficiency and low robustness during data processing and anomaly detection. In this regard, we propose an **Eth**ereum **T**ransaction **G**raph **C**ompression method named TGC4Eth, which assists malicious account detection by lightweighting both features and topology of the transaction graph. At the feature level, we select transaction features based on their low importance to improve the robustness of the subsequent detection models against feature evasion attacks; at the topology level, we employ focusing and coarsening processes to compress the structure of the transaction graph, thereby improving both data processing and inference efficiency of detection models. Extensive experiments demonstrate that TGC4Eth significantly improves the computational efficiency of existing detection models while preserving the connectivity of the transaction graph. Furthermore, TGC4Eth enables existing detection models to maintain stable performance and exhibit high robustness against feature evasion attacks.

Keywords: Ethereum · Malicious Account Detection · Compression

1 Introduction

The fintech sector is currently witnessing significant attention towards blockchain technology, driven by its attributes of anonymity, decentralization, and

D. He et al. (Eds.): BlockSys 2024, CCIS 2264, pp. 26–39, 2025.
https://doi.org/10.1007/978-981-96-1411-0_3

immutability. These attributes have captured the interest of a vast user base and propelled the growth of cryptocurrency transaction. Ethereum, being one of the most influential blockchain platforms, facilitates the creation and deployment of smart contracts, thereby further amplifying its influence in both financial and non-financial sectors. Recently, the widespread application of cryptocurrencies in the financial sector has also brought new security challenges, leading to malicious activities such as phishing attacks, Ponzi schemes, ICO frauds, and contract vulnerability manipulation. In the struggle against regulatory technologies, these malicious behaviors continue to evolve, with increasingly varied forms and enhanced concealment. Therefore, effectively identifying and monitoring malicious accounts, accurately detecting and promptly addressing these issues, are crucial not only for protecting user assets but also for maintaining the stable development of the blockchain ecosystem.

Existing methods primarily concentrate on manual feature engineering or transaction graph mining, combined with machine learning techniques, to detect malicious accounts. However, these methods have some limitations. On the one hand, manual feature engineering captures the behavioral patterns of malicious accounts through elaborate multi-dimensional features, which not only relies on expert knowledge, but is also easily circumvented by new malicious patterns. On the other hand, given the vast amount of transaction data, graph mining methods often rely on sampling techniques to balance the scale of data, which can compromise the integrity of transaction information.

To solve these issues, we propose a **T**ransaction **G**raph **C**ompression method for **Eth**ereum malicious account detection, named TGC4Eth, which lightweights the transaction graph at both the feature and topology levels. At the feature level, we first construct multi-dimensional transaction features and rank these features by importance, selecting those are difficult for attackers to evade for downstream detection tasks. At the topology level, we first capture the most relevant transaction subgraphs to the target nodes by graph focusing, and then perform graph coarsening to reduce the size of the transaction graph. By performing dual compression on the transaction graph, we maintain the connectivity of the graph while enhancing the concealment of transaction features during data processing. We conduct extensive experiments on Ethereum transaction data, which demonstrates that our TGC4Eth can improve the computational efficiency and robustness of existing detection models in malicious account detection, while simultaneously preserving the performance stability of these models.

2   Related Work

2.1   Traditional Detection Methods

Malicious account detection primarily concentrate on contract code [1] and transaction records [2–5]. The former mainly analyzes the logic of smart contracts to determine whether they contain malicious risks, offering the advantage of early identification. The latter utilizes vast transaction data to analyze behavioral patterns of accounts and thereby assess whether they are involved in malicious activities. This approach is relatively flexible but exhibits a lag compared to the former.

Early studies mainly detect malicious accounts through feature engineering combined with machine learning methods. Farrugia et al. [4] designed 42 transaction-related features to detect multiple malicious behaviors simultaneously and analyzed the contribution of different features to the detection model. Building on this, Ibrahim et al. [6] refined the number of features used for detection to six through correlation analysis. Luo et al. [7] employed statistical models, natural language processing techniques, and other machine learning models to detect emerging fraud related to DeFi (Decentralized Finance). Furthermore, some studies combine transaction features with contract code features for malicious account detection. Chen et al. [8] extracted account features and opcode features, applying ensemble learning methods such as Random Forest and XGBoost to identify Ponzi schemes. Zhang et al. [9] utilized account features, opcode features, and bytecode features, and enhanced the LightGBM [10] to detect Ponzi contracts. Galletta et al. [11] combined labeled data from the above three works and merged them to get 673 Ponzi accounts and analyzed the significance of 28 statistical features using the interface provided by the Etherscan website.

2.2 Graph-Based Detection Methods

The design of manual features relies heavily on expert knowledge and the detection effectiveness is limited by their expressive power. As a result, several studies have exploited the properties of blockchain data to construct code graphs or large-scale transaction graphs and combine them with graph intelligence algorithms to automatically mine account behavioral features and perform malicious account detection. Specifically, using traditional software engineering techniques, contract codes can be transformed into data flow graphs, control flow graphs [12,13], abstract syntax trees [14], etc.., forming graph-structured data with variables and functions as nodes, and control or data flows as edges. And transaction records can be naturally constructed as transaction graphs with accounts as nodes and transactions as edges. Bartoletti et al. [15] categorized Ponzi schemes into four transaction patterns: tree, chain, waterfall, and privilege transfer. Liang et al. [16] pioneered constructing a contract execution behavior graph, where transactions trigger variables forming edges. Chen et al. [17] extracted transaction subgraphs and used graph autoencoders to learn account features, ultimately identifying phishing accounts through LightGBM. Shen et al. [18] proposed an end-to-end GCN model based on transaction subgraphs to detect phishing accounts in Ethereum and bot accounts in EOSIO. Jin et al. [19] considered both code features and transaction features, building a dual-channel framework for Ponzi scheme alerts. Zhou et al. [5] proposed a de-anonymization model that integrates hierarchical attention and contrast mechanisms, effectively learning node-level account features and subgraph-level account behavior patterns, aiding in identifying account identity types. Jin et *al.* [20,21] constructed Ethereum transaction records into heterogeneous inter-action graphs and designed static and temporal meta-paths to capture account behavior patterns.

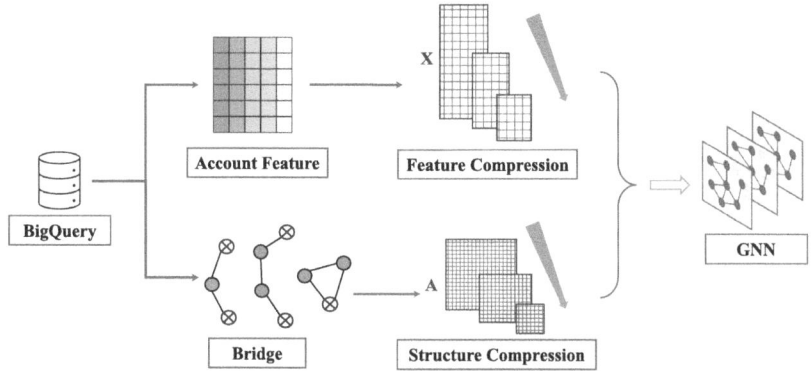

Fig. 1. Overall framework of TGC4Eth.

3   Method

In this section, we introduce our transaction graph compression method, as illustrated in Fig. 1, which assists malicious account detection by lightweighting both features and topology of the transaction graph.

3.1   Transaction Feature Compression

Feature Construction. Our study period spans from 2018-01-01 to 2020-01-01. During feature extraction, we select the intersection of the top 10 important features derived from the three studies [4,5,11]. It is worth noting that while these studies listed all features, they did not systematically categorize them from multiple perspectives. Therefore, we reclassify these features and conduct a comprehensive analysis of each. Additionally, we introduce several new statistics as transaction features. All monetary values in this paper are denominated in Ethereum (ETH). Lifecycle refers to the time span (in minutes) from the first transaction to the last transaction of an account within the study window. Different from previous studies, we count transaction frequency within the lifecycle rather than across the entire study period.

The manual features summarized in Table 1 encompass a comprehensive range of aspects, including balance, transaction amount, transaction frequency, income and expenditure. These features are more extensive compared to previous studies. Specifically, we summary a total of 29 features from seven perspectives. Transaction balances reflect the initial and final outcomes of the account.

Table 1. Summary of manual transaction features.

Feature Name	Description	Type
starting_balance_eth	Initial Balance	Balance-related
final_balance_eth	Ending Balance	
diff_balance_eth	Difference within the Research Window	
total_received_eth	Total revenue	Income-related
max_value_received_eth	Single Transaction Maximum Revenue	
min_value_received_eth	Single Transaction Minimum Revenue	
avg_value_received_eth	Single Transaction Average Revenue	
std_value_received_eth	Standard Deviation of Revenue per Transaction	
total_sent_eth	Total Expenditure	Expenditure-related
max_value_sent_eth	Single Transaction Maximum Expenditure	
min_value_sent_eth	Single Transaction Minimum Expenditure	
avg_value_sent_eth	Single Transaction Average Expenditure	
std_value_sent_eth	Standard Deviation of Expenditure per Transaction	
max_single_neighbor_count	Maximum Number of Transactions from a Neighbor	Neighbor-related (Undirected)
max_single_neighbor_value_eth	Total Amount of Transactions from a Neighbor	
avg_single_neighbor_count	Average Number of Transactions from a Neighbor	
avg_single_neighbor_value_eth	Average Total Amount of Transactions from a Neighbor	
num_received_single_neighbor	Number of Unique Payee Neighbors	Neighbor-related(Directed)
num_sent_single_neighbor	Number of Unique Payer Neighbors	
diff_rs_neighbor_count	Difference in the Number of Payee and Payer Neighbors	
std_dev_received	Standard Deviation of the Number of Payments between Unique Payer Neighbors	
std_dev_sent	Standard Deviation of the Number of Receipts between Unique Payee Neighbors	
lifecycle_min	Account Lifecycle	Lifecycle and Transaction Frequency
avg_min_between_sent_tnx	Average Number of Expenditures per Minute	
avg_min_between_sent_value_eth	Average Amount of Expenditure per Minute	
avg_min_between_received_tnx	Average Number of Incomes per Minute	
avg_min_between_received_value_eth	Average Amount of Income per Minute	
if_sc	Is it a Smart Contract?	Account Type
if_token	Is it a Token?	

Single transaction features enable the acquisition of fine-grained directed transaction characteristics. Life cycle-related features indicate the transaction frequency during the account's active period. Account-type features help bridge the gap between homogeneous and heterogeneous transaction graphs. Benefiting from the performance of BigQuery, the feature extraction method in this paper is capable of efficiently handling massive datasets and achieving real-time statistics.

Feature Selection. Due to the accessibility of machine learning-based detection models, adversaries might analyze the decision boundaries of these models and selectively adjust their behavioral patterns to weaken or even evade more significant features, thereby evading detection. To effectively counteract such potential feature evasion attacks, we adopt a low importance-based feature selection strategy that aims to compress transaction features to improve detection robustness. In this paper, we utilize the gain-based settings in LightGBM to quantify the importance of different features for detection, with the results illustrated in Fig 2. We conduct feature selection by evaluating feature importance and incorporating real-world analysis. For example, the balance difference at the beginning and end of the time window is a commonly utilized metric that reflects the net income of the account during the studied period. Malicious accounts typically transfer assets after being flagged, resulting in a significant alteration of this metric. However, malicious accounts are not labeled in the actual detection, resulting in no significant difference in this feature. Finally, We select 9 features out of the original 29 to characterize the attack based on their lower relevance to malicious behavior, including the following:

- *starting_balance_eth*
- *max_value_received_eth*
- *avg_value_received_eth*
- *std_value_received_eth*
- *max_single_neighbor_count*

- *max_single_neighbor_value_eth*
- *avg_single_neighbor_value_eth*
- *avg_min_between_sent_value_eth*
- *avg_min_between_received_tnx*

Although removing highly important features might somewhat impact detection performance, relying on the feature robustness of GNN-based models allows us to maintain relatively stable detection capabilities. By employing feature compression, we can effectively counter potential feature evasion attacks, thereby enhancing the robustness of existing detection models.

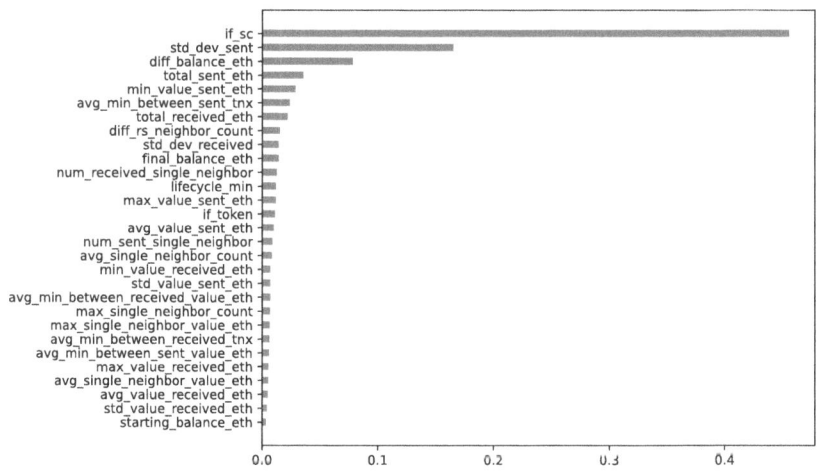

Fig. 2. The importance of the manual transaction features derived by LightGBM.

3.2   Transaction Topology Compression

After feature extraction, the information of multiple transactions between accounts has been embodied in these features, including transaction direction, amount, and frequency. Consequently, we only construct undirected transaction graphs. Moreover, since all internal transactions are essentially various cascading transaction behaviors triggered by external transactions, we only consider external transactions in this paper. The initial transaction graph is represented as $G_I = (\mathcal{V}_t, \mathcal{V}_{ba}, \mathcal{E})$, where $V_t \in \mathcal{V}_t$ represents the labeled accounts, referred to here as target accounts, while the others $V_{ba} \in \mathcal{V}_{ba}$ are called background accounts. We then define bridge accounts V_{br} as those that exist on the paths connecting any two target accounts, denoted as $\{V_{t_i}, V_{ba_1}, \cdots, V_{ba_n}, V_{t_j}\}$. The number of bridge accounts on the path is used to define the order of the bridge accounts. For instance, common neighbors of two target accounts can be considered as first-order bridge accounts V_{br}^1. If a path includes two bridge accounts, then both of them are considered second-order bridge accounts V_{br}^2. Note that some bridge accounts may be located on multiple paths between target accounts and are considered as hybrid bridge accounts. Accounts that are first-order neighbors of the target account but are not bridge accounts are defined as subordinate accounts V_s. Figure 3 illustrates the definition of initial transaction graph.

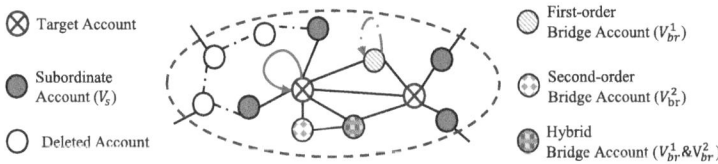

Fig. 3. The illustration of initial transaction graph and different types of accounts.

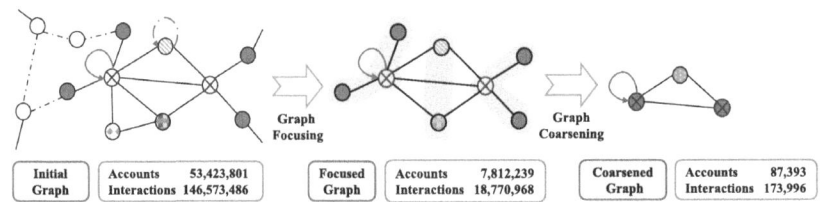

Fig. 4. A framework for graph structure compression, including graph focusing and graph coarsening. The meaning of nodes and edges is the same as in Fig. 3.

Graph Focusing. During graph focusing, we first extract the first-order neighbors of the target accounts, then identify and label the bridge accounts and subordinate accounts among them. To compress the graph topology while ensuring graph connectivity, we retain first-order and second-order bridge accounts among the first-order neighbors. Furthermore, if there are hybrid bridge accounts on the path between any two target accounts, i.e., these target accounts can be connected solely through first-order bridge accounts, we remove the redundant second-order bridge accounts. Ultimately, we obtain the focused graph G_F.

Graph Coarsening. The initial transaction graph contains approximately fifty million nodes. Although graph focusing has reduced this number to the millions, this scale remains computationally challenging for downstream detection models. Further analysis of the focused graph reveals that the importance of subordinate accounts is less than that of bridge accounts, but they are more numerous. To address this, we propose a graph coarsening method via account information aggregation to further compress the transaction graph topology. Specifically, we first aggregate the information of subordinate accounts into the target accounts, formalized as follows:

$$\hat{\boldsymbol{X}}_t = \frac{1}{|\mathcal{N}_s + 1|} \left(\boldsymbol{X}_t + \sum_{n \in \mathcal{N}_s} \boldsymbol{X}_{s_n} \right) \tag{1}$$

where $\mathcal{N}_s$ represents the set of subordinate accounts for the target account V_t, and $\boldsymbol{X}_*$ is the feature vector of account V_*, $\hat{\boldsymbol{X}}_t$ is a composite feature that aggregates the features of the target account and all subordinate accounts.

In addition, since bridge accounts serves as the key connecting module, we aggregate the information from all bridge accounts between two target accounts to form a new composite bridge account, formalized as follows:

$$\hat{\boldsymbol{X}}_{br}^1 = \frac{1}{|\mathcal{N}_{br}^1|} \left(\sum_{n \in \mathcal{N}_{br}^1} \boldsymbol{X}_{br_n}^1 \right)$$

$$\hat{\boldsymbol{X}}_{br}^{2-l}, \hat{\boldsymbol{X}}_{br}^{2-r} = \frac{1}{|2 \cdot \mathcal{N}_{br}^2|} \left(\sum_{n \in \mathcal{N}_{br}^{2-l}} \boldsymbol{X}_{br_n}^{2-l}, \sum_{n \in \mathcal{N}_{br}^{2-r}} \boldsymbol{X}_{br_n}^{2-r} \right) \tag{2}$$

where $\mathcal{N}_{br}^1$ represents the set of first-order bridge accounts between target accounts pair, $\mathcal{N}_{br}^2$ represents the set of second-order accounts, $-l$ and $-r$ indicate the relative positions of these second-order bridge accounts in the path connetcing the target account pair. Note that the aggregation of second-order bridge accounts between target account pairs will generate two composite second-order bridge accounts. Ultimately, we obtain the coarsened graph G_C. Figure 4 illustrates the processing of transaction topology compression.

3.3   Malicious Account Detection

After Transaction graph compression, we obtain a more lightweight transaction graph. When conducting malicious account detection, we input the graph into a GNN-based detection model. During message aggregation and feature updating, we obtain the final account representation, formulated as follows:

$$\boldsymbol{x}_i^{(k)} = \gamma^{(k)} \left(\boldsymbol{x}_i^{(k-1)}, \bigoplus_{j \in \mathcal{N}(i)} \phi^{(k)} \left(\boldsymbol{x}_i^{(k-1)}, \boldsymbol{x}_j^{(k-1)} \right) \right) \tag{3}$$

where ϕ and γ represent differentiable functions such as multilayer perceptrons (MLPs), $\oplus$ denotes the integration function, such as summation, averaging, and maximum. For classification problems, a softmax function is often required for normalization to output the predicted probabilities $\hat{\boldsymbol{y}}_i$.

$$\hat{\boldsymbol{y}}_i = \text{Softmax}\left(\boldsymbol{x}_i^{(k)}\right) = \frac{e^{\boldsymbol{x}_i^{(k)}}}{\sum_j e^{\boldsymbol{x}_j^{(k)}}} \tag{4}$$

We use cross-entropy loss function here.

$$\mathcal{L} = -\sum_i \boldsymbol{y}_i \log(\hat{\boldsymbol{y}}_i) \tag{5}$$

where $\boldsymbol{y}$ is the one-hot vector of account label.

Table 2. Statistics for each type of account in different compression graphs.

Account Role	Quantities	
	G_F	G_C
Target Account V_t	5,880	5,880
Subordinate Account V_s	2,349,274	0
First-order Bridge V_{br}^1	2,668,199	81,513
Second-order Bridge V_{br}^2	3,998,701	730,202

4   Experiment

4.1   Dataset

In this section, we primarily discuss the data preparation process. We obtain the labels for accounts from *Etherscan*[1] and *Cryptoscam*[2]. Since our study period is set from "2018-01-01" to "2020-01-01", we exclude accounts that had no transactions during this period, resulting in 5,880 labeled accounts that had transactions. The final dataset scale is shown in Table 2. We category malicious accounts into four types: 2,163 Phish/Hack, 1,257 Scamming, 18 Exploit, and 4 Unsafe, totaling 3,442. Normal accounts include platform, protocol, exchange, specific projects and applications, totaling 2,438. The total number of accounts and transactions acquired is 53,423,801 and 493,998,644, respectively. Additionally, we present the number of various bridge accounts during graph topology compression, as shown in Table 2. During graph focusing, we reduce the number of accounts from 50 million to 8 million and further decrease it to 800,000 through graph coarsening. Compared to the initial transaction graph, our graph compression method reduces the total number of accounts to approximately 1%.

---

[1] https://cn.etherscan.com.
[2] https://cryptoscamdb.org.

4.2   Experimental Setup

Since our proposed TGC4Eth aims to assist in detecting malicious accounts by lightweighting the transaction graph, we combine it with various GNN-based detection models, including GCN [22], SGC [23], SAGE [24], APPNP [25]. Meanwhile, we compare GNN-based detection methods with machine learning-based methods, including LightGBM and MLP, to illustrate the superiority of the former in handling compressed data. We set the number of layers for all GNN-based methods to 2, hidden layer dimension to 64, output head dimension to 2, training epochs to 500, and early stopping rounds to 100. We adopt the AdamW optimizer [26] and GeLU activation function, with the dropout set to 0 and the learning rate set to 0.05. The relevant parameters for LightGBM include *objective* is binary, *metric* is auc, *n_estimators* is 100. The data is standardized using z-score normalization before being inputted. Model-specific parameters are set to default. The dataset is divided into the training, validation and testing sets, with proportions of 60%, 20%, and 20% respectively. We report the average Accuracy and AUC with 5 repeated experiments.

Table 3. Detection performance under different compression settings.

Features	Feat-29				Feat-9			
Graph	G_F		G_C		G_F		G_C	
Metrics	ACC (%)	AUC (%)	ACC (%)	AUC (%)	ACC (%)	AUC (%)	ACC (%)	AUC (%)
LightGBM	92.79±0.54	92.68±0.61	92.79±0.54	92.68±0.61	89.01±0.87	88.92±0.96	89.01±0.87	88.92±0.96
MLP	88.64±0.45	87.57±0.64	88.64±0.45	87.57±0.64	86.21±0.50	84.07±0.31	86.21±0.50	84.07±0.31
GCN	90.19±1.16	89.61±1.15	89.68±0.95	89.42±1.06	88.06±0.68	86.59±0.77	88.04±0.58	86.95±0.72
SGC	90.24±0.80	89.64±0.65	90.00±0.84	89.30±1.28	88.33±0.62	87.00±0.62	88.09±0.53	87.06±0.76
SAGE	89.74±0.98	89.00±1.01	90.85±0.57	90.28±0.39	88.30±1.66	89.00±1.01	89.63±0.38	88.75±0.48
APPNP	87.04±0.92	87.01±0.68	89.37±0.72	88.25±0.56	80.75±4.09	81.42±4.08	88.17±0.44	87.39±0.56

4.3   Evaluation of Graph Compression

To validate the effectiveness of our graph compression method, we compare the detection performance of ML-based and GNN-based methods. Specifically, we conduct experiments using the Feat-29 and Feat-9 feature sets, respectively, in combination with focused and coarsened graphs. The feature sets are used to initialize the initial transaction graph features. The results are reported in Table 3, from which we can draw the following conclusions:

- ML-based methods are more sensitive to changes in features. With feature compression, the performance of LightGBM on the coarsened graph shows a decrease of 4.07% in ACC and 4.06% in AUC, while MLP exhibits reductions of 2.74% in ACC and 4.00% in AUC. In contrast, GNN-based methods suffer less performance loss, showing better robustness under feature variation;

- Feature compression on coarsened graphs has a smaller impact on the performance of GNN-based methods compared to focused graphs, indicating that the complete graph compression process can maintain the stability of the detection models' performance. However, APPNP suffers significant performance loss during the feature compression on focused graphs, which is due to the fact that the low importance features as well as the corruption of the transaction graph topology seriously affect the message aggregation process of APPNP, so that its retained initial features and the currently aggregated features cannot be effectively fused, which further highlights the importance of the graph coarsening process.
- In transaction graph detection after feature compression, GNN-based models generally perform better on coarsened graphs than that on focused graphs, and in most cases, slightly outperform ML-based models. This indicates the robustness of GNN-based models to graph compression, suggesting that our TGC4Eth can maintain the performance stability of GNN-based models.

4.4   Robustness Analysis Under Feature Evasion Attack

To further evaluate the robustness of existing detection methods when faced with feature evasion attacks, we generate five different feature sets (Feat-29, Feat-24, Feat-19, Feat-14, Feat-9) via two feature compression methods: random removal and evasion attack. For a fair comparison, all the experiments are performed on the coarsened graph, and the results are shown in Fig. 5.

- We compare random removal and evasion attacks, using the latter to simulate an adversary's behavior in evading features. We find that evasion attacks targeting feature importance have a greater impact on detection performance than random removal, with all methods showing a decline in performance when facing evasion attacks, while results fluctuated under random removal. This is consistent with our expectations and further underscores the serious threat that feature evasion poses to detection performance.
- As the number of features decreased from 29 to 9, the ACC of GNN-based methods drop only by 1%-2%. This may be due to their semi-supervised neighborhood aggregation mechanism, which partially compensates for the loss of features using graph topology information. In contrast, ML-based models that utilize labeled data exhibit significant performance fluctuations, with LightGBM's ACC decreasing by as much as 6% and 12% under the two settings, respectively. This difference highlights the superior robustness of GNN-based methods compared to ML-based methods and further emphasizes that feature evasion attacks are a matter of concern.

4.5   Graph Quality Analysis

To assess the superiority of our graph coarsening method over random sampling in maintaining graph connectivity, we conduct a quality comparison analysis

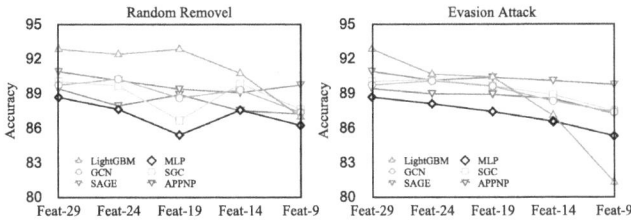

Fig. 5. Performance under feature random removal and evading attack.

between the coarsened transaction graph G_C and a sampled transaction graph G_R. We first define a connectivity metric that differs from the traditional one:

$$\text{Connectivity} = \frac{\text{The number of nodes in the maximum connected component}}{\text{The number of node in the graph}} \tag{6}$$

This metric assumes that a graph with better connectivity should have larger relative connected components. Table 4 shows the statistical differences between the coarsened and sampled graphs, from which it can be observed that, although random sampling yields more nodes, the number of edges is significantly lower, and the connectivity is also much less than that of the coarsened graph. This is because random sampling will generate many isolated communities, which are detrimental to message propagation. In contrast, our graph coarsening method effectively ensure graph connectivity while reducing the scale of transaction graph, which is beneficial for the training of subsequent detection models.

Table 4. Results of the comparison of graph structural integrity.

Indicators	G_F	G_R	G_C
Accounts	7,812,239	94,654	87,393
Transactions	18,770,968	99,409	173,996
Average Degree	4.8056	2.1004	3.9849
Connectivity	0.9999	0.3462	0.9862

5   Conclusion

This paper presents a transaction graph compression method that effectively reduces data scale from both feature and topological perspectives. Experimental results demonstrate that our method can significantly enhance the computational efficiency of GNN-based detection methods. Additionally, this paper analyzes feature compression from the perspective of feature evasion attacks, confirming the robustness of GNN-based detection methods when faced with such attacks. However, this study also has some limitations, including the need for efficiency optimization in the graph compression process and the design of selection strategies during the feature compression process. Furthermore, the paper lacks downstream detection models tailored for the compressed graphs, thus it cannot guarantee that the graph compression method will yield optimal detection performance.

Acknowledgments. This work was supported in part by the Key R&D Program of Zhejiang under Grants 2022C01018 and 2024C01025, by the National Natural Science Foundation of China under Grants 62103374 and U21B2001.

References

1. Shen, X., Jiang, S., Zhang, L.: Mining bytecode features of smart contracts to detect Ponzi scheme on blockchain. Comput. Model. Eng. Sci. **127**(3), 1069–1085 (2021)
2. Lin, D., Wu, J., Huang, T., Lin, K., Zheng, Z.: Who is who on Ethereum? Account labeling using heterophilic graph convolutional network. IEEE Trans. Syst. Man Cybern. Syst. (2023)
3. Chen, W., Zheng, Z., Ngai, E.C.H., Zheng, P., Zhou, Y.: Exploiting blockchain data to detect smart Ponzi schemes on Ethereum. IEEE Access **7**, 37575–37586 (2019)
4. Farrugia, S., Ellul, J., Azzopardi, G.: Detection of illicit accounts over the ethereum blockchain. Expert Syst. Appl. **150**, 113318 (2020)
5. Zhou, J., Hu, C., Chi, J., Wu, J., Shen, M., Xuan, Q.: Behavior-aware account de-anonymization on Ethereum interaction graph. IEEE Trans. Inf. Forensics Secur. **17**, 3433–3448 (2022)
6. Ibrahim, R.F., Elian, A.M., Ababneh, M.: Illicit account detection in the Ethereum blockchain using machine learning. In: 2021 International Conference on Information Technology (ICIT), pp. 488–493. IEEE (2021)
7. Luo, B., Zhang, Z., Wang, Q., Ke, A., Lu, S., He, B.: AI-powered fraud detection in decentralized finance: a project life cycle perspective. arXiv preprint arXiv:2308.15992 (2023)
8. Chen, W., Zheng, Z., Cui, J., Ngai, E., Zheng, P., Zhou, Y.: Detecting Ponzi schemes on Ethereum: towards healthier blockchain technology. In: Proceedings of the 2018 World Wide Web Conference, pp. 1409–1418 (2018)
9. Zhang, Y., Yu, W., Li, Z., Raza, S., Cao, H.: Detecting Ethereum Ponzi schemes based on improved LightGBM algorithm. IEEE Trans. Comput. Soc. Syst. **9**(2), 624–637 (2021)
10. Ke, G., et al.: LightGBM: a highly efficient gradient boosting decision tree. Adv. Neural Inf. Process. Syst. **30** (2017)
11. Galletta, L., Pinelli, F.: Sharpening Ponzi schemes detection on Ethereum with machine learning. arXiv preprint arXiv:2301.04872 (2023)
12. Zhu, D., Pang, J., Zhou, X., Han, W.: Similarity measure for smart contract bytecode based on CFG feature extraction. In: 2021 International Conference on Computer Information Science and Artificial Intelligence (CISAI), pp. 558–562. IEEE (2021)

13. Zhuang, Y., Liu, Z., Qian, P., Liu, Q., Wang, X., He, Q.: Smart contract vulnerability detection using graph neural networks. In: Proceedings of the Twenty-Ninth International Conference on International Joint Conferences on Artificial Intelligence, pp. 3283–3290 (2021)
14. Cai, J., Li, B., Zhang, T., Zhang, J., Sun, X.: Fine-grained smart contract vulnerability detection by heterogeneous code feature learning and automated dataset construction. J. Syst. Softw. **209**, 111919 (2024)
15. Bartoletti, M., Carta, S., Cimoli, T., Saia, R.: Dissecting Ponzi schemes on Ethereum: identification, analysis, and impact. Future Gen. Comput. Syst. **102**, 259–277 (2020)
16. Liang, R., et al.: PonziGuard: detecting Ponzi schemes on Ethereum with contract runtime behavior graph (CRBG). In: Proceedings of the 46th IEEE/ACM International Conference on Software Engineering, pp. 1–12 (2024)
17. Chen, L., Peng, J., Liu, Y., Li, J., Xie, F., Zheng, Z.: Phishing scams detection in Ethereum transaction network. ACM Trans. Internet Technol. (TOIT) **21**(1), 1–16 (2020)
18. Shen, J., Zhou, J., Xie, Y., Yu, S., Xuan, Q.: Identity inference on blockchain using graph neural network. In: Dai, H.-N., Liu, X., Luo, D.X., Xiao, J., Chen, X. (eds.) BlockSys 2021. CCIS, vol. 1490, pp. 3–17. Springer, Singapore (2021)
19. Jin, J., Zhou, J., Jin, C., Yu, S., Zheng, Z., Xuan, Q.: Dual-channel early warning framework for Ethereum Ponzi schemes. In: China National Conference on Big Data and Social Computing, pp. 260–274. Springer (2022)
20. Jin, C., Jin, J., Zhou, J., Wu, J., Xuan, Q.: Heterogeneous feature augmentation for Ponzi detection in Ethereum. IEEE Trans. Cir. Syst. II Express Briefs **69**(9), 3919–3923 (2022)
21. Jin, C., Zhou, J., Jin, J., Wu, J., Xuan, Q.: Time-aware Metapath feature augmentation for Ponzi detection in Ethereum. IEEE Trans. Netw. Sci. Eng. (2024)
22. Kipf, T.N., Welling, M.: Semi-supervised classification with graph convolutional networks. In: Proceedings of the 5th International Conference on Learning Representation,. pp. 1–14 (2017)
23. Wu, F., Souza, A., Zhang, T., Fifty, C., Yu, T., Weinberger, K.: Simplifying graph convolutional networks. In: International Conference on Machine Learning, pp. 6861–6871. PMLR (2019)
24. Hamilton, W.L., Ying, R., Leskovec, J.: Inductive representation learning on large graphs. In: Proceedings of the 31st International Conference on Neural Information Processing Systems, pp. 1025–1035 (2017)
25. Gasteiger, J., Bojchevski, A., Günnemann, S.: Predict then propagate: graph neural networks meet personalized PageRank. In: International Conference on Learning Representations, pp. 1–15 (2018)
26. Loshchilov, I., Hutter, F.: Decoupled weight decay regularization. In: International Conference on Learning Representations, pp. 1–18 (2018)

A Secure Hierarchical Federated Learning Framework Based on FISCO Group Mechanism

Xiaoli Li[1], Yizhe Zhao[1], Ting Cai[2], Lili Jiao[3(✉)], Degang Xu[1(✉)], and Qiong Gu[1]

[1] Computer School, Hubei University of Arts and Science, Xiangyang 441100, China
pcxinx@163.com
[2] School of Computer Science and Engineering, Hubei University of Technology, Wuhan 430000, China
[3] Police Officer College of the Chinese People, Chengdu 610000, China
lixli27@mail2.sysu.edu.cn

Abstract. Building a secure data joint analysis platform for multiple institutions, while protecting data privacy and data security is an urgent problem to be solved. Federated learning provides a feasible solution to the aforementioned problem. However, conventional federated learning frameworks require a central server to collect and aggregate models from all clients. Blockchain-based decentralized Federated Learning system brings huge communication, resulting in low efficiency of the entire system. To address the above issues, we integrate blockchain and hierarchical federated learning to improve system scalability while ensuring security. We propose a secure hierarchical federated learning framework based on FISCO group mechanism. First, we build a multi-layer and multi-group blockchain platform, and introduce multiple regulatory nodes with functions including verification, regulation, incentive allocation, and model aggregation. We also propose a malicious node filtering mechanism and incentive mechanism based on cosine similarity. The experimental results demonstrate the effectiveness and security of the framework.

Keywords: Blockchain · Hierarchical · Decentralized · Security · Federated Learning

1 Introduction

With the rapid development of big data and artificial intelligence, machine learning has been widely applied. Machine learning typically requires a large amount of data for training, however, conventional machine learning generally requires all data to be centralized on a central server for training. Due to data security and privacy issues, various institutions or individuals are unwilling to share data, resulting in data silos [1]. For example, the medical platform of a hospital gathers

D. He et al. (Eds.): BlockSys 2024, CCIS 2264, pp. 40–51, 2025.
https://doi.org/10.1007/978-981-96-1411-0_4

a large amount of patient data, which is a high-value production factor but also the most private personal data. Predicting the spread of infectious diseases and diagnosing rare diseases require joint analysis from multiple hospitals. However, the current situation is a lack of platforms for integrating and analyzing data from multiple hospitals. Firstly, joint analysis from multiple hospitals can easily leak patient privacy. Secondly, there is no fully trusted third party to conduct data fusion analysis.

Some biotechnology companies have developed auxiliary diagnostic instruments for certain diseases, collecting patient data by providing free auxiliary diagnoses to patients. If multiple hospitals use this instrument, the biotechnology company will collect a large amount of patient data, which can further optimize auxiliary diagnostic algorithms and improve the accuracy of disease diagnosis. However, this approach has the following drawbacks: firstly, it can only collect specific patient data for a specific disease, and other patient data cannot be utilized; Secondly, there is a lack of regulatory measures, and the issue of patient privacy leakage is very serious. Some patients may receive a large amount of false treatment advertising information after using the instrument, which seriously endangers the life and health safety of the disease; Thirdly, this approach poses certain obstacles to the development of medical technology. The time from data collection to model updates is relatively long, and the ownership of the trained model belongs to biotechnology companies, making it impossible for hospitals to modify or fine-tune the model. Therefore, building a secure data joint analysis platform for multiple hospitals, while protecting data privacy and data security, to solve the problem of obstacles to the value circulation of medical data, is an urgent problem to be solved.

Federated learning [2] provides a feasible solution to the aforementioned problem. In federated learning, each client uses its data to train locally, and then learns information from other clients through shared model parameters, allowing clients to jointly train a shared global model while ensuring data privacy. However, conventional federated learning frameworks require a central server to collect and aggregate models from all clients. This centralized federated learning framework has two issues: first, the credibility of the central server, where all operations of the central server are invisible and opaque to the client, and the client cannot verify whether its model is correctly received by the server; Secondly, all client models need to be uploaded to the server for aggregation, which requires high communication and computing power from the server. Once the server goes down, the entire federated learning process will be aborted. Therefore, due to the susceptibility of central servers to single point of failure and non neutrality, it greatly affects the willingness of clients to participate in federated learning. Meanwhile, due to legal, security, and competitive reasons, it may not be possible to elect a trusted third party as the central server that satisfies every client. Therefore, designing a decentralized federated learning framework to enhance the credibility of federated learning has become very important.

Some researchers [3–5] have proposed a decentralized federated learning framework based on blockchain, which is a serverless peer-to-peer federated learning framework. Blockchain is based on P2P networks, and all clients can directly interact with each other. Under this decentralized federated learning framework, using blockchain for model storage and transmission results in excessive communication overhead.

Based on the above considerations, we propose a secure hierarchical federated learning framework based on FISCO group mechanism. First, we build a multi-layer and multi-group blockchain platform, dividing clients into different layers and groups to ensure the privacy and scalability of the blockchain system. Then we introduce multiple regulatory nodes with functions including verification, regulation, incentive allocation, and model aggregation, achieving cross-institutional penetration supervision. We also propose a malicious node filtering mechanism and incentive mechanism based on cosine similarity.

The contributions of this paper are summarized as follows:

1. We introduce the multi-group mechanism of FISCO BCOS and build a blockchain platform with multiple layers and groups. We divide the client into different layers and groups, and isolate transaction processing, data storage, and block consensus between groups. Message exchange between groups will be accompanied by verification information, which is trustworthy and traceable. This multi-layer and multi-group framework can ensure the privacy and scalability of blockchain systems.
2. We add multiple regulatory nodes to achieve penetrative regulation. FISCO BCOS supports blockchain nodes to initiate multiple groups, each regulatory node joins multiple groups, one of which is the regulatory group and the others are the client groups it supervises. The functions of regulatory nodes mainly include verification, regulation, incentive allocation, and model aggregation.
3. We propose a malicious node filtering mechanism and incentive mechanism based on cosine similarity. The cosine similarity calculates the cosine value of the angle between the local model vectors of two clients, which is independent of the size of the model vectors, and therefore has better robustness than Euclidean distance.
4. To evaluate the advantages of our framework, we conduct some experiments on some datasets, and compare our approach with other state-of-the-art methods. Experimental results demonstrate the effectiveness of the proposed framework.

The remaining of this paper is organized as follows. Section 2 describes our framework. Section 3 summarizes the experimental results and analysis. Section 4 investigates related work. Finally, we conclude this paper in Sect. 5.

2   Our Framework

Our proposed framework is shown as Fig. 1. Assuming we divide all clients into L layers. Assuming there are a total of $N0$ groups in the highest layer 0, these $N0$ groups called $group-0-1$, $group-0-2$, ..., $group-0-i$,... $group-0-N0$, where the number of clients in $group-0-i$ is $n0_i$; The clients of the layer 1 form $N1$

groups:$group-1-1$, $group-1-2$, ..., $group-1-i$,... $group-1-N1$, where the number of clients in $group-1-i$ is $n1_i$; Similarly, the clients in the layer 2 form $N2$ groups according to a certain rule: $group-2-1$, $group-2-2$,...,$group-2-i$, ..., $group-2-N2$, where the number of clients in $group-2-i$ is $n2_i$. Following this process, we can divide clients into multiple layers and multiple groups based on the actual situation.

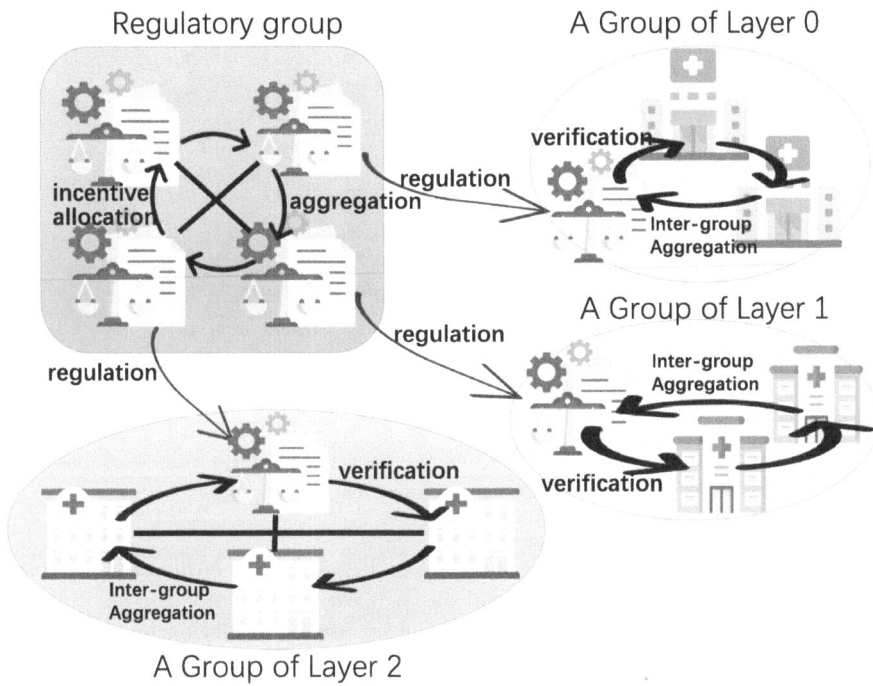

Fig. 1. The overview of the secure hierarchical federated learning framework based on FISCO group mechanism.

In addition, we also establish a regulatory group. We introduce regulatory nodes and divide them into multiple layers, where each layer of regulatory node needs to supervise the clients of its corresponding layer. Therefore, each regulatory node joins multiple groups simultaneously, one of which is the overall regulatory group, one of which is the regulatory group at the corresponding layer, and the others are the groups of the clients it supervises. It should be noted that if there are too many client groups, in order to reduce the number of regulatory nodes, the same regulatory node can supervise multiple client groups at the same time. Regulatory nodes need to join each client group they supervise.

The transaction processing, data storage, and block consensus between groups are isolated from each other. Each group independently executes the consensus process to maintain their own transactions and data unaffected by other groups, thereby achieving better privacy isolation. Cross-group message exchange carries verification information, which is trustworthy and traceable. Meanwhile, transactions between different groups can be executed in parallel, improving efficiency. The functions of regulatory nodes mainly include verification, regulation, incentive allocation, and model aggregation. The introduction of regulatory nodes can not only provide cross-group penetration supervision, but also greatly improve the efficiency of model aggregation.

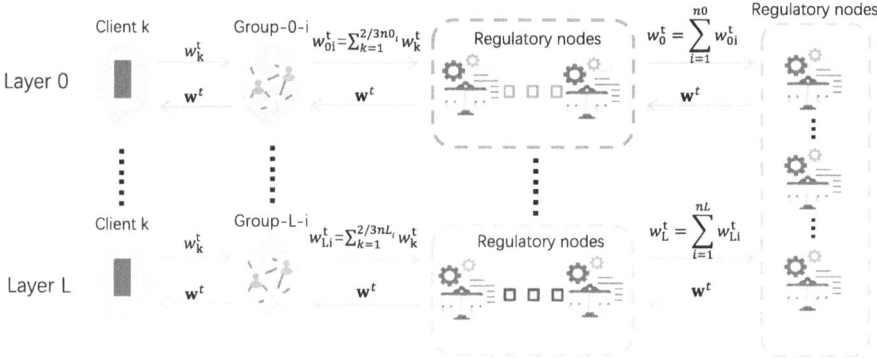

Fig. 2. The overview of The secure hierarchical federated learning framework based on FISCO group mechanism.

The process of the framework is shown as Fig. 2. In the t-th round of global iteration, each client first trains based on their own local data. For example, in the L layer, client k obtains the local model w_k^t after completing local training. The group $group - L - i$ where client k is located aggregates local models within the group for a certain period of time to obtain the model w_{Li}^t of the group. Due to the presence of a supervisory node within each group, this supervisory node can verify and supervise the effectiveness of model aggregation within the group. Afterwards, all the regulatory nodes of layer L also form a group, which will initiate inter-group messaging mechanisms, collect models of each group recorded by each regulatory node, and aggregate them again to obtain a new model w_L^t. After updating the models at all layers, one regulatory node is selected from each layer to form a global regulatory group, which is then aggregated again to form the global model $\mathbf{w}^t$. At the same time, the global regulatory group will also allocate rewards based on the contributions of each group. The detailed process introduction is as follows.

2.1 Local Training on the Client

Let's take client k as an example to introduce the local training process on the client side. The local loss function for client k is:

$$h_k\left(w_k^t, \mathbf{w}^t\right) = F_k\left(w_k^t\right) + \beta\left\|w_k^t - \mathbf{w}^t\right\|^2. \tag{1}$$

Assuming that client k participates in training in the t-th round and receives the global model $\mathbf{w}^t$ sent by the supervising node in its group. Client k first replaces its local model w_k^t with the global model $\mathbf{w}^t$, and then calculates about local updates:

$$\Delta h_k\left(w_k^t, \mathbf{w}^t\right) = \Delta F_k\left(w_k^t\right) + \beta\left(w_k^t - \mathbf{w}^t\right), \tag{2}$$

where ΔF_k is the gradient update obtained by client k using a random gradient descent algorithm to train the model w_k^t once based on local data. Equation 2 shows that while the client updates the local model, it also constrains the local model update not to deviate too far from the global model.

2.2   Model Aggregation of Inter-group

Clients within the same group can reach consensus based on the Practical Byzantine Fault Tolerance (PBFT) consensus mechanism without a central server, aggregating local models of clients within the group to generate local models.

Let's take group $group - L - i$ as an example to illustrate. In the t-th round of global iteration, after a certain period of time, the clients within the group complete local training, and the aggregated smart contracts within the group are triggered. In order to avoid dishonesty or attacks on some clients, whose uploaded local models deviate too far from the local models of other clients, forcing the aggregated models to move away from the global model and reducing the overall efficiency of the group, we have set up a malicious node filtering mechanism based on cosine similarity within the group.

The working principle of PBFT is to assume that less than one-third of blockchain nodes are dishonest, which means there should be at least $n = 3f + 1$ nodes to tolerate f malicious nodes. First, we use cosine similarity to measure the distance between the local models provided by two nodes. Because cosine similarity calculates the cosine value of the angle between two local models, which is independent of the model size; And Euclidean distance refers to the true distance between two points in high-dimensional space. The value of Euclidean distance is influenced by the dimension, and cosine similarity remains the same in high dimensions, with similarity being equal to 1 in low dimensions. Therefore, cosine similarity is more robust than Euclidean distance. Let $Cos\left(w_i, w_j\right) = \frac{w_i \cdot w_j}{|w_i||w_j|}$ be the cosine similarity of the local model between node i and node j within the group. For any node i, we use $i \longrightarrow j$ to indicate that node j belongs to the $n - f - 2$ nodes closest to node i. Then, we define the score $s(i) = \sum_{i \rightarrow j} Cos\left(w_i, w_j\right)$, and select the node with the lowest score and the local models of its nearest $n - f - 2$ nodes. We consider the local models of these nodes to be acceptable, and then generate a model within the group by averaging these local models: $w_{Li}^t = \sum_{k=1}^{2/3nL_i} w_k^t$.

2.3   Global Model Aggregation

In order to complete global model aggregation, we need two steps: model aggregation for groups on the same layer, and global model generation. Due to the fact that groups are independent of each other, we need to communicate messages between groups. Fisco has a strategy of on chain event subscription and notification, which can achieve fast message delivery between groups. Due to the presence of a supervisory node within each group, the supervisory nodes have the modes of client groups. Meanwhile, all the regulatory nodes of the corresponding layer form a group, the regulatory group sends an event subscription to all the client groups it supervises. Once a client group completes model aggregation, the supervisory nodes within the client group will record the generated model to its respective regulatory group. After the regulatory group of layer L collects models of client groups recorded by the regulatory node, the regulatory group aggregates them to obtain a new model $w_{\mathrm{L}}^{\mathrm{t}} = \sum_{i=1}^{nL} w_{\mathrm{L}i}^{\mathrm{t}}$.

One regulatory node is selected from each layer to form a global regulatory group, and the global regulatory group sends an event subscription to the regulatory groups of all layers. After the regulatory groups obtain new models, the selected regulatory node will record the models to the global regulatory group. Then, the global model is $\mathbf{w}^{\mathrm{t}} = \sum_{i=1}^{L} w_{\mathrm{L}}^{\mathrm{t}}$.

2.4   Incentive Mechanism

In order to encourage clients to participate in federated learning training, we need to set up a fair incentive mechanism, where nodes with greater contributions receive greater benefits. As mentioned above, cosine similarity is used to filter malicious nodes. Here, cosine similarity is used to motivate clients. The closer the client's model is to the global model, the greater the client's contribution, and the greater the profit should be.

Assuming that in the t-th round of the global model, the total return is $R(t)$. Firstly, the regulatory group needs to calculate the benefits of each provincial hospital model. Firstly, the global regulatory group calculates the benefits of each layer: $\mathrm{R_L(t)} = Cos\left(w_{\mathrm{L}}, \mathbf{w}\right) \frac{\mathrm{R(t)}}{\sum_{l=1}^{\mathrm{L}} Cos(w_l.\mathbf{w})}$ Afterwards, the global regulatory group sends the corresponding benefits to the regulatory groups at each layer through inter-group message notifications. Regulatory groups calculate the benefits of all groups that provide models: $\mathrm{R_{Li}(t)} = Cos\left(w_{\mathrm{L}i}, \mathbf{w}\right) \frac{\mathrm{R_L(t)}}{\sum_{i=1}^{\mathrm{nL}} Cos(w_i.\mathbf{w})}$ Then, the regulatory group sends the corresponding benefits to each client group through inter-group message notifications. After the client group receives the benefits, it calculates the benefits for each client: $\mathrm{R_k(t)} = Cos\left(w_{\mathrm{k}}, \mathbf{w}\right) \frac{\mathrm{R_{Li}(t)}}{\sum_{k=1}^{\mathrm{nL_i}} Cos(w_k.\mathbf{w})}$

3   Evaluation

3.1   Experiment Setting

We generated 500 clients and divided them into 10 groups, each with 50 clients. These groups are distributed in three different levels, with 3 groups in layer 0, 3 groups in layer 1, and 4 groups in layer 2. There is one regulatory node in each group, with a total of 10 regulatory nodes. Regulatory nodes $1 \sim 4$ supervise four groups in the second layer, regulatory nodes $5 \sim 7$ supervise three groups in the first layer, and regulatory nodes $8 \sim 10$ supervise three groups in layer 0. At the same time, each layer of regulatory nodes forms a hierarchical regulatory group, and all regulatory nodes form the global regulatory group.

The dataset is Mnist, which consists of a series of 28×28 pixel-sized grayscale images, each representing one of the ten digits from 0 to 9. Each image has a corresponding label that represents the number represented by the image. The dataset is divided into a training set and a testing set, with the training set containing 60000 images and the testing set containing 10000 images. The MNIST dataset has been preprocessed and the pixel value range of the images has been normalized to 0–1. We divide the dataset into different parts and assign them to each client. Mnist-IID represents that the labels and quantities of the dataset are evenly distributed to each client. Mnist-NonIID means that we divided the data into three layers based on labels, with different labels for each layer and varying sample sizes for each group in each layer.

3.2   Experiments Result Analysis

Figure 3 shows the testing accuracies of FedAvg and SHierFAVG under different datasets, the horizontal axis represents the global iteration rounds, and the vertical axis represents the testing accuracy.

(1) Accuracy. SHierFAVG has higher accuracy than FedAvg on both Mnist-IID and Mnist-NonIID. Especially on Mnist-NonIIDt, there is a greater difference in accuracy between SHierFAVG and FedAvg, indicating that SHierFAVG's method has a more significant advantage on the NonIID dataset. This is because SHierFAVG constrains the client's local model not to deviate too far from the global model, thereby reducing the impact of data heterogeneity.

(2) Convergence. The convergence speed of SHierFAVG is much faster than that of FedAvg on both Mnist-IID and Mnist-NonIID, and the convergence curve is more stable. The convergence curve of FedAvg exhibits significant oscillations, especially on the dataset Mnist-NonIID. This is because in each round of global iteration, only a portion of clients participate in training, and the heterogeneity of client data distribution leads to jitter in the convergence curve of the global model. This indicates that SHierFAVG can slow down data heterogeneity and improve convergence speed.

(3) Security. In the experiment, we set up 25% of malicious clients and perturbed the model updates of these clients. From the results, it can be seen that FedAvg is unable to filter malicious nodes, resulting in the inability to train the global model; and SHierFAVG can effectively identify and filter malicious nodes.

(4) Efficiency. Time complexity includes two aspects: communication and computation. Because all clients can train in parallel, we will only discuss communication time here. The communication time is equal to the amount of data transferred s divided by the transmission rate r. The communication time of a P2P-based decentralized federated learning framework is $T_{com} = O(N^2 * |w|/r)$, where N is the number of all clients, $|w|$ is the model size. The communication

time of SHierFAVG is $T_{com} = O((N_i^2 + L) * |w|/r)$, where N_i is the number of clients in one client group, and L is the number of layers. Because N_i is much smaller than N, SHierFAVG has higher efficiency and better scalability.

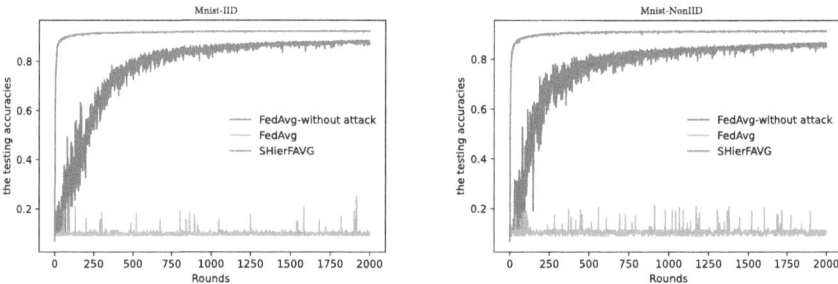

Fig. 3. The testing accuracies of FedAvg and SHierFAVG under different datasets.

4 Related Work

4.1 Decentralized Federated Learning

Decentralized Federated Learning can solve the problem of untrusted servers in conventional centralized Federated Learning. The implementation of decentralized Federated Learning is usually based on gossip, consensus, and communication methods. For example, Hu et al. [6] proposed a decentralized Federated Learning scheme using a segmented gossip aggregation method to improve the performance of federated data training. Lu et al. [7] proposed a graph based distributed Federated Learning scheme, which enables peer-to-peer communication between clients without the need for clients to transfer the model to a remote central server. However, the above scheme did not take into account the security issues of the system. To address security challenges, Kang et al. [8] integrated blockchain into federated settings and adopted blockchain to manage the reputation of Federated Learning clients. Jonathan et al. [9] integrate blockchain to achieve block consensus among participants, coordinate global model computation in an equal manner, and eliminate a single central server in model aggregation. Li et al. [10] proposed the use of blockchain in decentralized Federated Learning systems to prevent untrusted servers and external attacks. However, blockchain is based on the P2P network framework, which brings huge communication costs, resulting in low efficiency of the entire system.

4.2 Hierarchical Federated Learning

In conventional federated learning framework, clients directly send models to central servers. However, due to the dispersed location of clients and the remote location of central servers, a large number of clients simultaneously sending models to the central servers occupy huge bandwidth, causing network congestion [11]. With the development of edge computing technology, researchers have proposed an edge-based federated learning framework [12]. In edge based federated learning framework, clients send models to edge servers deployed nearby, reducing transmission distance. However, due to the limited number of clients that each edge server can connect to and the lack of sufficient information, the trained model performs poorly.

In view of the above reasons, researchers have proposed a hierarchical federated learning framework. The client uploads the model to the edge server, which collects the model from the client and aggregates it. Then, the aggregated model is sent to the cloud server, which aggregates again to form a global model and distributes it to the edge server and client. The hierarchical federated learning framework combines the advantages of conventional cloud federated learning framework and edge-based federated learning framework. It can not only access more clients, but also greatly improve training efficiency. Liu et al. [13] demonstrate the convergence of hierarchical federated learning framework and provide frequency analysis of model aggregation for two levels. Regarding the heterogeneity of the system, Wen et al. [14] believe that only a portion of edge servers will be able to upload models to cloud servers. Therefore, they focus on the scheduling and communication resource allocation issues of edge servers, transforming the problem into bit and subchannel allocation and auxiliary scheduling problems to achieve scheduling and resource allocation schemes; Abad et al. [15] proposed a communication efficient hierarchical federated learning framework that utilizes gradient sparsity and model period averaging to increase communication efficiency; Luo et al. [16] believe that edge servers can access multiple clients, and densely distributed clients can usually communicate with multiple edge servers. Therefore, they focus on edge server resource allocation and client association issues in hierarchical federated learning, and propose an effective resource debugging algorithm to reduce global costs; Wang et al. [17] defined the problem of resource efficiency in hierarchical federated learning framework and believed that the training time of clients is an important factor leading to communication resource overhead. Therefore, they divided clients into different clusters based on their communication overhead and model training ability. The clients in the cluster synchronously transfer the local model to the edge server, and all edge servers perform asynchronous update aggregation; Li et al. [18] proposed a hierarchical synchronous federated learning framework that classifies all available clients based on their computing power. clients in the same class transmit local models to each other based on a ring topology, reducing the impact of the dropout effect; Wang et al. [19] balanced the system cost and model performance in hierarchical federated learning by introducing incentive mechanisms.

Unlike the above work, we integrate blockchain and hierarchical federated learning to improve system scalability while ensuring security.

5   Conclusion

We integrate blockchain and hierarchical federated learning to improve system scalability while ensuring security. First, we introduce the multi-group mechanism of FISCO BCOS and build a blockchain platform with multiple layers and groups. Then we add multiple regulatory nodes to achieve penetrative regulation, the functions of regulatory nodes mainly include verification, regulation, incentive allocation, and model aggregation. In addition, we propose a malicious node filtering mechanism and incentive mechanism based on cosine similarity. We conduct some experiments, and the experimental results demonstrate the effectiveness and security of the framework.

Acknowledgments. The work described in this paper was supported by the National Natural Science Foundation of China (62306108,62302154), the Major Project of Hubei Province Science and Technology (2023BCA006), the Natural Science Foundation of Hubei Province in China (2023AFB042), and the Hubei Natural Science Foundation Innovation and Development Joint Fund Project (2022CFD102).

References

1. Yang, Q., Liu, Y., Chen, T., Tong, Y.: Federated machine learning: concept and applications. ACM Trans. Intell. Syst. Technol. **10**(2), 12:1-12:19 (2019)
2. McMahan, B., Moore, E., Ramage, D., Hampson, S., Agüera y Arcas, B.: Communication-efficient learning of deep networks from decentralized data. In: Proceedings of the 20th International Conference on Artificial Intelligence and Statistics, AISTATS 2017, Fort Lauderdale, USA, vol. 54, pp. 1273–1282. PMLR (2017)
3. Li, Y., Chen, C., Liu, N., Huang, H., Zheng, Z., Yan, Q.: A blockchain-based decentralized federated learning framework with committee consensus. IEEE Netw. **35**(1), 234–241 (2021)
4. Li, X., Du, E., Chen, C., Zheng, Z., Cai, T., Yan, Q.: Blockchain-based credible and privacy-preserving QoS-aware web service recommendation. In: Zheng, Z., Dai, H.-N., Tang, M., Chen, X. (eds.) Blockchain and Trustworthy Systems - First International Conference, BlockSys 2019, Guangzhou, China, December 7-8, 2019, Proceedings, vol. 1156 Communications in Computer and Information Science, pp. 621–635. Springer (2019)
5. Ghanem, M., Dawoud, F., Gamal, H., Soliman, E., El-Batt, T., Sharara, H.: FLoBC: a decentralized blockchain-based federated learning framework. In: Alsmirat, M.A., Aloqaily, M., Jararweh, Y., Alsmadi, I. (eds.) Fourth International Conference on Blockchain Computing and Applications, BCCA 2022, San Antonio, TX, USA, September 5-7, 2022, pp. 85–92. IEEE (2022)
6. Hu, C., Jiang, J., Wang, Z.: Decentralized federated learning: a segmented gossip approach. arXiv preprint arXiv:1908.07782 (2019)
7. Lu, S., Zhang, Y., Wang, Y.: Decentralized federated learning for electronic health records. In: 54th Annual Conference on Information Sciences and Systems, CISS 2020, Princeton, NJ, USA, March 18-20, 2020, pp. 1–5. IEEE (2020)
8. Kang, J., Xiong, Z., Niyato, D., Zou, Y., Zhang, Y., Guizani, M.: Reliable federated learning for mobile networks. IEEE Wirel. Commun. **27**(2), 72–80 (2020)

9. Passerat-Palmbach, J., et al.: Blockchain-orchestrated machine learning for privacy preserving federated learning in electronic health data. In: IEEE International Conference on Blockchain, Blockchain 2020, Rhodes, Greece, November 2-6, 2020, pp. 550–555. IEEE (2020)

10. Li, J., et al.: Blockchain assisted decentralized federated learning (BLADE-FL): performance analysis and resource allocation. IEEE Trans. Parallel Distrib. Syst. **33**(10), 2401–2415 (2022)

11. McMahan, B., Moore, E., Ramage, D., Hampson, S., y Arcas, B.A.: Communication-efficient learning of deep networks from decentralized data. In: Singh, A., Zhu, X. (eds.) Proceedings of the 20th International Conference on Artificial Intelligence and Statistics, AISTATS 2017, 20-22 April 2017, Fort Lauderdale, FL, USA, vol. 54, Proceedings of Machine Learning Research, pp. 1273–1282. PMLR (2017)

12. Nishio, T., Yonetani, R.: Client selection for federated learning with heterogeneous resources in mobile edge. In: 2019 IEEE International Conference on Communications, ICC 2019, Shanghai, China, May 20-24, 2019, pp. 1–7. IEEE (2019)

13. Liu, L., Zhang, J., Song, S., Letaief, K.B.: Client-edge-cloud hierarchical federated learning. In: 2020 IEEE International Conference on Communications, ICC 2020, Dublin, Ireland, June 7-11, 2020, pp. 1–6. IEEE (2020)

14. Wen, W., Yang, H.H., Xia, W., Quek, T.Q.S.: Towards fast and energy-efficient hierarchical federated edge learning: a joint design for helper scheduling and resource allocation. In: IEEE International Conference on Communications, ICC 2022, Seoul, Korea, May 16-20, 2022, pp. 5378–5383. IEEE (2022)

15. Abad, M.S.H., Ozfatura, E., Gunduz, D., Ercetin, O.: Hierarchical federated learning ACROSS heterogeneous cellular networks. In: 2020 IEEE International Conference on Acoustics, Speech and Signal Processing, ICASSP 2020, Barcelona, Spain, May 4-8, 2020, pp. 8866–8870. IEEE (2020)

16. Siqi Luo, X., Chen, Q.W., Zhou, Z., Shuai, Yu.: HFEL: joint edge association and resource allocation for cost-efficient hierarchical federated edge learning. IEEE Trans. Wirel. Commun. **19**(10), 6535–6548 (2020)

17. Wang, Z., Xu, H., Liu, J., Huang, H., Qiao, C., Zhao, Y.: Resource-efficient federated learning with hierarchical aggregation in edge computing. In: 40th IEEE Conference on Computer Communications, INFOCOM 2021, Vancouver, BC, Canada, May 10-13, 2021, pp. 1–10. IEEE (2021)

18. Li, G., et al.: FedHiSyn: a hierarchical synchronous federated learning framework for resource and data heterogeneity. In: Proceedings of the 51st International Conference on Parallel Processing, ICPP 2022, Bordeaux, France, 29 August 2022 - 1 September 2022, pp. 8:1–8:11. ACM (2022)

19. Wang, X., Zhao, Y., Qiu, C., Liu, Z., Nie, J., Leung, V.C.: InFEDge: a blockchain-based incentive mechanism in hierarchical federated learning for end-edge-cloud communications. IEEE J. Sel. Areas Commun. **40**(12), 3325–3342 (2022)

Research on Network Traffic Anomaly Detection Approach with Deep Learning

Wenlong Liu[1,2], Bin Wen[1,2(✉)], Mengshuai Ma[1,2], Feng Zhang[1,2],
and Xiaoxun Wei[1,2]

[1] Key Laboratory of Data Science and Smart Education,
Ministry of Education(Hainan Normal University), Haikou, China
`binwen@hainnu.edu.cn`
[2] School of Information Science and Technology, Hainan Normal University,
Haikou 571158, China

Abstract. Network traffic represents the volume of data sent and received during online website visits. Anomalies in network traffic indicate unusual variations in traffic, which are crucial to detecting timely and accurately in complex computer network systems to ensure efficient operation. Existing methods for anomaly detection in network traffic have rarely focused on effectively handling time-series data in the temporal dimension. Addressing the limitations of traditional Temporal Convolutional Networks in capturing local and significant features of time series, this paper proposes a network traffic anomaly detection method based on CAT-BiLSTM. CNN-Attention(CA) extract local features from sequences, while TCN learns abstract and high-level sequence patterns to capture long-term dependencies and hierarchical features. Bidirectional Long Short-Term Memory Networks (BiLSTM) capture long-term dependencies from both directions, incorporating attention mechanisms (Attention) in both TCN and BiLSTM modules. The CAT-BiLSTM model performs bidirectional temporal modeling of sequence features, capturing long-term dependencies and temporal patterns, thereby enhancing the capability to detect anomalous behaviors in network traffic. Experimental results indicate that the proposed method significantly improves anomaly detection performance compared to traditional machine learning approaches, showing more stable and accurate handling of time-series data.

Keywords: Anomaly detection · CAT-BiLSTM · Deep learning · CNN · BiLSTM

1 Introduction

The internet, as a crucial infrastructure of modern society, plays a pivotal role in people's lives and work. With the widespread adoption of the Internet and rapid technological advancements, abnormal network traffic has become a prominent issue. These attacks not only disrupt the normal operation of cyberspace but also

D. He et al. (Eds.): BlockSys 2024, CCIS 2264, pp. 52–65, 2025.
https://doi.org/10.1007/978-981-96-1411-0_5

inflict significant economic losses, and even pose a threat to national security [1]. In recent years, techniques like machine learning and deep learning have progressively found application in the field of network traffic anomaly detection. By comprehensively understanding the attributes of anomalous network traffic and effectively categorizing such deviations, it becomes possible to proactively identify the initial indicators of potential network attacks..

In the realm of traditional machine learning, which includes Convolutional Neural Network(CNN), Deep Neural Networks (DNN), and Long Short-Term Memory networks (LSTM), notable advancements have emerged in the context of network traffic anomaly detection. For instance, in reference [2] , a semi-supervised method for detecting network traffic anomalies, leveraging Gated Recurrent Unit (GRU) networks, exhibited superior performance when compared to conventional neural network methodologies. Reference [3] enhanced the conventional Recurrent Neural Network (RNN) for improved network traffic prediction. This research highlights the potential drawbacks of overly specialized machine learning models, which can result in information loss and overfitting issues. In recent years, a growing trend in research is to integrate various models to harness their complementary strengths and mitigate their weaknesses. The fusion model approach allows for a more in-depth capture of abnormal features, thus enhancing the effectiveness of network traffic detection. Vibekananda Dutta et al. [4] employed deep autoencoders and multiple deep decoders in their network traffic anomaly detection, which led to a notable improvement in detection accuracy. However, relying exclusively on this method to extract local features has certain limitations. Lingrui Yu [5] proposed an anomaly detection diagnostic model based on Transformer and Dual Temporal Convolutional Network(TCN), named DTAAD. Experiments on six public datasets demonstrated that DTAAD performs well in both detection and diagnostic capabilities. Wang Chenhui et al. [6] integrated CNN with BiLSTM to detect anomalies in operation and maintenance data collected from multiple data centers. The experiment demonstrated that this algorithm enhanced the performance of anomaly detection. However, a drawback of this algorithm is that it did not take into account the temporal dimension of time series data. Bai Wanrong et al. [7] employed the TCN BiLSTM algorithm for anomaly detection, incorporating the TCN, BiLSTM, and an attention mechanism. The results indicated the effectiveness of this approach, although it did not address certain limitations of TCN in extracting local features within the sequence. Fanhui Kong et al. [8] introduced a generative adversarial network construction model known as the Attention Mechanism Bidirectional GAN (AMBi GAN), which is based on bidirectional long short-term memory and an attention mechanism. The generator and discriminator structure employed bidirectional long short-term memory with an attention mechanism to capture time series dependencies, but it did not consider issues such as computational cost. Tae Young Kim et al. [9] utilized the C-LSTM method, which combines CNN, LSTM, and DNN to extract more intricate features and enhance accuracy. Experimental results have demonstrated that this method exhibits significant improvements in accuracy when compared to other machine-learning approaches. However, a drawback of this algorithm is its limited attention to critical time steps.

In response to the aforementioned challenges, this article presents a network traffic anomaly detection method founded on CAT-BiLSTM, featuring the following key innovations:

(1)Designed a convolutional neural network CA (CNN-Attention) based on the attention mechanism, integrating the attention mechanism between the convolutional and fully connected layers of the CNN. By applying attention weights to the outputs of convolutional layers, this method enhances the capture and utilization of local key features while reducing the impact of noise or redundant information on the model. This design improves the model's generalization ability and enhances its interpretability.

(2)Integrated CA with traditional TCN. Traditional TCN has limitations in extracting local features, hence CA is used for convolution and pooling operations, capturing critical factors of different local features through an attention mechanism. Subsequently, these extracted local features are fed into the TCN network for time-series feature extraction, aiming to comprehensively capture key information.

(3)Proposed the CAT-BiLSTM (CA+TCN+BiLSTM) model, combining the traditional TCN model with CA. The BiLSTM model learns long-term dependencies in sequences and integrates an attention mechanism within BiLSTM. CA extracts crucial local features from each sequence, while TCN learns more abstract and advanced sequence patterns from these features, aiding in capturing long-term dependencies and hierarchical features. The BiLSTM model weights information across all time steps using attention, emphasizing useful time steps for prediction. This model bi-directionally models sequence features, aiming to better capture long-term dependencies and temporal patterns in sequences.

2   Related Technologies

2.1   Convolutional Neural Networks

CNN is a feedforward neural network initially proposed by Lecunn et al. [10] for efficient extraction and processing of features in data, widely applied in deep learning for feature extraction tasks. A typical CNN includes an input layer for receiving raw pixel data, convolutional layers that generate feature maps to capture local features, activation layers like ReLU to enhance network learning capabilities, pooling layers to reduce feature map dimensions and alleviate computational burden while suppressing overfitting, fully connected layers to integrate features for final inference, and an output layer for producing results. This paper increases feature channel count through multiple convolutional layers to finely capture complex patterns and features in input data, reduces spatial dimensions via multiple pooling operations to enhance computational efficiency, suppress overfitting, and improve generalization ability. The integration of an Attention mechanism further enhances CNN's capability to capture crucial local information, resulting in shorter, multi-channel outputs that provide rich and concise information. The overall structure of the CNN model is illustrated in Fig. 1.

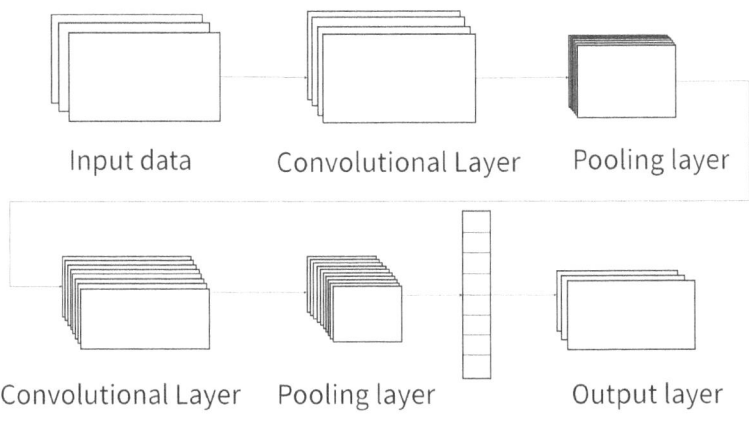

Fig. 1. CNN

2.2 Time Neural Networks

CNN excel at extracting local features but are constrained by their receptive fields. Consequently, Bai et al. [11] introduced TCN as an extension of CNN to address sequence modeling tasks. TCN aims to capture various temporal correlation ranges through multiple layers of convolutional operations while preserving temporal information, enabling a deeper understanding of complex time series patterns. The complete structure includes an input layer, multiple residual blocks, and an output layer. The input layer preprocesses raw data into a format compatible with the model's processing capabilities. Within each residual block, the input data undergoes two layers of Dilated Causal Convolution.The structure of the TCN residual module is shown in Fig. 2. Typically, after each convolution layer, weight normalization (WeightNorm), a non-linear activation function (ReLU), and optionally, dropout layers are applied to mitigate overfitting. The output layer transforms the final residual block's output into a prediction result.

2.3 Bidirectional Long Short-Term Memory Network

LSTM represents a significant improvement over traditional RNN by introducing gating mechanisms (such as input gates, forget gates, and output gates) that effectively address the gradient issues encountered in processing long sequence data. LSTM is particularly suited for tasks involving long-term dependencies,

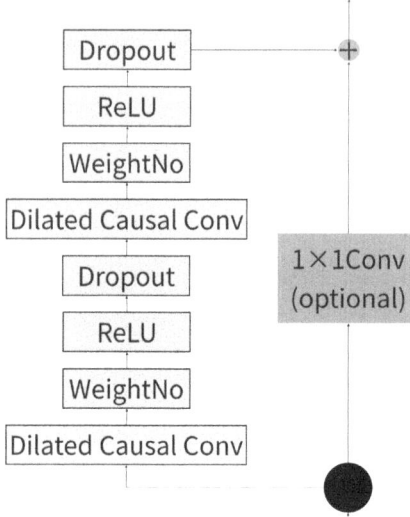

Fig. 2. Residual block structure

such as language modeling, text generation, and time series prediction.BiLSTM (Bidirectional Long Short-Term Memory), on the other hand, further advances LSTM by simultaneously considering both forward and backward sequence information to enhance the model's expressive power. It consists of two independent LSTM structures: one reads the sequence in chronological order, while the other reads the same sequence in reverse order. This bidirectional architecture enables the model to comprehensively capture and understand contextual information within the input data, significantly improving the accuracy and complexity of the tasks it handles.The BiLSTM model structure is shown in Fig. 3.

2.4   Attention Mechanism

The attention mechanism simulates selective attention behavior observed in human information processing. It enables neural networks to focus on the most relevant or important parts of the input while ignoring irrelevant information, thereby enhancing the efficiency and accuracy of complex data processing. Similar to how humans process information, this mechanism improves model performance and interpretability.

3   CAT-BiLSTM Model

This study provides a detailed description of a deep learning model specifically designed for time series analysis, optimized through a series of carefully designed steps. Initially, the model processes the data through cleaning and standardization to ensure consistency and quality. The processed data is then converted into a format suitable for model analysis and divided into training and testing sets. In the feature extraction phase, the model incorporates two parallel modules: CA and BiLSTM-Attention. The CA module uses convolutional neural networks to extract local features and emphasizes their importance through an attention mechanism; the BiLSTM-Attention module captures the temporal dependencies in the data using a bidirectional long short-term memory network and focuses on critical time points through attention mechanisms. The proposed model combines the advantages of traditional models, from local feature extraction and time series analysis to modeling long and short-term dependencies, achieving a comprehensive analysis of the data and effectively improving the efficiency of anomaly detection.The overall process of this model is depicted in Fig. 4.

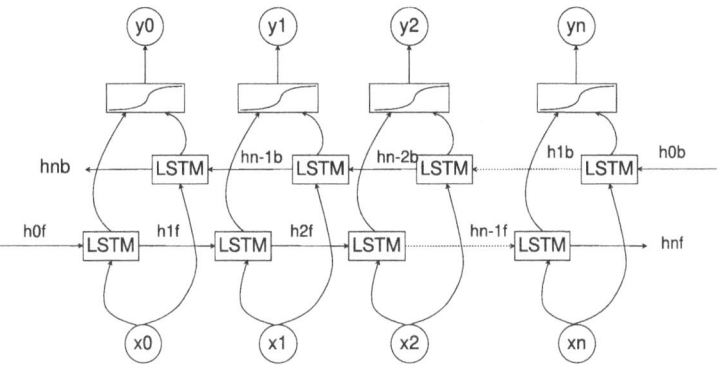

Fig. 3. BiLSTM

3.1 Data Preprocessing

Data processing involves four main stages: data cleaning, standardization, format conversion, and dataset splitting. These measures aim to improve data usage efficiency and ensure model performance and stability. Initially, to eliminate potential biases, data is randomized and any invalid or incorrect data is removed. Next, through standardization or normalization of the data, it is ensured that data is uniformly processed at all levels, thus aiding the model in more effective learning and analysis. Subsequently, the data is converted into a two-dimensional format that the model can handle, which is crucial for feature extraction and subsequent model building. Finally, the data is divided into training and testing sets, not only facilitating testing of the model on new data but also key in assessing the overall performance of the model. This series of meticulous steps ensures the quality of the data and the accuracy of model training.

(1) Data cleaning mainly targets data collected from real-world sources, aiming to remove invalid or incorrect entries. This process involves identifying these

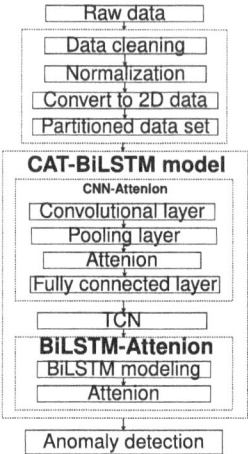

Fig. 4. CAT-BiLSTM Architecture

problematic data points and performing necessary replacements or deletions to ensure the quality of the dataset and the reliability of research results. Additionally, to avoid analysis errors due to data unevenness, data is often randomized to reduce biases that may arise from outliers.

(2) In the normalization step, the L2 norm method is used to standardize each feature of the data, which involves dividing each feature vector by its L2 norm to scale it to a uniform standard. The formula for calculating the L2 norm is as follows:

$$\|\mathbf{X}\| = \sqrt{x_1^2 + x_2^2 + \ldots + x_n^2} \tag{1}$$

Among them, x is the feature vector of the sample. This processing process causes the feature vectors of each sample to be scaled to a unit length. The normalization formula for the L2 norm is as follows:

$$\hat{x} = \frac{x}{\|x\|_2} \tag{2}$$

Among them,$\hat{x}$ represents the normalized feature vector, x is the feature vector of the sample, and | | x | | 2 is the L2 norm.

(3)To better handle time series data, this study reconstructs the original data into two-dimensional arrays, each containing 60 data points, and identifies and marks anomalies within these sequences. This step greatly facilitates the process of feature extraction and model training.

(4)In order to effectively train and evaluate the model, this paper collects the reconstructed two-dimensional data into a dataset and extracts feature data and their corresponding labels from it. The data is divided into two parts, with 70% used as the training set and the remaining 30% as the testing set. This division ratio helps ensure the breadth of model training and the representativeness of the tests.

After completing the data preprocessing, to address the imbalance between normal and anomaly data in the dataset, this study applied the SMOTE over-sampling technique to 70% of the training set data. SMOTE generates new synthetic samples instead of simply duplicating existing ones, effectively increasing the number of minority-class samples. This approach helps the model better learn decision boundaries, avoid overfitting, and significantly enhances its capability to handle imbalanced data. This step ensures the reliability and broad applicability of the research results.

3.2 Convolutional Neural Network Based on Attention Mechanism

The CA model proposed in this article significantly enhances the traditional CNN architecture to improve its efficiency in handling complex time series data. Although traditional CNN excel in extracting local features, their relatively small receptive fields make it challenging to effectively capture long-term dependencies, limiting their ability to identify key patterns and moments in time series. The CA model effectively resolves this issue by integrating the efficient feature extraction capabilities of CNN with the adaptability of attention mechanisms. In this model structure, two convolutional layers (Conv1 and Conv2) are used to precisely extract local features from the data, and two pooling layers (Pool1 and Pool2) reduce the spatial dimension of features, decreasing computational load and helping to prevent overfitting, thereby enhancing the model's generalization ability. The TCN Attention model is depicted in Fig. 5.

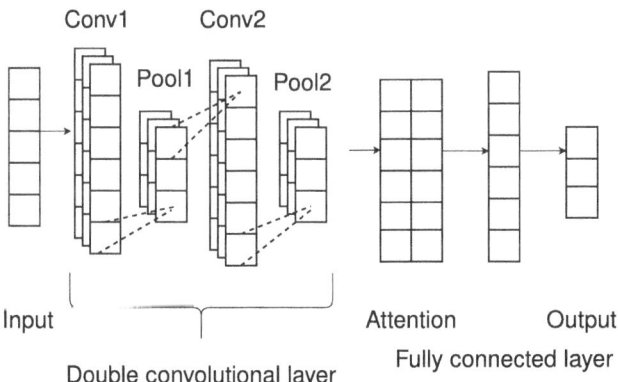

Fig. 5. CNN-Attention

3.3 Anomaly Detection Model Based on CAT-BiLSTM

This article presents a network traffic anomaly detection method based on the CAT-BiLSTM model, which not only relies on traditional feature extraction and long-term dependency capture but also enhances detection efficiency through in-depth analysis of time series data. The CAT-BiLSTM model initially extracts local features from data using the CA model and weights these key features to highlight their importance in anomaly detection. Subsequently, it uses TCN to deeply capture complex patterns in the time series and refines the understanding of time dynamics through multiple layers of convolution and nonlinear activation functions. Through BiLSTM, the model analyzes both forward and backward time dependencies, crucially understanding the interactions between different time points in the time series data. The introduced attention mechanism enables the model to more accurately identify and weigh the time steps that have the most significant impact on the prediction results, optimizing the decision-making process. Ultimately, all analyzed and weighted results are consolidated into a fully connected layer, which is responsible for outputting the final prediction results. Through this multi-level, multi-perspective feature analysis and data processing strategy, CAT-BiLSTM significantly enhances data feature recognition and analysis capabilities at various levels, greatly improving the accuracy and efficiency of network traffic anomaly detection. Additionally, the comprehensive and deep analytical capabilities of the model make it not only suitable for network traffic anomaly detection but also widely applicable to other fields that require in-depth analysis of time series data. The complete structure of CAT-BiLSTM is shown in Fig. 6.

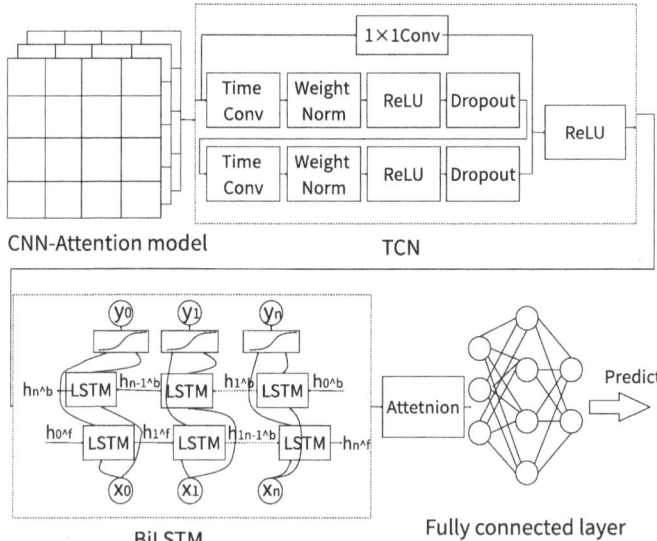

Fig. 6. CAT-BiLSTM

4   Experiments and Result Analysis

4.1   Experimental Environment

The development language for this experiment is Python 3.9, and a deep learning framework pytorch 2.0.0 + cu117 is used to build the model. The model is run in an environment with Windows 11 64-bit, Intel (R) Core (TM) i7-10700K processor, and 32GB of memory. GeForce RTX 3090 GPU is used to accelerate model training.

4.2   Experimental Data Description

This article conducts experiments using the Yahoo S5 public dataset [12] to validate the effectiveness of the proposed model. The Yahoo S5 dataset comprises 367 files, divided into four benchmarks from A1 to A4. The A1 benchmark showcases actual Yahoo production traffic, with each data point representing one hour of data. Benchmarks A2 to A4 are based on synthesized time series that include random seasonality, trends, and noise. This experiment only uses the value feature for training, as features other than values are not available. Detailed information for each benchmark is presented in Table 1.

Table 1. Experimental dataset

Dataset features	A1	A2	A3	A4
Realistic/Synthetic	Realistic	Synthetic	Synthetic	Synthetic
Time Series	67	100	100	100
Data Point	1462	1421	1680	1680
Number of Anomalies	178	200	939	835

4.3   Evaluation Indicators

Accuracy, precision, recall, and F1 score are important metrics for evaluating model performance. Accuracy reflects the proportion of correct predictions made by the model across the entire dataset, while precision evaluates the accuracy of the model's classifications. In anomaly detection, recall assesses the efficiency of the model in identifying actual positive cases. The F1 score balances accuracy and recall, evaluating the model's performance in avoiding false negatives and reducing false positives.The formula is:

$$Accuracy = \frac{TP + TN}{TP + TN + FP + FN} \tag{3}$$

$$Precision = \frac{TP}{TP + FP} \tag{4}$$

$$\text{Recall} = \frac{TP}{TP + FN} \tag{5}$$

$$\text{F1-Score} = \frac{2 \cdot \text{Precision} \cdot \text{Recall}}{\text{Precision} + \text{Recall}} \tag{6}$$

Among them, TP is the number of correctly predicted normal data, TN is the number of correctly predicted abnormal data, FN is the number of normal data predicted as abnormal, and FP is the number of abnormal data predicted as normal.

4.4 Experimental Settings

The model proposed in this paper involves several critical parameter configurations. In the CNN section, there are 64 filters, a kernel size of 3, and a stride of 2. The TCN comprises three residual blocks, each with an output channel size of 64. The convolutional layers have a kernel size of 5, and the dilation rates for the convolutional kernels are set to 1, 2, and 4, respectively, with a dropout rate of 0.5. In the LSTM, the number of hidden units is set to 64. The learning rate is set to 0.0001. ReLU serves as the activation function, and binary cross-entropy is chosen as the loss function to evaluate the model's performance.

4.5 Analysis of Experimental Results

Four preprocessed benchmark data, A1-A4, were placed into the model for training, and the test set was placed into the trained model for testing. The experimental results are shown in Table 2.

Table 2. Experimental Result

Evaluation indicators	A1	A2	A3	A4
Accuracy	0.98	0.99	0.99	0.99
Precision	0.94	0.99	0.99	0.98
Recall	0.95	0.99	1	0.99
F1-score	0.95	0.99	0.99	0.99

To verify the traffic anomaly detection performance of the CAT-BiLSTM model, CNN+BiLSTM, CA+BiLSTM, and CNN models were selected for comparison. The experimental results are shown in Figs. 7, 8, 9 and 10.

Figures 7, 8, 9 and 10 display the performance of our model on four benchmarks (A1-A4) of the Yahoo S5 public dataset, evaluated using accuracy, precision, recall, and F1 score. As a popular model for network traffic anomaly detection in recent years, CNN+BiLSTM often overlooks the temporal dimension when learning data features, leading to insufficient capture of time correlations and thus impacting detection results. Although the use of CA-BiLSTM enhances

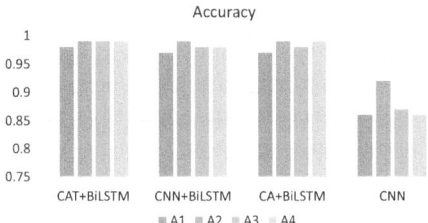

Fig. 7. Comparison chart of accuracy of different models

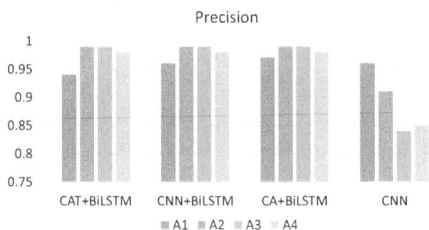

Fig. 8. Comparison chart of precision of different models

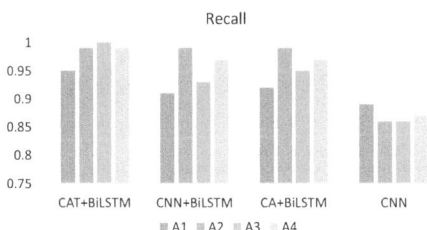

Fig. 9. Comparison chart of recall of different models

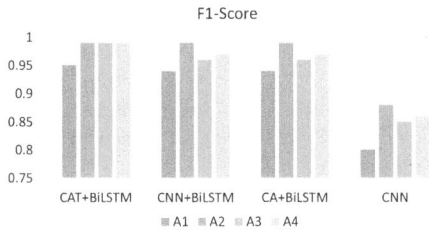

Fig. 10. Comparison chart of F1-Score of different models

the capture of key local features, this model still does not fully consider data anomalies from a temporal perspective, which limits its effectiveness. Traditional CNN models, as a type of machine learning model, also struggle with capturing long-term data characteristics, reducing the efficiency of network traffic anomaly detection. The model proposed in this paper not only considers local features but also analyzes data features from a temporal dimension, significantly enhancing detection efficiency. The experimental results further prove the effectiveness of this model.

5   Conclusion

This article addresses the shortcomings of existing data processing and the limitations of building single models by proposing an innovative approach that integrates a CAT-BiLSTM hybrid model with an attention mechanism. This method effectively combines the advantages of CNN, TCN, and BiLSTM, significantly enhancing the technology level of network traffic anomaly detection. Experimental results demonstrate that compared to traditional machine learning methods, this approach has improved the efficiency of network traffic anomaly detection. The findings of this study not only hold significant practical value for real-world applications but also introduce new innovative ideas to the field.

Acknowledgements. This work was supported by National Natural Science Foundation of China (No.62362029) and Hainan Provincial Natural Science Foundation of China (No.623RC485), and by a grant from Postgraduates' Innovative Research Projects of Hainan Province(Qhys2023-409).

References

1. Duan, X., Yun, F., Wang, K.: Network traffic anomaly detection method based on multi-scale residual classifier. Comput. Commun. **198**, 206–216 (2023)
2. Li, H., Wang, R., Dong, W.: One semi-supervised network traffic anomaly detection method based on GRU. Comput. Sci. **50**(3), 380–390 (2023)
3. He, X., Xing, W.: Research on network abnormal traffic detection based on improved RNN. Wirel. Internet Technol. **18**(22), 21–23+53 (2021)
4. Dutta, V., Pawlicki, M., Kozik, R., et al.: Unsupervised network traffic anomaly detection with deep autoencoders. Logic J. IGPL **30**(6), 912–925 (2022)
5. Yu, L.: DTAAD: dual TCN-attention networks for anomaly detection in multivariate time series data. arXiv preprint arXiv:2302.10753 (2023)
6. Wang, C., Wang, E., Gao, X.: Anomaly detection algorithm based on CNN-BiLSTM feature fusion. Comput. Appl. Softw. **39**(12), 272–277+340 (2022)
7. Bai, W., Wei, F., Zheng, G.Y.: Research on intrusion detection algorithm based on TCN-BiLSTM. Comput. Sci. **50**(S2)
8. Kong, F., Li, J., Jiang, B., et al.: Integrated generative model for industrial anomaly detection via bidirectional LSTM and attention mechanism. IEEE Trans. Ind. Inf. **19**(1), 541–550 (2021)
9. Kim, T.Y., Cho, S.B.: Web traffic anomaly detection using C-LSTM neural networks. Expert Syst. Appl. **106**, 66–76 (2018)

10. LeCun, Y., Bottou, L., Bengio, Y., et al.: Gradient-based learning applied to document recognition. Proc. IEEE **86**(11), 2278–2324 (1998)
11. Bai, S., Kolter, J.Z., Koltun, V.: An empirical evaluation of generic convolutional and recurrent networks for sequence modeling. arXiv preprint arXiv:1803.01271 (2018)
12. Yahoo! Webscope dataset ydata-labeled-time-series-anomalies-v1.0. https://webscope.sandbox.yahoo.com/catalog.php?datatype=s&did=70. Accessed 11 Dec 2023

Hyper-Parameter Optimization and Proxy Re-encryption for Federated Learning

Wanrong Du[1,2,3], Bin Wen[1,2,3(✉)], Mengshuai Ma[1,2,3], Wenlong Liu[1,2,3], and Xiaoxun Wei[1]

[1] Key Laboratory of Data Science and Smart Education, Ministry of Education, Hainan Normal University, Haikou 571158, China
[2] School of Information Science and Technology, Hainan Normal University, Haikou 571158, China
[3] Cloud Computing and Big Data Research Center, Hainan Normal University, Haikou 571158, China
binwen@hainnu.edu.cn

Abstract. Federated learning is a distributed machine learning paradigm that allows multiple participants to collaborate on training a shared model without revealing their own data. However, federated learning faces challenges such as data heterogeneity, communication overhead, security attacks, etc., which result in low efficiency of data training. To address these issues, this paper proposes a strategy to enhance the training efficiency of federated learning data through hyperparameter optimization and proxy re-encryption. A semi-supervised model of federated learning based on generative adversarial network is designed so that each participant can automatically adjust and optimize their own training parameters according to their own data distribution and environment in order to adapt to the data heterogeneity and dynamics of federated learning. Finally, experiments demonstrate that the proposed method can significantly improve the efficiency of data training and model performance compared with traditional federated learning methods across different datasets and scenarios. Experimental results show that the proposed strategy can achieve the same or even better accuracy than centralized machine learning while safeguarding data privacy and enabling ciphertext conversion.

Keywords: Federated Learning · Hyper-parameter Optimization · Proxy Re-encryption · Generative Adversarial Networks

1 Introduction

With the popularity of mobile devices and IOT devices, the generation and collection of data are characterized by distributed, heterogeneous and massive. These data contain rich information and value, which are important for the development of machine learning and artificial intelligence. However, due to the privacy sensitivity of the data, the restrictions of laws and regulations, and the

D. He et al. (Eds.): BlockSys 2024, CCIS 2264, pp. 66–77, 2025.
https://doi.org/10.1007/978-981-96-1411-0_6

constraints of network bandwidth, centralizing these data to a central server for training and analysis not only involves the risk of privacy leakage, but also causes huge communication overhead and waste of computational resources. Therefore, how to utilize distributed data for effective machine learning while protecting data privacy has become an important research issue.

Federated learning is a distributed machine learning paradigm that allows multiple participants to collaboratively train a shared model while protecting data privacy. The basic idea of federated learning is that each participant trains a local model locally using their own data, and then sends the parameters or gradients of the local model to a central server, which aggregates these parameters or gradients to obtain a global model and sends the parameters or gradients of the global model to each participant to update their local model. This process is repeated until a predetermined training goal or convergence condition is reached [1]. The advantages of federated learning are that it does not require data to be transmitted to a central server, which protects the privacy and security of the data, and it reduces the communication overhead and latency, which improves the efficiency and scalability of the computation.

Communication overhead refers to the transmission of parameters or gradients between the participants and the central server, which consumes a lot of network bandwidth and time and affects the speed and efficiency of model training. Security attack refers to the interference or theft of participants or the central server by malicious attackers, which leads to the tampering or leakage of the training results of the model [2].

To address these challenges, this paper proposes a strategy to improve the training efficiency of federated learning data based on hyper-parameter optimization and proxy re-encryption. Applying the method of hyper-parameter optimization to federated learning scenarios allows each participant to automatically adjust their training parameters according to their own data distributions and environments in order to adapt to the data heterogeneity and dynamics of federated learning.

2 Relevant Theoretical Foundations

2.1 Federal Learning

Federated learning is a distributed machine learning paradigm that allows multiple participants to collaboratively train a shared model while protecting data privacy. The basic idea of federated learning is that each participant trains a local model locally using their own data, and then sends the parameters or gradients of the local model to a central server, which aggregates these parameters or gradients to obtain a global model and sends the parameters or gradients of the global model to each participant to update their local model. This process is repeated until a predetermined training goal or convergence condition is reached. The advantages of federated learning are that it does not need to transmit data to a central server, which protects the privacy and security of the data, and it reduces the communication overhead and latency, and improves the efficiency and scalability of computation [3]. The challenge of federated learning is that participants' data are characterized by heterogeneity, imbalance, and sparsity, which leads to inconsistent model training and even negative migration. In addition, federated learning also suffers from interference or theft by malicious attackers, leading to tampering or leaking of model training results.

Architectures and protocols for federated learning are at the core of the research, aiming to design federated learning frameworks adapted to different application scenarios, such as horizontal federated learning for data features, vertical federated learning for different data sources, and cross-silicon federated learning. These architectural and protocol innovations are essential to achieve effective and secure model training [4]. Research on optimization algorithms for federated learning is dedicated to improving the efficiency and performance of model training. By designing optimization strategies such as federated averaging algorithms, federated momentum algorithms, and personalized federation learning algorithms based on attention-enhanced meta-learning [5],the model convergence can be accelerated and its learning effect in distributed environment can be improved.

2.2 Proxy Re-encryption

Proxy re-encryption is a technique used to enable secure transmission and sharing of data by allowing a third party (proxy) to convert one ciphertext into another without knowing the content of the data, allowing authorized access to the data without the original key holder needing to exchange keys directly with the new key holder [6]. The advantage of proxy re-encryption is that it reduces the complexity of key management and distribution and improves the security and availability of the data [7]. The challenge of proxy re-encryption is that the proxy can be exploited or coerced by malicious attackers, leading to data leakage or tampering.

In this paper, the technique of proxy re-encryption is applied to a federated learning scenario for achieving secure data transmission and sharing. Specifically, each participant encrypts his/her own data and stores it locally or in the cloud, and then sends a part of his/her public and private keys (namely re-encryption key) to the central server, which, according to the authorization policy of the participant, utilizes the algorithm of proxy re-encryption to convert the ciphertext of the participant's data to the ciphertext that can be decrypted by the other participants, so as to realize the secure sharing of data [8]. At the same time, the central server can also use the proxy re-encryption algorithm to convert the ciphertext of the global model into the ciphertext that each participant can decrypt, thus realizing the secure transmission of the model, as shown in Fig. 1. In this way, the privacy and security of participants' data and models are protected, and the data training efficiency of federated learning is improved.

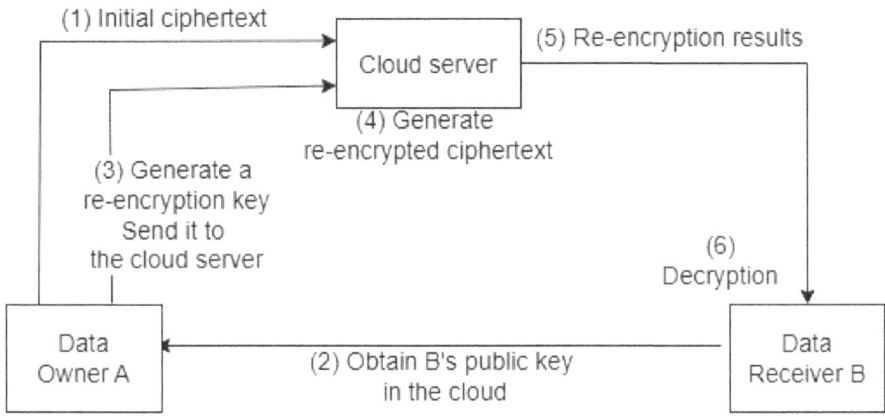

Fig. 1. Proxy re-encryption

2.3 Hyper-Parameter Optimization Method

Hyper-parameter optimization is a method used to automatically tune the training parameters of a machine learning model, such as learning rate, batch size, and number of iterations. The goal of hyper-parameter optimization is to find an optimal set of hyper-parameters that allows the model to achieve the best performance on a given data set and evaluation metrics [9]. There are many methods for hyper-parameter optimization, such as grid search, random search, Bayesian optimization, evolutionary algorithms, etc.

Lattice search is one of the simplest hyper-parameter optimization methods, which divides the range of values of each hyper-parameter into a number of discrete values, and then iterates through all the combinations of hyper-parameters, trains and evaluates the model for each combination, and then finally selects the combination with the best performance as the optimal hyper-parameters [10,11]. The advantages of grid search are that it can guarantee to find the optimal hyper-parameters and it can be parallelized to improve the efficiency of the search. The disadvantages of grid search are that it requires a predefined range of values for the hyper-parameters, and when the number and dimension of hyper-parameters are large, the space and time for searching grows exponentially, leading to excessive search overheads [14].

3 Semi-supervised Model Design for Federated Learning Based on Hyperparameter Optimization and Proxy Re-encryption

3.1 Multi-task Sharing in Federated Learning Collaborative Training

In federated learning for collaborative training, multi-task sharing is achieved by sharing a portion of the model among multiple participants. This usually involves a multi-task learning framework [15], where each task corresponds to a local dataset of one participant. A federated learning model for multi-task sharing can be represented using the following equation:

$$L(\theta) = \sum_{k=1}^{K} w_k L_k(\theta_k) \qquad (1)$$

where, $L(\theta)$ is the global loss function, and $L_k(\theta_k)$ is the local loss function for the first task, and w_k is the weight of the first k task, and θ is the global model parameter, and θ_k is the local model parameter of the first k task.

3.2   Semi-supervised Model Design for Federated Learning Based on GAN Algorithm

Generative adversarial networks (GAN) were first proposed by Goodfellow et al. [12].in 2014, aiming to solve the problem of how to train new samples from existing samples, thereby expanding the dataset. The core of GAN technology is to learn the data distribution of the training sample, so as to discover the mapping function of the evolution of random variables to the training sample. GAN mainly consists of two parts, namely generator model (G) and discriminator model (D). The generator is a neural network model composed of multi-layer perceptrons, whose function is to convert random one-dimensional noise into a new data sample. The discriminator is the probability of determining whether the sample is a real sample or a fake sample generated by the generating network [13].

In this paper, a semi-supervised model algorithm of federation learning is implemented based on GAN algorithm, which combines hyperparameter optimization and proxy re-encryption. The generator G of GAN is used to generate a large amount of pseudo-data, and the discriminator D is used to distinguish between real data and pseudo-data. The goal of the GAN algorithm is to train the generator G to maximize the error rate of the discriminator D. This can be expressed by the following min-max formula:

$$L(\theta) \min_{G} \max_{D} V(D, G) = E_{x \sim p_{data}(x)}[\log D(x)] + E_{z \sim p_z(z)}[\log(1 - D(G(z)))] \qquad (2)$$

Dynamic aggregation is a mechanism that dynamically adjusts the weight of model updates for each participant in federated learning. This adjustment is achieved by introducing an aggregate weight that changes dynamically based on the quality and quantity of data for each participant, as illustrated in the design model in Fig. 2.

The approach involves splitting each client's local network into a private feature extractor and a public classifier, with the feature extractor kept local to protect privacy. The feature extractor shares the client's generator with the server to aggregate shared knowledge, thereby enhancing the performance of the client's local network. Privacy protection between the server and the client is realized through the fusion of proxy re-encryption technology during federal learning and training process.

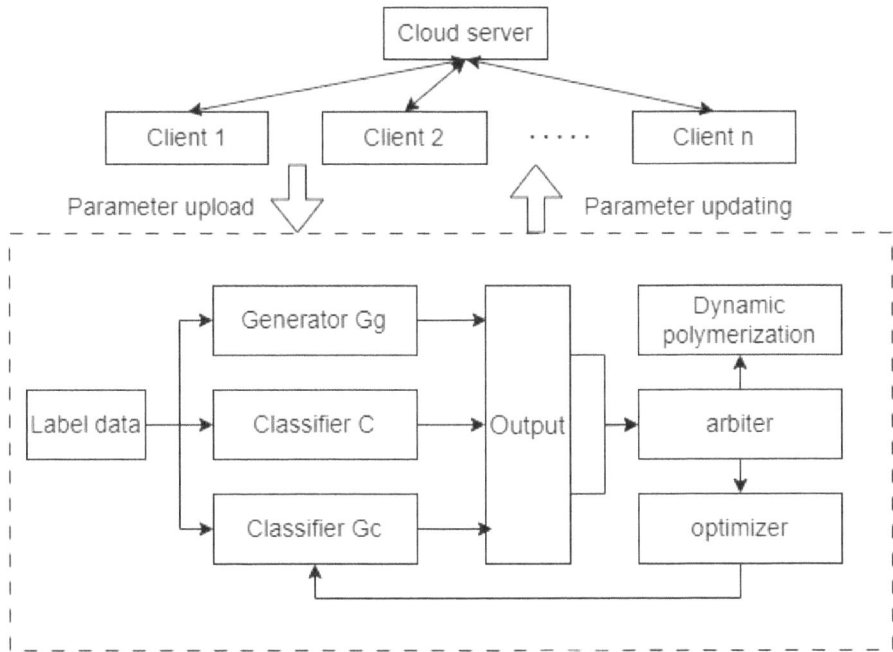

Fig. 2. Semi-supervised model design for federated learning based on GAN algorithm

3.3   Design Flow of Proxy Re-encryption

Proxy reencryption is a secure method for transforming ciphertext. In proxy reencryption, the ciphertext encrypted using the delegator's public key can be converted to another ciphertext, while the corresponding plaintext remains unchanged. The converted ciphertext can then be decrypted by the delegate's private key. This conversion process is carried out by a semi-trusted proxy. Prior to executing the conversion process, the proxy must possess a conversion key from an authorized party. Typically, this conversion key is obtained by the authorized party and then provided to the agent. Throughout the entire process of converting ciphertext, it is important to note that the agent cannot access any information about the plaintext corresponding to the ciphertext, as depicted in Fig. 3.

The specific steps are as follows:Each participant generates its own public key (pk) and private key (sk). This can be expressed by the following equation:

$$(pk, sk) \longleftarrow KeyGen() \tag{3}$$

The participants generate a re-encryption key (rk) that allows the agent to re-encrypt data from one participant's public key (pk−i) to another participant's public key (pk−j). This can be expressed by the following equation:

$$rk_{i \to j} \longleftarrow ReKeyGen(sk_i, pk_j) \tag{4}$$

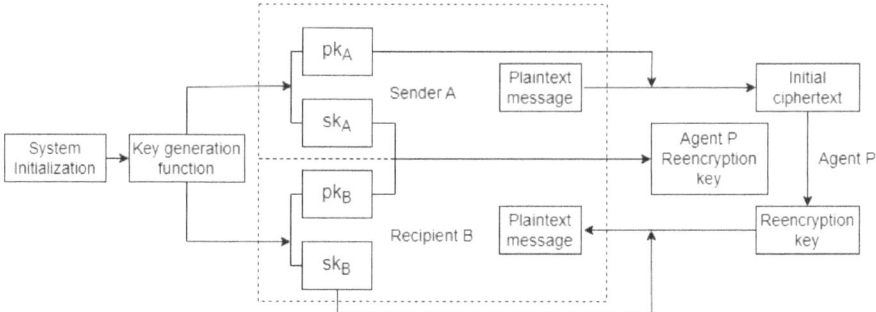

Fig. 3. Proxy re-encryption process

Participants use their own public key (pk) to encrypt the data (m). This can be expressed by the following equation:

$$c \longleftarrow Encrypt(pk, m) \tag{5}$$

The agent uses a re-encryption key to convert the encrypted data (c) into a form (c') that can be decrypted by other participants. This can be expressed by the following equation:

$$c' \longleftarrow ReEncrypt(rk_{i \rightarrow j}, c) \tag{6}$$

The receiving participant decrypts the data (c') using his own private key (sk). This can be expressed by the following equation:

$$m \longleftarrow Decrypt(sk, c) \tag{7}$$

At the center of this process is the re-encryption key, which allows data to be securely transferred from one participant to another without exposing the original content. In this way, data can flow securely through the Federated Learning Network even in the absence of a direct trust relationship between participants [8].

4   Experimental Analysis

4.1   Experimental Environment

To evaluate the semi-supervised model for federated learning based on hyperparameter optimization and proxy re-encryption, the experiments were performed in a computing environment with the following specifications: CPU: Intel(R) Core(TM) i7-10700K CPU @ 3.80GHz, GPU: NVIDIA GeForce RTX 3090, and RAM: 64GB. using Python 3.7, TensorFlow 2.4.1, PyTorch 1.8.0, and corresponding scientific computing libraries such as NumPy and Pandas.

4.2   Data Sources and Processing

This paper selects MNIST and CIFAR-10, two widely used benchmark datasets.to cover different data types and application scenarios. The MNIST dataset contains grayscale images of handwritten digits, while the CIFAR-10 dataset contains color images of 10 categories.

Data cleaning is the first step in ensuring data quality. It begins by automatically detecting and removing any corrupted or incomplete image data. For example, for the MNIST dataset, each image was checked for missing pixel values; for the CIFAR-10 dataset, the image files were checked for completeness. In addition, a portion of the data was manually reviewed to ensure the accuracy of the automatic cleaning process.

Normalization is done to eliminate lighting, contrast and scale differences between different images. Normalizing the pixel values of all images to the interval [0,1] helps to speed up the convergence of the model and improves the generalization ability of the model. Specifically, the mean and standard deviation of the pixel values were calculated for each dataset and then normalized using the following formula:

$$x_{norm} = \frac{x - \mu}{\sigma} \tag{8}$$

4.3   Methods of Comparison

In federated learning research, in order to validate the effectiveness of a proposed model, it is common to compare it with several contrasting methods. These methods include the traditional basic federated learning model, which does not include hyper-parameter optimization and proxy re-encryption mechanisms, and thus can be used as a benchmark to evaluate the performance of other complex models.

In addition, the federated learning model with hyper-parameter optimization alone is used to demonstrate the impact on model performance by optimizing the hyper-parameters only, which helps to understand the role and importance of hyper-parameter tuning in federated learning.

Similarly, the federated learning model of proxy re-encryption alone is used to evaluate the contribution of introducing only the proxy re-encryption mechanism to security and privacy protection. Comparisons with these approaches provide a clearer picture of the combined improvements in hyper-parameter optimization and security enhancement of the proposed model, and how these improvements work together to enhance the overall performance and security of federated learning.

4.4   Semi-supervised Model Evaluation of Federated Learning Based on GAN Algorithm

In this section, we compare and evaluate the Accuracy, Recall rate, F1 Fractional and Training time of the traditional federal learning algorithm FedAvg before and after adding proxy re-encryption and hyper-parameter optimization respectively. The algorithm parameters were set as follows: Global model iteration rounds (epochs) E=80, the total number of participants N=10, the number of participants selected to participate in the training in each round n=4, and the local training rounds of the user party participating in the training e=4. Accuracy results under different methods are shown in Fig. 4, and other evaluation indicators are shown in Table 1.

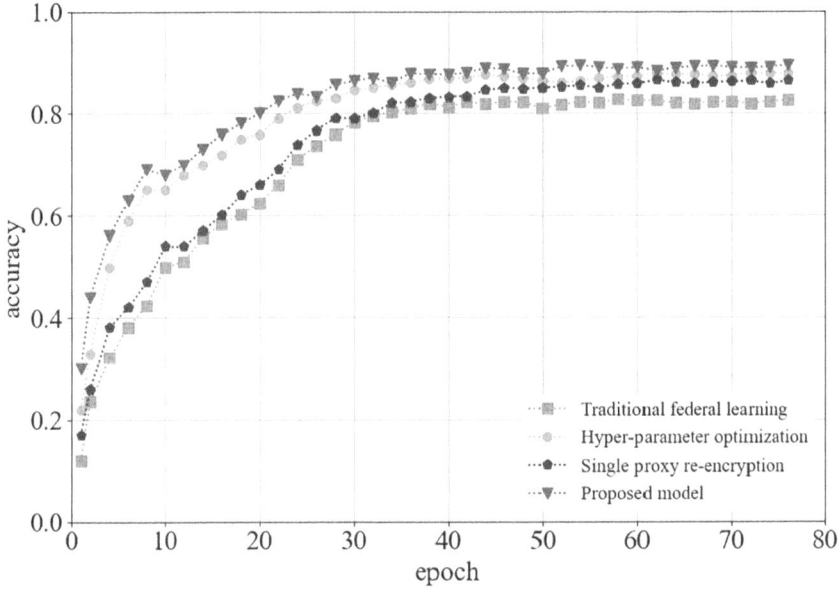

Fig. 4. Accuracy results of different schemes

Table 1. Comparative analysis.

Method	Accuracy	Recall rate	F1 fractional	Training time
Traditional federal learning	82.3%	81.7%	81.9%	2 h
Hyper-parameter optimization	87.5%	87.0%	87.2%	1.5 h
Single proxy re-encryption	86.3%	85.8%	86.0%	1.75 h
Proposed model	89.4%	89.1%	89.2%	1.25 h

As can be seen from the table above, the proposed model outperforms the comparison method in all evaluation indexes, especially in the accuracy and training time. This proves the effectiveness of hyper-parameter optimization and proxy re-encryption mechanisms in improving federated learning efficiency.

4.5   Performance Evaluation of Training Efficiency for Federal Learning Data

The number of communication rounds serves as an important indicator of the efficiency of model training, which reflects the number of communications required from the beginning of training to the convergence of the model.

A reduction in the number of communication rounds means that the communication efficiency during model training is improved, thus speeding up the overall training speed. The communication volume metric measures the amount of data transmitted in each communication round, and a reduction in the volume of communication directly correlates to a reduction in communication overhead, which is especially important in bandwidth-constrained environments. The communication time metric focuses on the time required for data transmission in each communication round, and a reduction in communication time indicates a reduction in communication latency, which is especially critical for real-time demanding application scenarios.

Through the comprehensive consideration of these metrics, the training efficiency of the federated learning model can be comprehensively and accurately evaluated, and the results are shown in Table 2.

Table 2. Performance evaluation of training efficiency.

Method	Number of communication rounds	communications volume	communication time
Traditional Federal Learning	50	100MB	10 s
Individual hyper-parameteroptimization	40	80MB	8 s
Single proxy re-encryption	45	60MB	6 s
Proposed model	30	40MB	4 s

From the above table, it can be seen that the proposed model outperforms the comparison methods in all the evaluation metrics, especially in terms of the number of communication rounds, the amount of communication, and the communication time showing a significant reduction. This proves the effectiveness of hyper-parameter optimization and proxy re-encryption mechanism in reducing the factors affecting the training efficiency of federated learning data.

The proposed model requires only 30 communication rounds, which is 20 rounds less than traditional federated learning, 10 rounds less than hyper-parameter optimization alone, and 15 rounds less than proxy re-encryption alone. This demonstrates that the proposed model can effectively use hyper-parameter optimization to automatically adjust the training parameters of the model, thus speeding up the convergence of the model and reducing the training time of the model.

The proposed model requires only 40 MB in communication volume, which is 60 MB less than traditional federated learning, 40 MB less than hyper-parameter optimization alone, and 20 MB less than proxy re-encryption alone.This illustrates that the proposed model can effectively utilize the proxy re-encryption mechanism to achieve secure transmission and sharing of data, which reduces the amount of communication data of the model and reduces the communication overhead of the model.

In terms of communication time, the proposed model takes only 4 s in communication time, which is 6 s less than the traditional federated learning, 4 s less than the individual hyper-parameter optimization, and 2 s less than the individual proxy re-encryption.This illustrates that the proposed model can effectively utilize the proxy re-encryption mechanism to achieve the fast conversion and decryption of the data, which reduces the communication time of the model and decreases the communication delay of the model.

5   Conclusion

In this paper, we propose a method to improve the training effect of federated learning data based on hyper-parameter optimization and proxy re-encryption, aiming to address the challenges of data heterogeneity, communication overhead and privacy protection under security attacks in federated learning, and the results of the study are as follows:

(1) The proposed strategy, which is based on hyperparameter optimization and proxy re-encryption, effectively addresses the issue of data heterogeneity among different participants in federated learning. Hyperparameter optimization allows each participant to automatically adjust and optimize their training parameters according to their own data distribution and environment, thus enabling them to adapt to the dynamic nature of federated learning. Meanwhile, proxy re-encryption technology can effectively safeguard data privacy, mitigate the risk of security attacks, and facilitate secure and efficient conversion of ciphertext stored on the cloud server.

(2) A federated learning semi-supervised model based on the GAN algorithm is designed to utilize the ability of generative adversarial networks to generate high-quality pseudo-data, thus enhancing the diversity and representation of the data. At the same time, the relationship between global and local models is balanced through a dynamic aggregation mechanism to ensure that the model has a better generalization ability.

(3) Through experimental verification using different benchmark datasets and scenarios, the proposed method has been shown to significantly reduce model communication time and delay while ensuring data privacy protection. This improvement in efficiency enhances the training process of federated learning data and better accommodates data heterogeneity during training, when compared with the traditional federated average learning method. These findings offer new ideas and methods for advancing the field of federated learning.

Acknowledgements. This work was supported by National Natural Science Foundation of China (No.62362029) and Hainan Provincial Natural Science Foundation of China (No.623RC485), and by a grant from Postgraduates' Innovative Research Projects of Hainan Normal University.

References

1. McMahan, B., Moore, E., Ramage, D., et al.: Communication-efficient learning of deep networks from decentralized data. Artif. Intell. Stat., 1273–1282 (2017)
2. Jingwu, H.: Differential privacy based privacy security technique for federated learning data privacy. Commun. Technol. **55**(12), 1618–1625 (2022)
3. Dong, Z.J.: Research on privacy protection methods for federated learning data across data Silos. Hebei University (2022). https://doi.org/10.27103/d.cnki.ghebu. 2022.000958
4. Fu, S.M.: Research on robust federated learning methods for personalized privacy. Beijing Jiaotong University (2022). https://doi.org/10.26944/d.cnki.gbfju. 2022.003564
5. Gao, Y., Wang, P., Liu, L., et al.: Configure your federation: hierarchical attention-enhanced meta-learning network for personalized federated learning. ACM Trans. Intell. Syst. Technol. **14**(4), 1–24 (2023)
6. Zhou, D.H.: Research on proxy re-encryption system. Shanghai Jiao Tong University (2013)
7. Qin, Z., Xiong, H., Wu, S., et al.: A survey of proxy re-encryption for secure data sharing in cloud computing. IEEE Trans. Serv. Comput. **1939**, 1 (2016). https://doi.org/10.1109/TSC.2016.2551238
8. Li, R., Jia, C., Wang, Y.: Multi-key homomorphic proxy re-encryption scheme based on NTRU and its application. J. Commun. **42**(03), 11–22 (2021)
9. Zhang, R., Pan, J., Bai, X., et al.: Agent model for hyperparameter self-optimization of deep classification model. J. Comput. Appl. (2024)
10. Zhang, X., Li, Y., Li, Z.: Research about pruning hyper-parameter optimization method based on transfer learning in geographic information system. Arab. J. Geosci. **14**(5), 1–11 (2021). https://doi.org/10.1007/s12517-021-06465-0
11. Du, X., Xu, H., Zhu, F.: Understanding the effect of hyperparameter optimization on machine learning models for structure design problems. Comput. Aided Des. **135**(5), 103013 (2021). https://doi.org/10.1016/j.cad.2021.103013.
12. Goodfellow, I.J., Shlens, J., Szegedy, C.: Explaining and harnessing adversarial examples. arXiv preprint arXiv:1412.6572 (2014)
13. Jia, W.U., Senpeng, C.H.E.N., Xiuyun, C.H.E.N., et al.: Model selection and hyper-parameter optimization based on reinforcement learning. J. Univ. Electr. Sci. Technol. **49**(2), 7 (2020). https://doi.org/CNKI:SUN:DKDX.0.2022-02-015
14. Lei, W., Li, G., Wang, F.Y.: Improved attribute encryption combined with proxy re-encryption for secure access control policy in cloud computing. Comput. Appl. Softw. **2019**(007), 036 (2019)
15. Smith, V., Chiang, C.-K., Sanjabi, M., Talwalkar, A.S.: Federated multi-task learning. Adv. Neural Inf. Process. Syst., pp. 4424–4434 (2017)

Data Security and Anomaly Detection

Exploring Embedded Content in the Ethereum Blockchain: Data Restoration and Analysis

Mingdong Tang[✉], Xingyu Feng, and Weili Chen

School of Information Science and Technology, Guangdong University of Foreign Studies, Guangzhou 510006, China
mdtang@126.com

Abstract. Blockchain technology is celebrated for its transparency and immutability, revolutionizing trust models. However, its decentralized nature raises concerns about potential inclusion of malicious or illegal content. This study focuses on Ethereum's blockchain, proposing an algorithm for data identification and restoration. We successfully recovered 175 files, 296 images, and 91,206 texts. Employing FastText for sentiment analysis, we achieved 0.9 accuracy after parameter tuning. Classification revealed 70,189 neutral, 5,208 positive, and 15,810 negative texts, aiding in identifying sensitive or illicit information. Our findings expose benign and harmful content coexisting on Ethereum, including personal data, explicit images, divisive language, and racial discrimination, notably targeting Chinese government officials. This study provides valuable insights for public understanding and regulatory guidance on blockchain technology.

Keywords: Blockchain · Data Embedding · Ethereum · Privacy and security

1 Introduction

In recent years, blockchain technology has attracted widespread attention from academia and industry and is hailed as a new technology that will trigger social changes. Simply put, blockchain technology is a new type of distributed ledger technology that can realize trusted transactions without intermediaries in an environment of mutual distrust. Different from the traditional information system, the blockchain system has many characteristics such as user anonymity, transaction traceability, anti-counterfeiting, non-tampering, and the ability to realize smart contracts. It has been widely used in health care, financial contracts, enterprise operation management, data management, auditing [1], and many other fields, showing an explosive growth trend.

The blockchain mainly realizes the reliable accounting of digital events, such as the application of financial applications and asset certification services via the blockchain [2]. But at the same time, due to the anonymous, open and immutable nature of the blockchain, anyone can embed all kinds of information in Ethereum transactions. In earlier studies, researchers found that child abuse, pornography [3], etc. existed in Bitcoin transactions, which seriously affected the reputation of the Bitcoin system. Due to the limitations of Bitcoin transaction fields, a large amount of information cannot be embedded in a Bitcoin transaction at one time. In the Ethereum blockchain, the amount of information a transaction can embed is greatly increased. A natural question is: Is there any behavior of illegal, sensitive, malicious information embedding in Ethereum transactions? What specific harmful information is embedded and what impact it might have? The answers to these questions will help us to further understand the application status of the blockchain system, and then strengthen the supervision measures of the system during its application.

At present, blockchain technology has been incorporated into the construction of new infrastructures in countries around the world. In the future, blockchain technology will become an important supporting technology for the global digital economy. Strengthening the supervision of blockchain platforms and technologies is an inevitable measure for blockchain applications. In this context, this paper conducts a comprehensive analysis of the possible malicious information embedding behavior on the Ethereum platform for the first time.

Compared with existing blockchain-based data analysis work, the main contributions of this paper are:

1) In this study, for the first time, the data embedded in the Ethereum blockchain was analyzed and restored comprehensively (as of the 13 millionth block), and a total of 175 common types of files, 296 image files, and 91,206 pieces of text data were found.
2) The study proposed recognition and restoration algorithms for ordinary text, file data, and image data in blockchain transactions based on feature codes and text-encoding methods.
3) The research utilized natural language processing algorithms to classify the text data embedded in the blockchain and identify pornographic images. The study discovered various embedded sensitive and illegal information, pointing out the potential risks of the Ethereum network and providing robust evidence for the necessity of blockchain supervision.

The paper's structure is as follows: Sect. 2 provides technical background on the Ethereum blockchain. Section 3 discusses data collection methods. Section 4 details the design and implementation of three proposed algorithms for identifying and restoring embedded data. In Sect. 5, we analyze the content of restored data, explore common embedded data types. Section 6 further analyzes the Information Embedding Network. Section 7 reviews related work. Finally, Sect. 8 concludes with findings and suggestions for future research.

2   Background

In Ethereum transactions, the "value" field denotes transferred ether, while "Gas limit" specifies the maximum gas allocation for a transaction [4]. "Gas price" determines the cost per gas unit. Transaction fees are computed as Gas Limit * Gas Price and can vary based on data field contents [5]. The "input" field accommodates up to 700KB of data, while others store up to 32KB. Only the "input" field is discussed herein. It contains a hexadecimal string capable of representing various data types. Images, videos, or files can be converted into hexadecimal and embedded in the "input" field for transmission. Once on the blockchain, this data is immutable. Platforms like Etherscan.io can display text from the "input" field, facilitating blockchain data dissemination.

3   Data Collection

To collect input field data, we utilized the Parity client provided by Openethereum, constructing a local Ethereum full node. Open Ethereum offers JSON-RPC APIs for local data retrieval. Using the trace_block API, we accessed transaction details from 13 million Ethereum blocks, spanning November 1, 2015, to August 10, 2021. This dataset encompasses approximately 3.4 billion transactions. Our analysis focused on extracting content from the input field.

Since Ethereum imposes no constraints on input field data, we identified three potential types: files (e.g., images, PDFs), plain text (e.g., languages, URLs), and "meaningless" content (e.g., random characters, bytecode). Designing algorithms to recognize these types and restore embedded data is essential. Additionally, data may be split across transactions due to gas price and field limitations, necessitating algorithms to address this scenario. We elaborate on these algorithms in the subsequent section.

4   Data Restoration Algorithm

This article uses the UTF8 encoding method in the Unicode encoding rules to decode text data. When the data embedded in Ethereum does not use the sub-encoding method, there will be some "gibberish characters" during the decoding process, that is, characters that are not included in the UTF8 encoding. To filter out these "gibberish characters", according to the principle of UTF8 encoding, "gibberish characters" filtering rules are designed: if the continuous bytes satisfy the UTF-8 encoding, they are kept, otherwise, they are directly discarded. In this paper, for the sake of familiarity, this paper only considers decoding Chinese and English texts. The specific text restoration algorithm is shown in Algorithm 1.

Algorithm 1. Text Restore Algorithm

    Input: Hex string *hex*
    Output: Restored *text*
1: Define Chinese UTF-8 range c_utf8
2: Define English UTF-8 range e_utf8
3: Convert *hex* to byte array *bytes*
4: $filtered$ = FilterUTF8(*bytes*)
5: **if** $filtered$ contains characters in c_utf8 **then**
6:    $text$ = ConvertToChinese(*filtered*)
7: **else if** $filtered$ contains characters in e_utf8 **then**
8:    $text$ = ConvertToEnglish(*filtered*)
9: **end if**
10: **return** *text*

4.1　File Restoration Algorithm

The method for identifying file types based on their hexadecimal signatures is crucial for restoring files with modified extensions. Such as "ffd8ffe0", "ffd8ffe1", and "ffd8ffe8" for jpg files, and "89504e47" for png files. Additionally, some image files have end signatures, like $0 \times 003B$ for gif files, indicating the end of the file. To identify files likely embedded in the data, we employ regular expression matching to detect signatures, discarding preceding data if necessary. Then, utilizing Java stream tools, we convert the remaining data into byte streams. Finally, we restore the byte streams to their corresponding file types based on the identified signatures, completing the initial file data restoration. The detailed implementation is outlined in Algorithm 2.

Algorithm 2. File Restore Algorithm

    Input: Hex string *hex*
    Output: Restored *file*
1: Find *head* and *tail* in *hex*
2: **if** *head* is found **then**
3:    hex = Hex between *head* and *tail* if both found, else hex after *head*
4: **end if**
5: Convert *hex* to byte array *bytes*
6: $file$ = Restore file from *bytes*
7: **return** *file*

4.2　Multi-transaction-Based File Segmentation and Embedding Restoration Algorithm

Considering that a file may be divided into multiple transactions and embedded separately because of its size, this paper designs a segmentation and embedding restoration algorithm. That is, once a transaction that embeds incomplete files is recognized, multiple transactions sent by the same sender after the first transaction are searched. Algorithm 2 is called to restore possible files by synthesizing data from multiple transactions. In this article, considering that Ethereum generates a block in about 13 s, a relatively complete file is restored by looking for 6700 blocks later, that is, all transactions sent by the sender within about 24 h after sending the initial transaction. The detailed implementation is shown in Algorithm 3.

Algorithm 3. File Split Embedded Restore Algorithm

    Input: Incomplete file data *input*; Current *block*
    Output: Restored file *output*
 1: Load header signature *header*
 2: Load trailer signature *trailer*
 3: **if** *header* is found in *input* **then**
 4:    $i \leftarrow block$
 5:    **while** $i \geq 0$ **do**
 6:        **if** *trailer* is found in *input* **then**
 7:            Extract substring between *header* and *trailer*
 8:            **return** Call restore Algorithm 2
 9:        **else**
10:            $input \mathrel{+}= input$
11:        **end if**
12:        $i \leftarrow i - 1$
13:    **end while**
14:    **return** Call restore Algorithm 2
15: **end if**

---

5   Data Embedding Analysis

Using the aforementioned data acquisition methods and data restoration algorithms, about 3.4 billion transaction data were analyzed, and various forms of data were decoded, including 175 common types of files and 296 images. Table 1 summarizes the types and quantities of text data. Among them are 73,180 English texts; 17,053 Chinese texts; 944 email addresses and 831 links. The restored data will be analyzed in detail in the following part.

Table 1. Restoration result statistics

Com files	Img	English	Chinese	Mail	Link
175	296	74163	17043	944	831

5.1   File Data Analysis

The Ethereum network hosts a diverse array of file types, with the most prevalent being images, comprising 63% of the embedded files. Notably, 30 of these images are NFT-encrypted artworks destined for the CreepyCryptos contract address. Additionally, 55 files contain personal images, raising privacy concerns due to the potential exposure of Ethereum address holder information. Detection of seven pornographic images, including prohibited content such as a Nazi flag emblem, underscores ethical and legal implications.

Apart from images, the remaining 37% of embedded files encompass a range of formats categorized as "other types of files." This category includes 72 compressed files, 79 HTML files, 19 PDF files, and a small number of EXE and DOCX files. Notably, 30 encrypted compressed files hint at potential illicit activities, while the presence of EXE files raises concerns about virus dissemination, with two files having an 80% likelihood and one an 87% likelihood, as analyzed by VirusTotal.

The examination underscores the complexity of content hosted on the Ethereum network, posing challenges in addressing illicit activities. From encrypted NFT artworks to prohibited imagery, the diversity of files demands nuanced strategies for regulation and mitigation. Moreover, the presence of potentially malicious files highlights the importance of robust security measures to safeguard network integrity and user safety (Figs. 1 and 2).

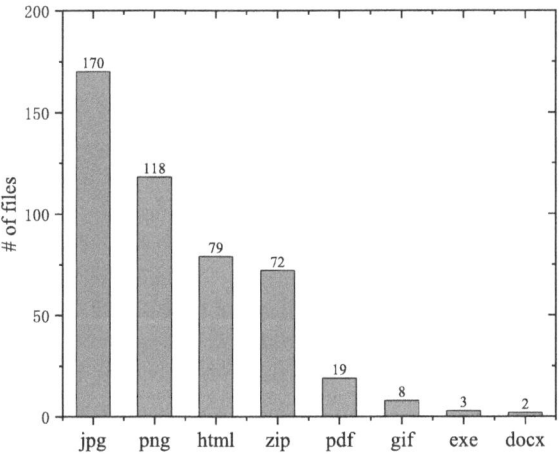

Fig. 1. The file types and quantities are restored

5.2   File Segmentation Embedding Analysis

Large files can be embedded in the blockchain through multiple transactions due to field capacity limits. We developed the file segmentation and embedding restoration algorithm (Algorithm 3). Figure 3 demonstrates its application,

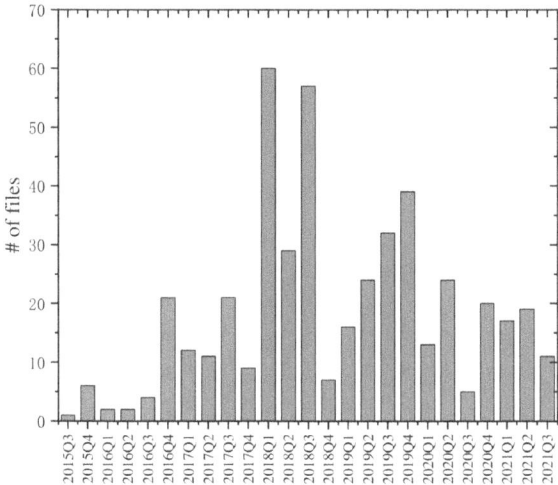

Fig. 2. Number of embedded files per quarter (2015–2021).

restoring a segmented image of East Africa. Despite segmentation, the original image size is restored using header file information. However, incomplete connections and color variations are observed in the restored image. Transactions sent to a smart contract with an upload function caused this. As Algorithm 3 relies on header and tail feature codes, middle file data is unidentified, resulting in incomplete connections. The reason for color changes is unclear, possibly due to smart contract function calls altering the input field. This validates our speculation on multi-transaction file embedding. Our algorithm effectively restores segmented files.

After further analysis, we found 54 incomplete pictures, among which 10 pictures were segmented and embedded. After applying the file segmentation and embedding restoration algorithm, six complete pictures were obtained, including 1 blockchain proof of work map, 1 map of East Africa, 1 picture of human eyes, two landscape pictures, and one cartoon bird. At the same time, in the pdf file that cannot be opened, three files are successfully restored, which are the Ethereum white paper, a research paper about gorillas, and the Foxit software advertisement.

5.3 Text Data Analysis

In this section, we classify directly embedded text data into four types: Chinese, English, URLs, and emails. We analyze the temporal features of text embeddings by categorizing the number of embeddings per every one million blocks. Figure 4 illustrates a notable surge in text embeddings between 5 to 10 million blocks (spanning 2017 to 2021). English texts constitute the predominant portion, with Chinese texts also showing a substantial presence. Further analysis of the content and characteristics of these text categories will be conducted subsequently.

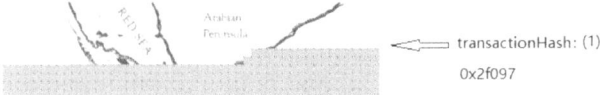

(a) Incomplete image files

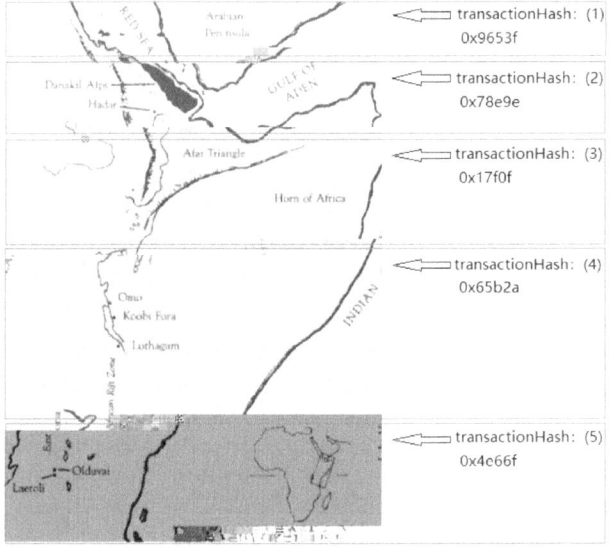

(b) Algorithm3 restores the image files

Fig. 3. Incomplete image restoration using file segmentation embedded restore algorithm (Algorithm 3), (a) incomplete image file found, and (b) image file restored using Algorithm 3. The image file is split 5 times for embedding, and the top 5 bits of the hash value of each transaction are marked in the figure.

Link Type Text Analysis. Among the 720 email addresses sent by participants in the ICO, 96 contain "http" in the URL, and 218 share the URL "podcrypt.app." Additionally, 93 emails contain the URL "ddblock.io," the official website of slideshow software. Notably, one URL ends with ".onion," indicating dark web access. We refrain from further analysis due to potential undesirable content associated with dark web URLs.

Text Sentiment Classification. Facebook introduced the FastText text classification model in 2016. This model computes document vectors by averaging word vectors and N-gram model vectors, enabling efficient multi-class classification with high accuracy. We train the FastText model on emotion-labeled datasets from Chinese Weibo and English Twitter. After parameter optimization, the model achieves a Chinese classification accuracy of 0.925 and an English accuracy of 0.949.

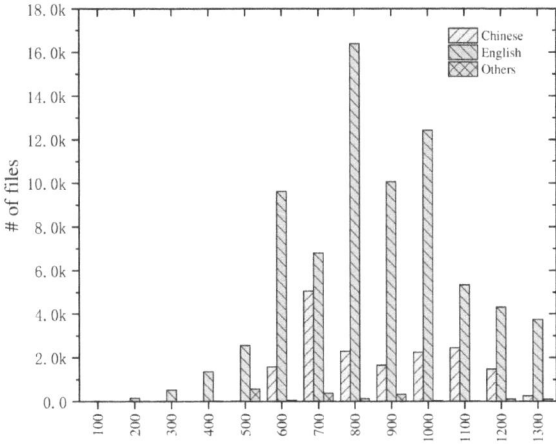

Fig. 4. Number of embedded texts per 1 million blocks in the Ethernet blockchain.

We classify 17,050 Chinese and 74,163 English texts restored in this study. Results show 3,479 negative, 4,155 positive, and 9,450 neutral emotions in Chinese texts, and 12,331 negative, 1,093 positive, and 60,739 neutral emotions in English texts (Table 2).

Table 2. Text Sentiment Classification Results

Category	All	Neutral	Positive	Negative
Chinese	17043	9450	4115	3479
English	74163	60739	1093	12331

Chinese Text Analysis. After decoding, we obtained 17,043 Chinese text files, predominantly related to finance and blockchain. Analysis of text messages received by active addresses revealed varied content, with the top addresses receiving wishes, copyright certification, logistics traceability, financial analysis, and sexual harassment records. The sentiment classification experiment identified neutral and positive sentiments in wishes and logistics-related messages, alongside negative views on current affairs, politics, social issues, and COVID-19 concerns. Notably, some texts contained separatist political rhetoric, highlighting the permanent recording and dissemination nature of blockchain.

English Text Analysis. Following the decoding process, 74,163 English text files were unveiled, totaling 85.7M in size. Among these, EOS tokens emerged as the predominant content, with 31,958 occurrences. Moreover, 9,337 records were linked to Over-the-Counter (OTC) transactions, while 6,892 pertained to token offering and marketing promotions. Following thorough cleaning and word separation, word frequency analysis unveiled a prevalence of terms associated with tokens, transactions, and smart contracts. The term "EOS" appeared over 400,000 times, with "token" following closely at over 360,000 instances, largely attributed to token issuance crowdfunding. Notably, "OTC" surfaced over 240,000 times, likely driven by heightened token offerings, resulting in increased transaction volumes, elevated fees, and network congestion. Consequently, users opted for OTC transactions to bypass soaring fees.

In the sentiment classification of English text, neutral and positive sentiments are observed in token advertisements, token applications, blessings, and event records. However, racially discriminatory remarks were detected in negative sentiment texts. Additionally, instances of users recording incidents of being cheated on the blockchain network were found. For example, information regarding a fake token investment scam based on the Alpha Finance protocol was stored on the chain, exposing the scam. The hash value of this transaction is $0 \times 4ef4$. Alpha Finance is a cross-chain DeFi protocol connecting users to various financial services. The address 0xc88f[1] purchased ALPHA tokens with ether invested by other users but failed to transfer the investment return, indicating fraudulent activity on the Ethereum network. This corroborates with previous research on phishing scams and Ponzi scheme identification [6] in Ethereum.

5.4   Sensitive Information Embedding Analysis

In October 2020, sensitive personal information of several deputy ministerial-level cadres and national leadership team members was embedded into the Ethereum network. The authenticity of this information was verified through public channels, raising concerns about personal privacy and safety. Address A (0×8562) had 15 transactions embedding information related to 29 officials from 12 departments, including China's Ministry of Commerce and the United Front Work Department of the CPC.

Tracing the source of funds, address B $(0 \times 7A34)$ initially transferred Ether to address A, exhibiting suspicious behavior. Address B was found to be associated with the ChangeNow exchange, and it was linked to fund transfers following the KuCoin cryptocurrency exchange hack on September 25, 2020[2]. This suggests that the embedding of sensitive information on the Ethereum network by address A may have been funded by a hacker group.

Embedding such information on Ethereum poses privacy challenges and potential threats to national security if utilized by lawbreakers.

6   Information Embedding Network

Firstly, we constructed the Ethereum Information Embedding Network (IEN) based on information embedding transaction fields. We defined a set

---

[1] 0xc88fdbcaa45142c0cdd1da4eea79ed40022f15da.
[2] https://pastebin.com/r7rJH0g2.

⟨from, to, input⟩ consisting of these fields. Then, we built IEN with the following detailed definitions:

$$IEN = (V, E, W) | E = (v_i, v_j), v_i, v_j \in V$$

Here, V represents the set of addresses of all embedded messages. E consists of ordered edges formed by groups of information embedding behaviors between addresses. Each edge signifies that node v_i embeds information in node v_j. The function $w : E \rightarrow \mathbb{R}^+$ associates each edge with a weight, representing the sum of embeddings. Thus, IEN is a weighted directed graph.

The information embedding network comprises 44,887 nodes and 91,206 edges, categorized into four graphs based on embedded information types (Fig. 5).

In the file embedding network (Fig. 5(a)), most senders and receivers share addresses. Notably, 30 addresses send NFT artwork to the CreepyCryptos contract. In the link information embedding network (Fig. 5(b)), some users widely disseminate advertisements, e.g., for "podcrypt.app" and "ddblock.io". In the Chinese (Fig. 5(c)) and English (Fig. 5(d)) networks, clustering of addresses is evident. In Chinese, addresses cluster for copyright authentication, order records, logistics, blessings, and financial analysis. English text embedding primarily relates to token issuance, notably EOS tokens, followed by FTC, ATOM token ads, and commodity transaction certification.

Additionally, total degree, in-degree, and out-degree distribution were analyzed. The degree distribution follows a power-law, observed across all information-embedded graphs (Figure 6). Most addresses are inactive in embedding information, while a few frequently embed for specific tasks. The address with highest in-degree, $0xc68b$, received 31,958 texts related to EOS tokens. The highest out-degree address, $0x0920$, sent 4,407 texts advertising Polkadot (DOT) and Kusama (KSM), platforms enabling independent blockchain operation.

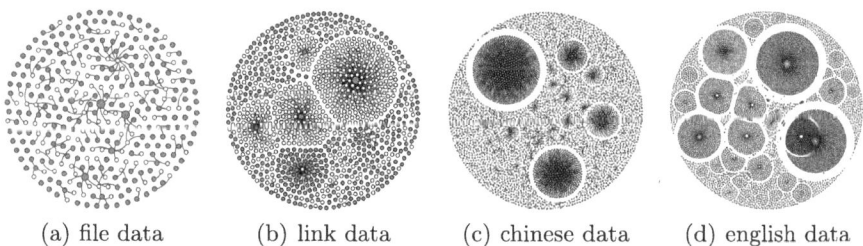

(a) file data   (b) link data   (c) chinese data   (d) english data

Fig. 5. Information embedding network visualization: (a) File data embedding network, (c) Chinese data embedding network, (d) English data embedding network, (e) New data embedding network

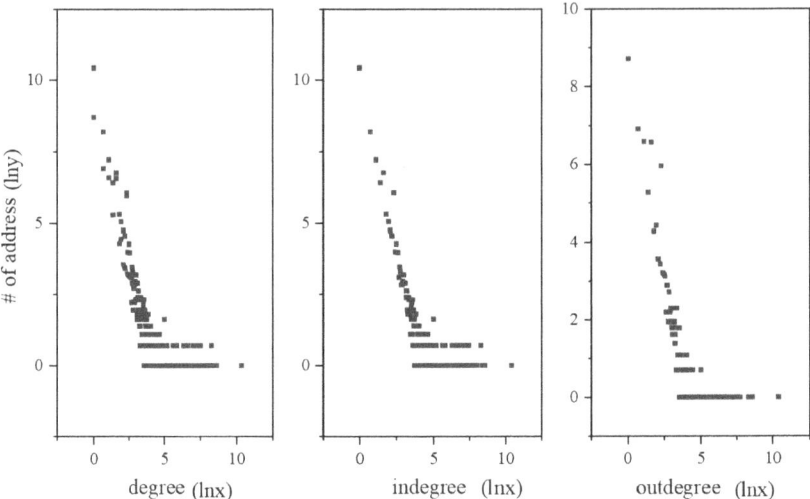

Fig. 6. The degree, in-degree, and out-degree distribution of various types of information embedded in the Ethereum blockchain.

7   Related Work

Since the emergence of Bitcoin, extensive literature has explored blockchain data mining. This paper focuses on data embedding in the Ethereum blockchain. Tian et al. [7] explore techniques for constructing covert channels in networks, with blockchain emerging as a new covert channel type. Du et al. [8] propose applying blockchain to covert communication due to limitations in traditional methods, categorizing it into four types. Chen et al. [9] review core technologies for applying blockchain to covert communication and discuss privacy issues, suggesting future research directions. Zhang et al. [10] summarize covert channels in blockchain and blockchain-based communication schemes. Matzutt et al. [11] identify inappropriate content embedded in the Bitcoin blockchain, while Henze et al. [12] propose countermeasures against embedding such content. Liu et al. [13] investigate embedding covert information in Ethereum transactions. Sato et al. [14] analyze Ethereum transaction data and recover files using a carving tool, prompting the development of algorithms to detect embedded files in blockchain data.

8 Conclusion and Future Work

This paper investigates data embedding in the Ethereum blockchain network, decoding approximately 3.4 billion transaction records to restore various types of information. It identifies sensitive and illegal content, emphasizing risks within the Ethereum network. Future efforts should focus on enhancing privacy protection, refining data restoration algorithms, implementing robust review mechanisms, educating communities, and establishing global collaborative frameworks to mitigate these risks.

Acknowledgments. The work was supported by the Guangdong Philosophy and Social Science Foundation (Grant No. GD24CXW05).

References

1. Khan, A.A., et al.: A drone-based data management and optimization using meta-heuristic algorithms and blockchain smart contracts in a secure fog environment. Comput. Electr. Eng. **102**, 108234 (2022)
2. Chaleenutthawut, Y., Davydov, V., Kuzmin, A., Yanovich, Y.: Practical blockchain-based financial assets tokenization. In: Proceedings of the 2021 4th International Conference on Blockchain Technology and Applications, pp. 51–57 (2021)
3. Matzutt, R., et al.: A quantitative analysis of the impact of arbitrary blockchain content on bitcoin. In: Meiklejohn, S., Sako, K. (eds.) FC 2018. LNCS, vol. 10957, pp. 420–438. Springer, Heidelberg (2018). https://doi.org/10.1007/978-3-662-58387-6_23
4. Laurent, A., Brotcorne, L., Fortz, B.: Transaction fees optimization in the Ethereum blockchain. Blockchain Res. Appl. **3**(3), 100074 (2022)
5. Buterin, V., et al.: A next-generation smart contract and decentralized application platform. White Paper **3**(37) (2014)
6. Chen, W., Zheng, Z., Cui, J., Ngai, E., Zheng, P., Zhou, Y.: Detecting Ponzi schemes on Ethereum: towards healthier blockchain technology. In: Proceedings of the 2018 World Wide Web Conference, pp. 1409–1418 (2018)
7. Tian, J., Xiong, G., Li, Z., Gou, G.: A survey of key technologies for constructing network covert channel. Secur. Commun. Netw. **2020**, 1–20 (2020)
8. Du, B., He, D., Luo, M., Peng, C., Feng, Q.: The applications of blockchain in the covert communication. Wirel. Commun. Mob. Comput. **2022**(1), 4618007 (2022)
9. Chen, Z., et al.: Blockchain meets covert communication: a survey. IEEE Commun. Surv. Tutorials (2022)
10. Zhang, T., Li, B., Zhu, Y., Han, T., Wu, Q.: Covert channels in blockchain and blockchain based covert communication: overview, state-of-the-art, and future directions. Comput. Commun. (2023)
11. McReynolds, E., Lerner, A., Scott, W., Roesner, F., Kohno, T.: Cryptographic currencies from a tech-policy perspective: policy issues and technical directions. In: Brenner, M., Christin, N., Johnson, B., Rohloff, K. (eds.) FC 2015. LNCS, vol. 8976, pp. 94–111. Springer, Heidelberg (2015). https://doi.org/10.1007/978-3-662-48051-9_8

12. Matzutt, R., Henze, M., Ziegeldorf, J.H., Hiller, J., Wehrle, K.: Thwarting unwanted blockchain content insertion. In: 2018 IEEE International Conference on Cloud Engineering (IC2E), pp. 364–370. IEEE (2018)
13. Liu, S., et al.: Whispers on Ethereum: blockchain-based covert data embedding schemes. In: Proceedings of the 2nd ACM International Symposium on Blockchain and Secure Critical Infrastructure, pp. 171–179 (2020)
14. Sato, T., Imamura, M., Omote, K.: Threat analysis of poisoning attack against Ethereum blockchain. In: Information Security Theory and Practice: 13th IFIP WG 11.2 International Conference, WISTP 2019, Paris, France, December 11–12, 2019, Proceedings 13, pp. 139–154. Springer (2020)

Task Allocation and Process Optimization for Weather Services

Yifan Li[2] and Lei Yu[1(✉)]

[1] Department of Computer Science, Inner Mongolia University, Hohhot, China
`yuleiimu@163.com`
[2] Service Center, Inner Mongolia Meteorological Bureau, Hohhot, China

Abstract. With the rapid acceleration of information processing and the increasing volume of digital content, there is a growing demand for intelligent processes across various fields. When dealing with complex business tasks, the traditional static task assignment approach proves to be ineffective and inefficient. We investigate task allocation method of Flowable (an open-source software) and highlight the limitations of its static binding strategy in terms of adaptability and rationality. Based on this analysis, a comprehensive multi-criteria task allocation strategy is proposed, considering factors such as task type, urgency, employee workload, capacity, availability, and workload balance. The multi-objective optimization problem is solved using Hybrid Particle Swarm and Gray Wolf Optimization (HPSGWO), and a multi-dimensional evaluation task allocation model is constructed. In conjunction with the time-constrained push model, an optional time interval is set, allowing employees to proactively choose tasks. If the deadline is reached and the task list remains unallocated, the system automatically reassigns suitable employees based on the multi-criteria strategy. Flowable's Application Programming Interface (API) is extended to enhance flow control, enabling dynamic routing, task deletion, and re-triggering functionalities. Finally, the optimized Flowable workflow is applied to the management system. The improved Flowable not only enhances user work efficiency and relieves the system from repetitive and tedious task allocation, but also provides more time for complex and intricate business processing.

Keyword: Flowable; Multi-criteria task allocation strategy; Workflow

1 Introduction

Business processes represent the execution of various logical abstractions and processes between interconnected organizations [1]. Initially, business processes were primarily used for file transfers. However, as the market environment continues to change and enterprise needs evolve, there has been an increasing urgency for business process automation. This gave rise to workflow technology, which automates business processes, enhancing efficiency and accuracy. Workflow technology is a computerized business process management system that automates and coordinates various steps within business processes, enabling effective process management and control [2]. With the continuous development and innovation in technology, workflow technology is constantly improving and expanding, becoming an essential component of modern enterprises.

Workflow pertains to the process of decomposing work into a series of orderly tasks and assigning these tasks to different individuals or systems for processing [3]. The study of workflow originated primarily in Western countries. Initially, workflow aimed to manage and optimize complex workflows, while providing an electronic foundation for storage and retrieval of vast amounts of process data. As internal business requirements continued to expand and the significance of information management grew, the scope of workflow in enterprise applications gradually broadened.

DIKW represents a hierarchical model that describes the different stages of information processing and understanding. Each tier represents the progress in transforming raw data into valuable insights. Data: Data refers to unprocessed raw facts and figures, including discrete elements such as numbers, text, images, or measurements. Data lacks context and meaning; Information is derived by organizing, structuring, and meaningfully presenting data to provide context and relevance. It makes data easier to understand and use. Information answers questions such as who, what, when, and where; Knowledge is gained by analyzing and interpreting information to identify patterns, relationships, and insights. It involves applying expertise, experience, and understanding to comprehend information. Knowledge answers how and why questions, enabling individuals to draw conclusions and make informed decisions; Wisdom represents the highest level of understanding and insight. It goes beyond knowledge and includes judgment, ethical values, and a broader perspective. Wisdom involves applying knowledge in a meaningful and ethical manner, considering long-term consequences and societal implications. The DIKW model applies to various fields and industries. It provides a framework to help us understand and exploit the hierarchical relationships of data, information, and knowledge to generate valuable insights and wisdom that drive the development of individuals, organizations, and societies.

2   Related Work

Nowadays, countries worldwide are actively promoting the adoption of enterprise management information. In response to this developmental demand, workflow has undergone a progressive evolution, moving from superficial to comprehensive integration within organizations. Over several decades, the advancement of workflow technology has traversed three distinct stages, starting from its initial role in document delivery and processing and gradually evolving into a comprehensive business process management system. During the first stage, workflow, which had yet to be deeply integrated into an organization's internal system, primarily focused on document delivery and processing. IBM's Domino Notes, as an exemplary product, set a precedent in the enterprise collaboration market [4]. Subsequently, workflow transitioned into the second stage, where it functioned as an independent management system platform within enterprises. This stage featured underlying communication infrastructure and collaboration capabilities, exemplified by products like TIBCO iProcess Suite and Staffware, which catered to the requirements of file management and other relevant aspects [5, 6]. Ultimately, workflow progressed to the third stage, maturing into a comprehensive Business Process Management (BPM) system applicable to a broader range of application scenarios. At this stage, representative products such as the Pega Platform, Oracle BPM Suite, and IBM Business Automation Workflow emerged. These products effectively manage the relationships among various business processes, personnel, and resources, offering comprehensive monitoring capabilities for overseeing the execution of the entire process [7–9]. The deployment of these products enhances efficiency and productivity within enterprises and propels the continued advancement of workflow technology, paving the way for its broader application prospects.

To commercialize workflow management systems, several technology giants have collaborated with universities or research institutes to establish dedicated institutes. Oracle Corporation introduced Oracle Workflow as a comprehensive workflow management system that offers a complete suite of solutions for designing, implementing, and managing business processes within an enterprise. Its primary objective is to enhance operational efficiency, reduce costs, and expedite decision-making processes. Oracle Workflow adopts a server-centric architecture that combines a workflow engine with a robust database, providing a reliable and high-volume environment. Additionally, it incorporates a sophisticated Internet monitoring tool based on the Internet model, designed for compatibility with Oracle Application Server or OracleWebDB [10]. Being a pure Java language open-source software, Oracle Workflow boasts notable flexibility, enabling users to concentrate fully on business and rule definition. IBM Business Automation Workflow (BAW), launched by IBM, is a comprehensive workflow management and automation solution. BAW seamlessly integrates BPM and case management functions on a unified platform, enabling enterprises to automate, optimize, and monitor business processes. This results in increased efficiency, cost reduction, and improved decision-making quality [11]. Microsoft's Windows Workflow Foundation is a framework built on the concept of workflow, providing application solutions within the .Net Framework environment [12]. This framework not only offers a standardized workflow design system but also provides a suite of unified development tools. Windows Workflow Foundation exhibits excellent flexibility and scalability, supporting model-based workflow development. Users can write code to construct business processes and utilize custom activities within workflows to meet specific process requirements. Huang et al. [13] exploited the differences between DIKWP models to define and measure fairness and justice issues. Huang et al. [14] proposed a content-filled Data, Information, Knowledge, and Purpose (DIKP) modeling approach. This method transforms the compiler and the content of the form into data, information, knowledge, and purpose, and establishes the DIKP system. Hu et al. [15] proposed an approach to intrinsic computation and reasoning, stemming from the fact that there are computational layers and relations defining everything in the semantic model, by merging cross-modal and available DIKW or mesoscale capabilities to synchronize cross-modal processing to minimize uncertainty. Marco et al. [16] utilized the DIKW hierarchy as a framework for modeling scientific data generated during large-scale assessment activities of information retrieval systems to design a digital library system capable of managing and supporting the process of such assessment activities. Duan et al. [17] proposed a formalization of the DIKW elements, where the central idea is to model data as multidimensional hierarchical types associated with observable properties, information as the identification of data with explicit differences, knowledge as the integrity of applied types, and wisdom as the prediction of variability. The DIKW can be applied in conjunction with or in place of other technical behavioral or social context models to inform the components of oral health education delivery [18]. Duan et al. propose a DIKW-based [19] approach to emotional communication, which addresses possible misunderstandings caused by the limitations of the expressive space and individual cognitive differences [20].

3   Intelligent Task Allocation and Process Improvement

This study introduces a hybrid algorithm named Hybrid Particle Swarm and Gray Wolf Optimization (HPSGWO) that amalgamates the merits of Particle Swarm Optimization (PSO) and Gray Wolf Optimization (GWO) to achieve efficient optimization based on knowledge [21, 22]. Initially, HPSGWO generates an initial population comprising individuals with randomly assigned positions and velocities. Subsequently, the algorithm iteratively updates the positions of particles by integrating the search mechanism of PSO with the hunting behavior of GWO. This hybrid algorithm continues to iterate until a predefined number of iterations or a convergence condition is met. Finally, it yields an optimal solution along with its corresponding objective function values.

In PSO, the velocity and position of each particle i are updated and calculated based on its current position, velocity, and the optimal position of the group.

$$v_i^{t+1} = w * v_i^t + c_1 * r_1 * \left(pbest_i^t - x_i^t\right) + c_2 * r_2 * \left(gbest^t - x_i^t\right) \tag{1}$$

$$x_i^{t+1} = x_i^t + v_i^{t+1} \tag{2}$$

Among them, v_i^t represents the velocity of particle i at time t, x_i^t denotes the position of particle i at time t, $pbest_i^t$ signifies the individual optimal solution for particle i, $gbest^t$ represents the global optimal solution, w denotes the inertia weight, c_1 and c_2 are acceleration coefficients, and r_1 and r_2 are random numbers chosen from the interval [0,1].

In GWO, the hunting behavior of gray wolves encompasses three primary stages: stalking, chasing, and approaching the prey; chasing, surrounding, and harassing the prey until it ceases movement; and ultimately, attacking the prey.

(1) Encircling prey: During the search for prey, gray wolves employ a gradual approach and encircling technique to capture their target.

$$D = \left|C * X_p(t) - X(t)\right| \tag{3}$$

$$X(t+1) = X_p(t) - A * D \tag{4}$$

In formula (3), D represents the distance between the individual and the prey, and $X(t+1)$ in formula (4) represents the updated position of the gray wolf. Here, t represents the current iteration, A and C are coefficient vectors, Xp denotes the position vector of the prey, and X represents the position vector of the gray wolf.

$$A = 2a * r_1 - a \tag{5}$$

$$C = 2 * r_2 \tag{6}$$

Formulas (5) and (6) are utilized for the computation of the coefficient vectors A and C, correspondingly. Here, the convergence factor is denoted by a. As the number of iterations decreases linearly toward 0, the modulus of r_1 and r_2 is assigned a random number selected from the range [0,1].

(2) Hunting: Gray wolves rely on the guidance of the three optimal gray wolves (α, β, δ) to identify possible optimal positions of prey during the search process. Due to the unknown characteristics of the solution space, the gray wolf cannot precisely determine the location of the prey (the optimal solution). In the simulation of search behavior, it is assumed that α, β and δ possess a strong ability to identify potential prey locations. During the iterative process, the positions of the three optimal gray wolves (α, β, δ) in the current population are preserved, while the positions of other search agents (including ω) are updated based on the information derived from these optimal positions.

$$D_\alpha = |C_1 * X_\alpha - X|, D_\beta = |C_2 * X_\beta - X|, D_\delta = |C_3 * X_\delta - X| \tag{7}$$

$$X_1 = X_\alpha - A_1 * (D_\alpha), X_2 = X_\beta - A_2 * (D_\beta), X_3 = X_\delta - A_3 * (D_\delta) \tag{8}$$

$$X(t+1) = \frac{X_1 + X_2 + X_3}{3} \tag{9}$$

D_α, D_β, and D_δ in formula (7) denote the distances between α, β and δ, and other individuals, respectively. X_α, X_β and X_δ represent the current positions of α, β and δ, respec.ively. C_1, C_2 and C_3 are random vectors, and X represents the current position of the gray wolf. Formula (8) represents the step size and heading of the ω gray wolf individuals within the wolf pack towards α, β and δ, respectively. Formula (9) represents the final position of the ω gray wolf individual within the wolf pack.

(3) Attacking Prey: During the construction of the attacking prey model, the value of A fluctuates in accordance with the decrease of a, as indicated by formula (5).

The steps of the HPSGWO algorithm are as follows:

Step 1: Parameter Initialization: Set various parameters, including the size of the particle swarm, size of the gray wolf group, maximum number of iterations, inertia weight, individual best position weight, global best position weight, etc.

Step 2: Random Generation of Initial Particle Swarm and Gray Wolf Group: Randomly generate a group of particles and gray wolves within the problem's search space. Each particle and gray wolf is represented by a position vector, which corresponds to a potential solution.

Step 3: Fitness Evaluation: Calculate the fitness value for each individual in the particle swarm and gray wolf group.

Step 4: Update Individual Best and Global Best: For each particle in the particle swarm, compare its current position with its historical best position and update the individual best position accordingly. Simultaneously, update the global best position based on the fitness values of all particles and gray wolves.

Step 5: Update Particle Position and Velocity: Update the velocity of each particle using the inertia weight, individual best position weight, and global best position weight. Then, update the particle position based on the new velocity.

Step 6: Update Gray Wolf Position: Utilize the GWO technique to update the position of each gray wolf. The positions of the other gray wolves are primarily guided by the positions of the three optimal gray wolves: α, β, and δ.

Step 7: Merge Particle Swarm and Gray Wolf Group: Merge the particle swarm and gray wolf group into a single large group. Select individuals with better fitness to update the global best position (G_best) and individual best position (P_best).

Step 8: Separate the Large Group into Particle Swarm and Gray Wolf Group: Split the large group back into the particle swarm and gray wolf group for the next iteration.

Step 9: Convergence Check: If the maximum number of iterations is reached or other convergence conditions are met, terminate the algorithm. Otherwise, return to Step 3 and continue iterating.

The two methods of task assignment in Flowable workflow are depicted as follows. Firstly, a task node is created in the flowchart and configured as a manual task type, such as UserTask, indicating that this node requires manual assignment of tasks to specific users or user groups. The task node is given an ID and name, and the task executor is specified using the setAssignee() method, while the task candidate group is set using setCandidateGroups(Arrays.asList("sales", "engineering")). A listener is attached to the task node to trigger corresponding events when the task is completed or enters the waiting state, enabling appropriate processing through TaskCreateListener() and TaskCompleteListener(). For instance, upon task completion, the listener can assign the task to the next node or update the task status. When the task node enters the waiting state, it becomes necessary to select a specific person from the candidate or candidate group as the task executor. This can be achieved using Flowable API or a custom task assignment strategy. The TaskService is utilized to obtain the task service and create a task query through createTaskQuery(). Finally, the task is assigned to a specific executor using setAssignee(), and the executor completes the task process, bringing it to an end. Through the aforementioned process of assigning tasks in a Flowable workflow, it becomes evident that there are certain limitations in solely assigning tasks to roles or role groups. The need for developers to manually assign each task not only increases their code workload but also presents challenges in maintenance. In the event of personnel changes in the future, developers would have to modify the code accordingly. Frequent code modifications can result in a poor experience in practical scenarios.

The task assignment method in Flowable workflow has certain limitations, leading to a heavy workload for developers and challenges in meeting enterprise requirements. The multi-criteria strategies consider multiple influencing factors and objectives, aiming to achieve more comprehensive and effective problem-solving. To address these issues, a task assignment model based on multi-criteria is proposed. The model is solved using HPSGWO, and a well-designed workflow allocation mechanism is incorporated, taking into account the time-constrained push model.

Definition 1 There are N tasks to be assigned, denoted as $T_1, T_2, \cdots, T_N$, and K employees as $E_1, E_2, \cdots, E_K$. We define an N-dimensional vector $t = (t_1, t_2, \cdots, t_N)$, where t_i represents the type of task i. The task type is converted into a numerical value, i.e., $t_i \in [1, T]$, where T represents the total number of task types.

Similarly, we define an N-dimensional vector $u = (u_1, u_2, \cdots, u_N)$, where u_i represents the urgency of task i. The task urgency is also converted into a numerical value, i.e., $u_i \in [1, U]$, where U represents the total number of urgency levels.

Furthermore, we define an N-dimensional vector $p = (p_1, p_2, \cdots, p_N)$, where p_i represents the workload of task i.

Definition 2 We introduce a matrix $S = (s_{ij})$ with K rows and T columns, where s_{ij} indicates whether the skill level of employee i is suitable for handling tasks of type j. A value of 1 denotes suitability, while a value of 0 denotes unsuitability.

Additionally, we define a K-dimensional vector $v = (v_1, v_2, \cdots, v_K)$, where v_i represents the availability of employee i. The availability is converted into numerical values, i.e., $v_i \in [0, 1]$.

Moreover, we define a K-dimensional vector $z = (z_1, z_2, \cdots, z_K)$, where z_i represents the maximum quantity of tasks that employee i can handle. The task assignment should satisfy the requirement of workload balance, aiming to distribute the total workload among all employees as evenly as possible.

Taking all the aforementioned factors into comprehensive consideration, a Multi-Objective Optimization Problem (MOP) model is formulated. The objective of this optimization problem is to minimize the cost associated with task assignments. The cost is composed of three key components: the workload of employees, the urgency of tasks, and the availability and skills of employees. This model aims to find an optimal assignment solution that achieves a balance between these factors, leading to efficient and effective task allocation.

Definition 3 A K-dimensional vector $w = (w_{E_1}, w_{E_2}, \cdots, w_{E_k})$, where w_{E_i} represents the workload of employee E_i. To achieve a balanced workload distribution among employees, the variance of employee workloads is utilized as an objective function. The objective is to minimize the variance, indicating that the workload should be spread as evenly as possible among the employees.

$$f_1(w) = \frac{1}{K} \sum_{i=1}^{K} \left(w_{E_i} - \overline{w}\right)^2 \tag{10}$$

Definition 4 An N-dimensional vector $q = (q_1, q_2, \cdots, q_N)$, where q_i represents the urgency of the current task i. To prioritize tasks based on their urgency, an objective function is defined as the number of tasks that do not meet the required urgency level. The objective is to minimize this number, indicating that a higher number of tasks should meet the urgency criteria.

$$f_2(q) = \sum_{i=1}^{N} max(0, u_i - q_i) \tag{11}$$

Definition 5 A matrix $x = (x_{ij})$ with M rows and K columns, where x_{ij} represents the probability of assigning task i to employee j. The objective is to assign tasks to employees who possess suitable skills and high availability. To achieve this, an objective function is defined as the summation of probabilities for all unassigned tasks. The goal is to minimize this objective function, indicating that a higher number of tasks should be successfully assigned to suitable employees.

$$f_3(x) = \sum_{i=1}^{M} \max_{j=1}^{K} (0, 1 - x_{ij}) \tag{12}$$

In summary, the problem can be formulated as a Multi-Objective Optimization Problem (MOP), considering the objectives of minimizing the variance of employee workload, reducing the number of tasks that do not meet urgency, and maximizing the assignment probabilities for unassigned tasks. The goal is to find an optimal task assignment solution that balances workload, meets task urgency, and maximizes task assignment probabilities.

$$f(w, q, x) = min[f_1(w), f_2(q), f_3(x)] \tag{13}$$

$$s.t. \quad \sum_{j=1}^{K} x_{ij} = 1, \quad i = 1, \cdots, N$$

$$\sum_{i=1}^{N} x_{ij} p_i \leq z_j, \quad j = 1, \cdots, K$$

$$x_{ij} \in [0, 1], \quad i = 1, \cdots, N, \ j = 1, \cdots, K$$

Among them, w, q, and x represent the workload of employees, the urgency of tasks, and the task assignment, respectively. The constraints dictate that each task must be assigned to an employee, the workload of each employee must not exceed their maximum capacity, and the task assignment must satisfy the probability limit.

Time constraints are crucial in task assignments as they can greatly affect the workflow. The push model based on time constraints ensures tasks are completed within the specified time, enabling the smooth progress of the entire workflow. By assigning tasks in advance, the task assigner allows executors to prepare, resulting in faster task completion and improved efficiency. This model reduces complexity in task assignment, guarantees timely task completion, and optimizes workflow management, leading to smoother operations and increased efficiency. The multi-criteria-based strategy in HPSGWO follows a series of steps for effective optimization.

Step 1: Obtain the TaskQuery object through TaskService to retrieve information on unfinished tasks and generate a task list.

Step 2: Initiate a timer and set the initial values for relevant parameters.

Step 3: Calculate the workload of candidates in the candidate set, the number of tasks that do not meet the urgency level, and the probability of unassigned tasks.

Step 4: Utilize the HPSGWO algorithm to solve the problem and identify the employees best suited to handle the tasks.

Step 5: Upon completion of the timer, for tasks that remain unclaimed by any employee, employ the recommendation mechanism to assign these tasks to the most suitable employees, ensuring task completion.

The process instance typically follows a predefined route, reaching each node in sequential order until it reaches the termination node, where it stops. In the case of starting a process, the start node is first directed to node a, followed by node b, and subsequently nodes c, d, and e based on the gateway conditions. Finally, the process reaches the termination node, concluding the process. However, in scenarios where a more urgent event arises during the process execution, it may be necessary to skip certain intermediate nodes or backtrack from one node to another to save time and enhance process efficiency. The dynamic routing improvement scheme is shown by following steps:

Step 1: Retrieve the ID of the currently running task node and the target task node ID.

Step 2: Obtain the TaskEntity object of the current runtime task and retrieve the current node object (sourceFlowNode) and target node object (targetFlowNode) based on the TaskEntity object and the target node ID.

Step 3: Obtain the current node ID (sourceRealId) and target node ID (targetRealId) that should be operated on, according to sourceFlowNode and targetFlowNode.

Step 4: Obtain the current list of parallel gateways (sourceGatewayList) and the list of parallel gateways (targetGatewayList) where the target node is located.

Step 5: Divide the positions of the current node and the target node into the following four scenarios:

1. When neither the target node nor the current node is in a parallel gateway, add the current sourceRealId to the sourceRealIds collection.
2. When the target node is not in a parallel gateway and the current node is in a parallel gateway, add the sourceGatewayList node in the current gateway to the sourceRealIds collection.
3. When the target node is in a parallel gateway and the current node is not in a parallel gateway, add the current sourceRealId to the sourceRealIds collection, and find the closest parallel gateway to the current node.
4. When both the target node and the current node are in a parallel gateway, if they are on the same layer and the same branch of the parallel gateway, perform the same operation as in case 1. If they are not in the same branch of the same layer and the current node is outside the parallel gateway relative to the target node, performing the same operation as in case 1. Otherwise, perform the same operation as in case 2. If they are not in the same branch of the same layer and the target node is in the parallel gateway relative to the current node, the target node gateway and the current node gateway need to be classified as the same layer and the same branch gateway, otherwise no processing is performed.

Step 6: Filter out the executions that need to be processed based on sourceRealIds [23] and use the internal function moveExecutionToSingleActivityId() within Flowable to execute the jump to the target node.

Step 7: Special processing is required if the target node is in a parallel gateway relative to the current node, and manual generation of execution data for the sink node of the parallel gateway is needed.

The Flowable engine provides an internal task deletion API interface [24]. However, directly calling taskService.deleteTask() often results in the exception "The task cannot be deleted because it is part of a running process." Deleting a task requires meeting two conditions: 1. The task's status must be completed or deleted. 2. The process instance where the task resides must be in a non-running state (e.g., suspended or ended). In this paper, the ExecutionEntityManager class is utilized to manage entities of the Execution class. The deleteExecution() method is used to delete an Execution entity and all its sub-Execution entities. This resolves the issue of exceptions when using the taskService.deleteTask() method. The improved algorithm for task deletion is shown by following steps:

Step 1: Retrieve the entity ID (executionId) and the reason for deleting the task (deleteReason).

Step 2: Acquire the ExecutionEntityManager object and retrieve the ExecutionEntity object based on the executionId.

Step 3: Utilize the deleteExecutionAndRelatedData method from the executionEntityManager object, passing the executionEntity and deleteReason as parameters.

The improved algorithm for task retriggering is shown by following steps:

Step 1: Retrieve the identification business key (businessKey) and target node (targetActivityId).

Step 2: Determine the current node id (sourceRealId) and target node id (targetRealId) based on the businessKey.

Step 3: Perform the node jump operation, where the current node jumps to the target node (following the node jump step).

4   Conclusion

Through a comprehensive analysis of common task assignment methods, this paper identifies the limitations of static assignment and single-factor assignment and proposes improvement measures. It introduces a task assignment method based on a multi-criteria strategy that takes into account various conditions influencing task assignment. The method incorporates HPSGWO optimization and the time-constrained push model to establish a multi-criteria task allocation model. Additionally, the paper explores Flowable workflow, enhances its API, and improves task deletion, dynamic routing, and task re-triggering functionalities, offering a more flexible and efficient solution. The improved Flowable workflow is applied to a mobile device management system, specifically the report review process, illustrating the execution process in detail to achieve efficient operations and cater to diverse business requirements. In conclusion, the proposed method enables more rational and efficient task allocation under multi-criteria conditions, providing enterprises with scalable and adaptable workflow solutions.

Acknowledgement. This work was supported by Natural Science Foundation of Inner Mongolia Autonomous Region (No. 2022MS06024).

References

1. Beheshti, A., Benatallah, B., Motahari-Nezhad, H.R.: Processatlas: a scalable and extensible platform for business process analytics. Softw.: Pract. Experience **48**(4), 842–866 (2018)
2. Chen, M., Zhang, D., Zhou, L.: Empowering collaborative commerce with Web services enabled business process management systems. Decis. Support. Syst. **43**(2), 530–546 (2007)
3. Kulkarni, A., Can, M., Hartmann, B.: Collaboratively crowdsourcing workflows with turkomatic. In: Proceedings of the acm 2012 Conference on Computer Supported Cooperative Work, pp. 1003–1012 (2012)
4. Mohan, C.: A database perspective on lotus domino/notes. In: SIGMOD Conference, vol. 507 (1999)
5. Pourshahid, A., Mussbacher, G., Amyot D, et al.: An aspect-oriented framework for business process improvement. In: E-Technologies: Innovation in an Open World: 4th International Conference, MCETECH 2009, Ottawa, Canada, May 4–6, 2009. Proceedings 4. Springer Berlin Heidelberg, pp. 290–305 (2009)
6. Brown, C.: Workflow management in staffware. Process-Aware Inf. Syst.: Bridging People Softw. through Process Technol. 343–362 (2005)
7. Dunie, R.,Schulte, W.R., Cantara, M., et al.: Magic Quadrant for intelligent business process management suites.Gartner Inc (2015)
8. Bluck, A.S.: Configuring java custom components. In: IBM Software Systems Integration: With IBM MQ Series for JMS, IBM FileNet Case Manager, and IBM Business Automation Workflow. Berkeley, CA: Apress, pp. 143-334 (2023)
9. Bluck, A.S.: IBM FileNet case manager 5.3. 3 case builder solution development steps for the audit system. In: IBM Software Systems Integration: With IBM MQ Series for JMS, IBM FileNet Case Manager, and IBM Business Automation Workflow. Berkeley, CA: Apress, pp. 1–141 (2023)
10. Panzarasa, S., Stefanelli, M.: Workflow management systems for guideline implementation. Neurol. Sci. **27**, s245–s249 (2006)
11. Walker, L.: IBM business transformation enabled by service-oriented architecture. IBM Syst. J. **46**(4), 651–667 (2007)
12. Fairman, M.J., Price, A.R., Xue, G., et al.: Earth system modelling with windows workflow foundation. Futur. Gener. Comput. Syst. **25**(5), 586–597 (2009)
13. Huang, Y., Duan, Y.: Fairness modelling, checking and adjustment for purpose driven content filling over DIKW. In: 2021 IEEE 23rd Int Conf on High Performance Computing & Communications; 7th Int Conf on Data Science & Systems; 19th Int Conf on Smart City; 7th Int Conf on Dependability in Sensor, Cloud & Big Data Systems & Application (HPCC/DSS/SmartCity/DependSys). IEEE, pp. 2316–2321 (2021)
14. Huang, Y., Duan, Y.: Towards purpose driven content interaction modeling and processing based on DIKW. In: 2021 IEEE World Congress on Services (SERVICES), pp. 27–32. IEEE (2021)
15. Hu, S., Duan, Y, Song M. Essence computation oriented multi-semantic analysis crossing multi-modal DIKW graphs. In: Collaborative Computing: Networking, Applications and Worksharing: 16th EAI International Conference, CollaborateCom 2020, Shanghai, China, October 16–18, 2020, Proceedings, Part I. Cham: Springer International Publishing, pp. 320−339 (2021)
16. Dussin, M., Ferro, N.: The role of the dikw hierarchy in the design of a digital library system for the scientific data of large-scale evaluation campaigns. In: Proceedings of the 8th ACM/IEEE-CS Joint Conference on Digital Libraries, pp. 450–450 (2008)
17. Duan, Y., Zhan, L., Zhang, X., et al.: Formalizing DIKW architecture for modeling security and privacy as typed resources. In: Testbeds and Research Infrastructures for the Development of

Networks and Communities: 13th EAI International Conference, TridentCom 2018, Shanghai, China, December 1–3, 2018, Proceedings 13. Springer International Publishing, pp. 157–168 (2019)

18. Aukett, J.: The DIKW pathway: a route to effective oral health promotion? Br. Dent. J. **226**(11), 897–901 (2019)

19. Hu, T., Duan, Y.: Modeling and measuring for emotion communication based on DIKW. In: 2021 IEEE World Congress on Services (SERVICES), pp. 21–26. IEEE, (2021)

20. Hu, T., Duan, Y., Mei, Y.: Purpose driven balancing of fairness for emotional content transfer over DIKW. In: 2021 IEEE 23rd Int Conf on High Performance Computing & Communications; 7th Int Conf on Data Science & Systems; 19th Int Conf on Smart City; 7th Int Conf on Dependability in Sensor, Cloud & Big Data Systems & Application (HPCC/DSS/SmartCity/DependSys), pp. 2074–2081. IEEE (2021)

21. Liang, L., Li, Y., Wen, M., Liu, Y.: KG4Py: A toolkit for generating Python knowledge graph and code semantic search. Connect. Sci. **34**(1), 1384–1400 (2022)

22. Chen, E., Zhao, H., Li, B., Zha, X., Wang, H., Wang, S.: Affective feature knowledge interaction for empathetic conversation generation. Connect. Sci. **34**(1), 2559–2576 (2022)

23. Fan, Y., Xu, B., Zhang, L., Song, J., Zomaya, A., Li, K.C.: Validating the integrity of convolutional neural network predictions based on zero-knowledge proof. Inf. Sci. **625**, 125–140 (2023)

24. Chen, Y., Chen, S., Li, K. C., Liang, W., Li, Z.: DRJOA: intelligent resource management optimization through deep reinforcement learning approach in edge computing. Cluster Comput. 1–15 (2022)

Location Data Sharing Method Based on Blockchain and Attribute-Based Encryption

Xueping Sun[2], Peng Liu[1,2], Bingjie Liao[2], and Qian He[1,2(✉)]

[1] State and Local Joint Engineering Research Center for Satellite Navigation and Location Service, Guilin University of Electronic Technology, Guilin 541004, China
heqian@guet.edu.cn

[2] Guangxi Key Laboratory of Cryptography and Information Security, Guilin University of Electronic Technology, Guilin 541004, China

Abstract. With the development of communication technology and the prevalence of mobile smart devices, location-based services have been widely applied in various scenarios. However, the data typically provided by location-based services includes sensitive information such as personal identity, posing a risk of privacy leakage. Due to the limited resources of mobile smart devices, data is typically uploaded to semi-trusted cloud servers for storage and sharing, leading to the possibility of malicious access and abuse of data. To address these issues, we propose a location data sharing method based on blockchain and attribute-based encryption scheme. By combining blockchain technology with ciphertext-policy attribute-based encryption technology, the shared data is authenticated with trust while providing fine-grained access control. The immutability and traceability features of blockchain are utilized to enhance the security of the entire system. Furthermore, local differential privacy is employed to locally perturb the data before sharing, ensuring that individual privacy in location data remains uncompromised by untrusted third parties. Security analysis and performance evaluation indicate that our scheme is superior to the existing solutions.

Keywords: Location-Based Service · Blockchain · Attribute-Based Encryption · Access Control · Local Differential Privacy

1 Introduction

With the adoption of GPS and wireless technologies, Location-Based Services (LBS) greatly ease daily activities by allowing data owner (DO) to send location and query data to Location-based Service Provider (LSP) for information services. This data often includes sensitive personal details beyond mere geographical information. Due to limited mobile device capacities, LSPs frequently store this data on semi-trusted cloud servers (CS), risking unauthorized access

© The Author(s), under exclusive license to Springer Nature Singapore Pte Ltd. 2025
D. He et al. (Eds.): BlockSys 2024, CCIS 2264, pp. 107–117, 2025.
https://doi.org/10.1007/978-981-96-1411-0_9

and misuse [1,2]. Thus, DO must encrypt their data before upload, necessitating stringent access controls and effective searchability of encrypted data.

Attribute-based encryption (ABE) enhances encrypted data access control. Introduced by Sahai et al. [3], ABE has evolved from identity-based schemes to more complex models such as the Key-Policy ABE (KP-ABE) and Ciphertext-Policy ABE (CP-ABE), which ties access structures to ciphertexts. Only if a Data User's (DU) attributes meet the access policy can decryption occur. Zheng et al. [4] proposed a verifiable attribute-based keyword searchable encryption scheme prone to single point failures in cloud storage. Subsequent research in location privacy [5,6] and cloud storage [7–9] offered similar schemes, yet none addressed privacy protection for shared data.

Since the introduction of the Bitcoin network by Satoshi Nakamoto in 2008 [10], blockchain (BC) technology has expanded into numerous sectors [11,12]. Research has leveraged BC to enhance the reliability of various systems [13,14]. However, existing studies often provide only coarse-grained control over encrypted data, which may be inadequate for detailed data sharing needs. Sammy et al. [15] incorporated BC into access control, developing a user-centric CP-ABE scheme with BC, though it lacks search functionality. Additionally, Wang et al. [16] introduced a blockchain-based medical data sharing scheme that ensures data integrity and searchability but suffers from high Gas costs and inefficiency, rendering it impractical for location data sharing.

Local Differential Privacy (LDP) [17,18] enables local anonymization of data before it is sent to a CS or third party. Widely applied since its inception, Google's RAPPOR [19] uses randomized responses to collect Chrome user settings anonymously. Liu et al. [20] employed RAPPOR to minimize real location exposure by perturbing location data, and Zhang et al. [21] refined LDP to protect both location and query privacy of DO. Nonetheless, LDP's use in LBS has mostly focused on location trajectories, typically overlooking the privacy of DO's sensitive data during sharing.

It is evident that although numerous data sharing schemes exist, most primarily focus on privacy protection or access control within shared data, rarely addressing both issues concurrently. Additionally, location data often contains sensitive personal information, with existing schemes mostly concentrating on the privacy protection of locations. To address these concerns, this paper summarizes its main contributions based on related work as follows:

(1) To address the risk of privacy leakage in centralized cloud servers, this scheme employs BC for its decentralization, immutability, and verifiability. BC stores URLs of encrypted data and access structures, and collaborates with CS to verify and ensure trustworthy search results.
(2) A ciphertext-policy attribute-based keyword searchable encryption scheme was designed, with smart contracts on BC handling data retrieval operations. ABE is applied to enforce fine-grained access control, while LDP is used to randomly perturb sensitive information in location data, guarding against untrusted third-party attacks.

(3) Security analysis demonstrates that our scheme possesses additional features to safeguard data during the sharing process. Performance evaluations confirm the scheme's effectiveness and practicality.

The remainder of this paper is organized as follows. Section. 2 briefly introduces the related preliminaries. Section 3 describes the system overview and specific implementation of the scheme. Then, section four analyzes the security and performance. Finally, the paper concludes in sect. 5.

2 Preliminaries

(1) **Bilinear Mapping.** Suppose that G and G_1 are cyclic multiplicative groups of the order p, and g is a generator of G_T. If the mapping $e : G \times G \rightarrow G_T$ defined on G, G satisfies the following properties, then e is a bilinear mapping.

a) Bilinearity: For any $g_1, g_2 \in G$, and for any $u, v \in Z_p$, we have $e(g_1^u, g_2^v) = e(g_1^v, g_2^u) = e(g_1, g_2)^{uv}$.
b) Non-degeneracy: There exists $g_3, h \in G$ such that $e(g_3, h) \neq 1$.
c) Computability: For any $a, b \in G$, there exists an efficient algorithm to compute $e(a, b)$.

(2) **Access Structure Tree.** For an access policy tree T, each node within the tree is denoted as x. The leaf nodes represent attribute values set by the DO, while non-leaf nodes represent access threshold values. In this paper, $parent(x)$ is used to denote the parent node of x, $index(x)$ is used to denote the index value for locating the parent node of x, and $Attribute(x)$ is used to denote the attribute value of the node x.

3 System Overview

3.1 System Model

The system model contains five entities, namely: DO, DU, BC, CS, attribute center (AC), as shown in Fig. 1.

(1) DO: DO perturbs the original data and establishes an access policy, subsequently encrypting the perturbed data using the system's public key. The DO is also responsible for uploading the encrypted data to the CS.
(2) DU: DU generates a search trapdoor and submits a search request to the BC. Upon verification by the BC, the encrypted data are retrieved from the CS, and the data is decrypted using a symmetric key.
(3) CS: CS stores encrypted data from DO and communicates with BC to jointly verify the accuracy of the data. It returns the corresponding encrypted data to DU upon request.

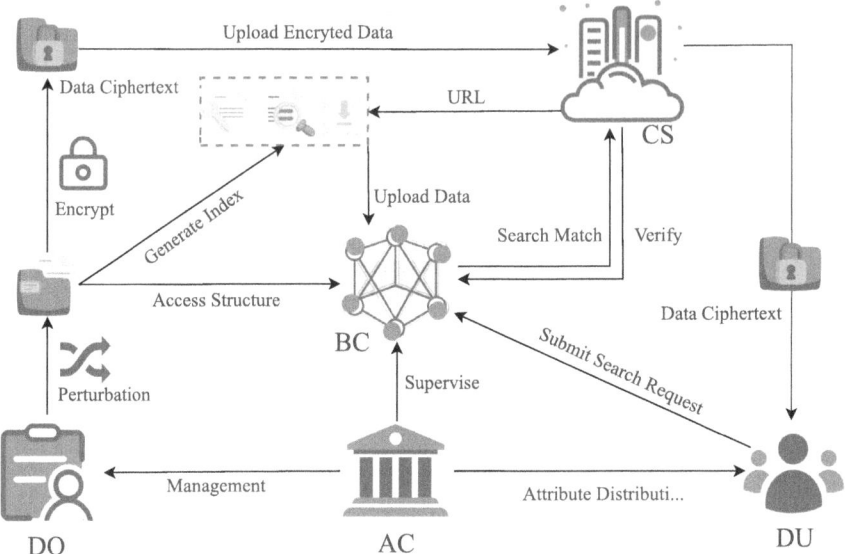

Fig. 1. Data Sharing System Model

(4) *BC*: *BC* is maintained collaboratively by multiple parties and utilizes smart contracts to store data indices and access control rules formulated by *DO*. It is responsible for data retrieval.

(5) *AC*: *AC* are honest and trustworthy entities in the system and are responsible for generating system parameters and generating keys for *DU*.

The *AC* establishes the system, generating a *PK* and a *MK*. *DO* first perturb their data using *LDP* techniques before encrypting the perturbed data with searchable symmetric encryption. This encrypted data is then uploaded to *CS*, which return a corresponding address. *DO* encrypts this address and uploads it, along with the specified access control policy, to a smart contract deployed on the *BC*. When a *DU* wishes to search for data associated with a specific keyword, they must apply to *AC* for an attribute-related *SK* and submit it to *BC* for verification. Once verified, *CS* sends the data's ciphertext to *DU*, who then decrypts the data using a symmetric key.

3.2   Implementation

(1) **System Initialization.** $Setup(\lambda) \rightarrow (PK, MK)$: The process is performed by *AC*, this process inputs a security parameter λ and generates a bilinear map $e : G_1 \times G_1 \rightarrow G_2$, defining G_1, G_2, G_T as cyclic groups of prime order p with generator g. *AC* selects secure hash functions $H : \{0,1\}^* \rightarrow G_1$ and random coefficients $\alpha, \beta \in Z_p$, creating public key $PK = (G_1, G_2, p, g, e(g,g)^a, h = g^b, f = g^{1/b})$ and master key $MK = (g^a, \beta)$.

(2) **Key Generation.** $KeyGen(PK, MK, S) \rightarrow SK$: The process is performed by AC, this process creates a private key for DU based on their attribute set $S = \{s_1, s_2, \ldots, s_n\}$. AC selects a random $r \in Z_p$. For each attribute x in S, AC selects a random $r_x \in Z_p$, computes $d_x = g^r \cdot H(x)^{r_x}$ and $d'_x = g^{r_x}$. The private key $SK = \{d = g^{(\alpha+r)/\beta}, d_x, d'_x$ for each $x \in S\}$ is then securely delivered to DU.

(3) **Data Perturbation.** The process is performed by DO using the RAPPOR method from LDP to perturb the original data. Given n data users U, each ith user U_i holds a sensitive attribute value $x_i \in \chi$ with $|\chi| = k$. The objective is to tally the occurrences of $x_i(1 \leq i \leq k)$. Initially, Bloom filter technology converts x_i into a binary vector M of length h. Each element of M is then perturbed to create a randomized vector M'. The perturbation method follows a probability $f \in [0, 1]$.

$$p(M') = \begin{cases} 0.5f, & x = 1 \\ 0.5f, & x = 0 \\ 1 - f, x = M_i \end{cases} \tag{1}$$

Subsequently, a second perturbation is applied to each bit of the vector M' to generate a transient random response result D. The probability of setting D_i to 1 is specified by the following formula, where M_i takes values of 1 and 0, with the probabilities $p \in [0, 1]$ and $q \in [0, 1]$, respectively.

$$p(D_i = 1) = \begin{cases} p, M'_i = 1 \\ q, M'_i = 0 \end{cases} \tag{2}$$

In RAPPOR, D_i represents the instantaneous random response. The probability of the ith bit being 1 is influenced by p or q. A 1 in the original data remains 1 after perturbation with probability $p^* = \frac{1}{2}f(p+q) + (1-f)p$, and a 0 becomes 1 with probability $q^* = \frac{1}{2}f(p+q) + (1-f)q$.

(4) **Data Encryption.** $Encrypt(PK, T, D) \rightarrow (C, CT)$: Performed by DO employs n to perturb plaintext D, this process uses m random numbers, i.e., $K_i(i \in [1, m])$. Before sending shared data to CS, DO needs to encrypt the data locally. DO randomly selects $K_{mac} \in Z_p^*$ and encrypts the perturbed plaintext D to obtain the ciphertext C, sends C to CS. DO generates a message authentication code set $MAC_C = \{H(K_{mac}, C)\}$ for the ciphertext C and sends MAC_C and K_{mac} to AC.

DO constructs an access control tree T. In this tree, each node x is associated with a polynomial q_x of degree d_x, where $d_x = l_x - 1$ and l_x is the threshold of node x. If node x is a leaf node, then $d_x = 0$. For the root node r of T, randomly select $s \in Z_p$ and set $q_x(0) = s$. For non-root nodes x, set $q_x(0) = q_{parent(x)}(index(x))$. Get the ciphertext $CT = (T, C = K_{sym} \cdot e(g, g)^{\alpha x}, \tilde{C} = h^s, \forall y \in Y : C_y = g^{q_y(0)}, C'_y = H(Attribute(y))^{q_y(0)})$, K_{sym} represents the symmetric key for perturbed plaintext D. $Attribute(y)$ denotes the attribute associated with node y, and Y denotes the set of leaf nodes.

(5) **Data Query.** Assume that the keyword set $W = \{w_1, w_2, \ldots, w_m\}$, for the given keyword $w_i \in W(i \in [1, m])$. DO create an empty array $D(w_i)$ of

length n, if the keyword w_i exists in the j-th file, then $D(w_i)[j] = 1$, otherwise $D(w_i)[j] = 0$. Subsequently, randomly select a search key $K_{sear} \leftarrow \{0,1\}^k$ for each keyword w_i, calculate $A_{w_i} = F_{k_{ran}}(w_i)$ and send A_{w_i} to AC. DO send A_{w_i} and $D(w_i)$ to BC. AC transmits K_{sear}, K_{mac}, and MAC_C to DU. $TokenGen(PK, K_{sear}, \hat{w}) \to A_{\hat{w}}$: The process is performed by DU. Input the PK, search key K_{sear} and the keyword $\hat{w}$ with the query keyword, then randomly selects number $u \in Z_p$, and compute search token $A_{\hat{w}}$.

$Search(PK, A_{w_i}, D(w_i)) \to D(\hat{w})$: The process is performed by the BC. DO sends A_w to the smart contract. Upon inputting keyword index I_x and A_w, if the A_w matches the keywords in the index, it indicates a successful match and the results are returned to DU, Otherwise it returns $\perp$.

$Validation(D(W_i), K_{mac}, MAC_C) \to C_{\hat{w}}$: The process is performed by BC and CS. Upon receiving $D(\hat{w})$, the DU iteratively processes the array $D(\hat{w})$ and establishes a set MAC_{ID}. For each instance where $D(\hat{w})[j] = 1$, $j \in MAC_{ID}$. Following this, DU navigates through MAC_{ID} to compile and return the complete set of message authentication $MAC_{\hat{w}}$, which are associated with keyword i. DO transmits $MAC_{\hat{w}}$ alongside K_{mac} to the BC deployed smart contract. Upon reading $D(\hat{w})$, CS initializes a set B_{ID} and iterates through array $D(\hat{w})$. If $D(\hat{w})[j] = 1$, j is added to B_{ID}. Based on the set B_{ID}, it retrieves the ciphertext stored on the CS, and outputs all qualifying ciphertexts $CT_{\hat{w}}$. Subsequently, CS sends $CT_{\hat{w}}$ to the verification contract to verify the accuracy of the CS returns results.

(6) **Data Decryption.** $Decrypt(PK, SK, CT) \to PM_{\hat{w}}$: The process is performed by DU. Upon receipt of the correct ciphertext, the DU must verify whether it has decryption authorization. The ciphertext can only be decrypted when S possessed by the DU satisfies the access policy T. The decryption process is recursive, discussed below in two cases:

$a)$ Assume that node x is a leaf node in the access policy tree and if there exists $i \in S$, then the following Eq. (3) is satisfied:

$$DecNode(CT, SK, x) = \frac{e(d_i, C_x)}{e(d'_i, C'_x)} = e(g, g)^{rq_x(0)} \tag{3}$$

If $i \notin S$, then it will output $\perp$, which means that the attributes of DU are not included in the attribute collection of the access control structure, then the decryption key it holds will not meet the requirements of the access control structure and cannot decrypt the ciphertext.

$b)$ Assuming that node x is a non-leaf node within the access control tree, the function $DecNode(CT, SK, ch)$ is invoked for each child node ch of node x, storing the computed results in F. The set of child nodes, denoted as C_h, must fulfill the condition $F_{ch} \neq \perp$. If no such set exists, the function returns $\perp$. Conversely, if a set meeting the condition is identified, the corresponding computational operation is executed:

$$F_x = \prod_{ch \in C_h} F_{ch}^{\Delta_{i,C_h'}(0)} = \prod_{ch \in C_h} \left(e(g,g)^{r \cdot q_{parent(ch)}(index(ch))} \right)^{\Delta_{i,C_h'}(0)}$$
$$= \prod_{ch \in C_h} e(g,g)^{r \cdot q_x(i) \cdot \Delta_{i,C_h'}(0)} = e(g,g)^{r \cdot q_x(0)} \tag{4}$$

where $i = index(ch)$, $C_h' = \{index(ch) : ch \in C_h\}$. For non-leaf nodes, compute $e(g,g)^{r \cdot q_x(0)}$. Invoke the $DecNode(CT, SK, ch)$ function for each child node ch of node x, resulting in F_{ch}. Subsequent iterations lead to the computation of the root node's polynomial, thereby disclosing the concealed secret value s at the root node, denoted as $q_x(0)$ in the aforementioned formula.

Subsequently, it is necessary to compute the symmetric key K_{sym} for decrypting the perturbed plaintext D. This can be accomplished by executing the following algorithm using SK, where $A = e(g,g)_{rs}$:

$$\frac{C}{\frac{e(\tilde{C},d)}{A}} = \frac{K_{sym} \cdot e(g,g)^{\alpha s}}{\frac{e\left(h^s, g^{\frac{\alpha+r}{\beta}}\right)}{e(g,g)^{rs}}} = \frac{K_{sym} \cdot e(g,g)^{\alpha s+rs}}{e\left(g^{\beta s}, g^{\frac{\alpha+r}{\beta}}\right)} \tag{5}$$
$$= \frac{K_{sym} \cdot e(g,g)^{\alpha s+rs}}{e(g,g)^{\alpha s+rs}} = K_{sym}$$

Finally, the DU utilizes K_{sym} to further decrypt $C_{\hat{w}}$, thereby retrieving the perturbed plaintext $PM_{\hat{w}}$ containing the query keyword $\hat{w}$.

4 Performance Evaluation

4.1 Theoretical Evaluation

(1) **Feature Analysis.** The scheme presented in this paper is compared with the features proposed in references [7,8,15]. The comparison results are shown in Table 1.

Table 1. Functional comparison of programs

Features	[7]	[8]	[15]	Our
Cloud Storage	✓	✓	✓	✓
Tamper-proof	×	×	✓	✓
Resist Untrusted Third-Party Attacks	×	✓	×	✓
Secure Search	×	×	×	✓
Prevent Collusion Attacks	×	×	×	✓

It can be seen that the introduction of BC makes our solution have richer functions than existing similar works such as resist untrusted third-party attacks, tamper-proof, secure search and secure prevent collusion attacks.

(2) **Time Complexity Analysis.** The encryption and decryption time complexity of the scheme presented in this paper is analyzed and compared with the schemes proposed in other literature [7,8,15].

For better description, let T_p denote the operation of the bilinear pairing, T_e represent the exponentiation operation on the multiplicative cyclic group G, $|B|$ denote the number of attributes declared in the access policy, and $|C|$ represent the number of attributes possessed by the user. Compared to the computational cost of exponentiation and pairing operations, the cost of multiplication and hashing operations is relatively low and can be neglected. The comparison results are shown in Table 2. It can be observed that, theoretically, our scheme outperforms the other schemes.

Table 2. Time complexity comparison

Scheme	Encryption time	Decryption time
[7]	$(6|B|+4)T_e$	$(2|C|+2)T_p + 2|C|T_e$
[8]	$(2|B|+3)T_e$	$(2|C|+2)T_p + T_e$
[15]	$(2|B|+2)T_e$	$T_e + (|C|+2)T_p$
Our	$(2|B|+1)T_e$	$T_e + 2|C|T_p$

4.2   Experimental Evaluation

To better compare the performance of the proposed scheme with other similar works, we simulated the computation time of the selected schemes based on the Type-A curves from the Charm-crypto library. The simulation platform utilized Linux Ubuntu 18.04, equipped with an Intel(R) Xeon(R) Silver 4114 CPU @ 2.20 GHz and 4 GB of memory. To mitigate random effects, the operation time was determined by averaging over 1000 runs. The computation time for bilinear pairing operations P was measured at 10.323 ms, and for exponentiation operations E at 15.639 ms. The computational overhead of other operations was significantly lower than these two, thus negligible.

We focused on studying the impact of the number of attributes on the efficiency of data encryption and decryption, and selected variations in the number of attributes within the access control policy tree from 5 to 50 for comparison with the schemes presented in references [7,8], as shown in the following Fig. 2.

As shown in Fig. 2(a), encryption time increases proportionally with the number of user attributes, indicating that an increase in attributes complicates the encryption process. Nevertheless, our method still outperforms the schemes presented in references [7,8] in terms of encryption efficiency. Figure 2(b) demonstrates that our scheme is superior to the other two in terms of decryption time. Although the increase in attributes leads to a slight increase in decryption time,

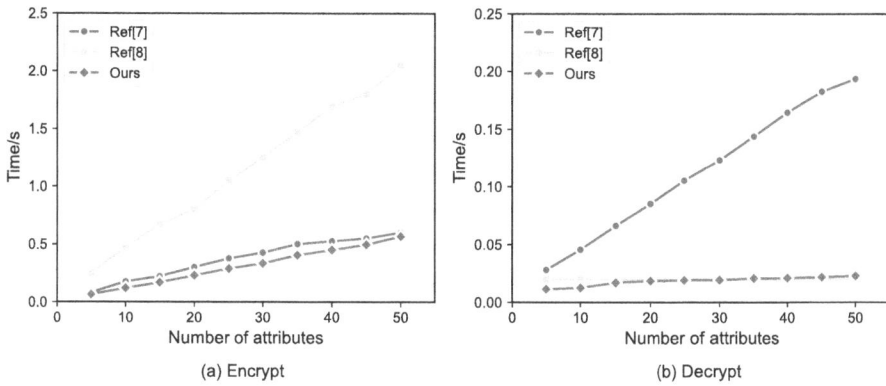

Fig. 2. Comparison of computation overhead

our scheme maintains a shorter decryption time compared to the scheme in reference [8]. Even when the number of attributes continues to grow, the decryption time of our scheme, while approaching that of reference [8], remains significantly lower than that of reference [7].

5   Conclusion

This paper presents a location data sharing scheme that incorporates blockchain and CP-ABE to address the access control challenges posed by untrusted third parties during the sharing process. To enhance fairness and transparency in user-cloud interactions, data verification and retrieval are conducted via blockchain, thereby improving system security and trustworthiness. Additionally, LDP is employed for local perturbation of sensitive data to ensure privacy protection, while CP-ABE provides fine-grained access control for shared data. Theoretical and experimental results confirm the effectiveness of this scheme in protecting data security during the sharing process.

Acknowledgments. This work was supported in part by the National Natural Science Foundation of China (62162018, 61967005); The Natural Science Foundation of Guangxi (2023JJD170008).

References

1. Tang, L., He, M., Xiong, L., Xiong, N., Luo, Q.: An efficient and privacy-preserving query scheme in intelligent transportation systems. Inf. Sci. **647**, 119448 (2023)
2. Wang, L., Lin, Y., Yao, T., Xiong, H., Liang, K.: Fabric: fast and secure unbounded cross-system encrypted data sharing in cloud computing. IEEE Trans. Dependable Secure Comput. **20**, 5130–5142 (2023)
3. Song, D.X., Wagner, D., Perrig, A.: Practical techniques for searches on encrypted data. In: Proceeding 2000 IEEE Symposium on Security and Privacy. S&P 2000, pp. 44–55. IEEE (2000)
4. Zheng, Q., Xu, S., Ateniese, G.: VABKS: verifiable attribute-based keyword search over outsourced encrypted data. In: IEEE INFOCOM 2014-IEEE Conference on Computer Communications, pp. 522–530. IEEE (2014)
5. Huang, Q., Du, J., Yan, G., Yang, Y., Wei, Q.: Privacy-preserving spatio-temporal keyword search for outsourced location-based services. IEEE Trans. Serv. Comput. **15**(6), 3443–3456 (2021)
6. Zhang, L., Kan, H., Wang, Y.: Privacy-preserving AGV collision-resistance at the edge using location-based encryption. IEEE Trans. Serv. Comput. **16**, 2868–2878 (2023)
7. Zhang, W., Zhang, Z., Xiong, H., Qin, Z.: PHAS-HEKR-CP-ABE: partially policy-hidden CP-ABE with highly efficient key revocation in cloud data sharing system. J. Ambient. Intell. Humaniz. Comput. **13**, 1–15 (2022)
8. Hong, X.: Cloud data security sharing mechanism based on differential privacy and attribute based encryption. Guilin University Of Electronic Technology, Guilin (2020)
9. Chen, N., Li, J., Zhang, Y., Guo, Y.: Efficient CP-ABE scheme with shared decryption in cloud storage. IEEE Trans. Comput. **71**(1), 175–184 (2020)
10. Nakamoto, S.: Bitcoin: a peer-to-peer electronic cash system (2008)
11. Tian, Z., Gao, X., Su, S., Qiu, J.: Vcash: a novel reputation framework for identifying denial of traffic service in internet of connected vehicles. IEEE Internet Things J. **7**(5), 3901–3909 (2019)
12. Wang, N., et al.: When energy trading meets blockchain in electrical power system: the state of the art. Appl. Sci. **9**(8), 1561 (2019)
13. Wang, L., Tian, Y., Xiong, J.: Achieving reliable and anti-collusive outsourcing computation and verification based on blockchain in 5G-enabled IoT. Digit. Commun. Netw. **8**(5), 644–653 (2022)
14. Zhou, Y., Cao, Z., Dong, X., Zhou, J.: BLDSS: a blockchain-based lightweight searchable data sharing scheme in vehicular social networks. IEEE Internet Things J. **10**(9), 7974–7992 (2022)
15. Sammy, F., Vigila, S.M.C.: An efficient blockchain based data access with modified hierarchical attribute access structure with CP-ABE using ECC scheme for patient health record. Secur. Commun. Netw. **2022**, 1–11 (2022)
16. Wang, S., Zhang, D., Zhang, Y.: Blockchain-based personal health records sharing scheme with data integrity verifiable. IEEE Access **7**, 102887–102901 (2019)
17. Duchi, J.C., Jordan, M.I., Wainwright, M.J.: Local privacy and statistical minimax rates. In: 2013 IEEE 54th Annual Symposium on Foundations of Computer Science, pp. 429–438. IEEE (2013)
18. Yang, M., Guo, T., Zhu, T., Tjuawinata, I., Zhao, J., Lam, K.-Y.: Local differential privacy and its applications: a comprehensive survey. Comput. Stand. Inter. **89**, 103827 (2023)

19. Erlingsson, Ú., Pihur, V., Korolova, A.: RAPPOR: randomized aggregatable privacy-preserving ordinal response. In: Proceedings of the 2014 ACM SIGSAC Conference on Computer and Communications Security, pp. 1054–1067 (2014)
20. Liu, Z., Miao, D., Liu, Q., Li, R., Li, X.: Location privacy protection through local differential privacy under k-anonymity. Appl. Res. Comput. **39**(08), 2469–2473 (2022)
21. Zhang, Q., Zhang, X., Wang, M., Li, X.: DPLQ: location-based service privacy protection scheme based on differential privacy. IET Inf. Secur. **15**(6), 442–456 (2021)

Implicit White-Box Implementations of Efficient Double-Block-Length MAC

Hengxing Liu, Yupeng Zhang, Luoqi Chen, and Zheng Gong[✉]

School of Computer Science, South China Normal University, Guangzhou, China
cis.gong@gmail.com

Abstract. In recent years, message authentication codes (MAC) have been typically applied in the blockchain system and the Internet of Things (IoT), where the environments have constrained security and limited resources. However, little research pays attention to designing a secure and efficient MAC implementation. Following the construction of double-block-length compression functions proposed by Hirose, this paper proposes an implicit white-box MAC implementation (WB-HDBL-MAC). With the resistance of existential forgery, WB-HDBL-MAC can also mitigate the algebraic, side-channel, and code-lifting attacks in the white-box attack context. Furthermore, the efficiency of WB-HDBL-MAC is compared with other MAC schemes. The experimental results demonstrate that WB-HDBL-MAC can improve the security of MAC implementation with acceptable performance.

Keywords: Blockchain · White-box cryptography · Implicit implementation · Message authentication codes · Double block length

1 Introduction

In recent years, message authentication codes (MAC) have been utilized to ensure data integrity and authenticity in blockchain technology. In vehicular ad-hoc networks (VANETs), Noh *et al.* [1] introduced public-private key and message authentication codes for secure identification information. Wu *et al.* [2] proposed a blockchain-based IoT sensor data privacy protection scheme, which applied HMAC to ensure data integrity. In 2023, to address the issue of excessive resource consumption in blockchain, Panasenko [3] proposed a lightweight blockchain solution built upon hash-based message authentication codes. Panasenko [4] also proposed a lightweight blockchain scheme based on HMAC to process data in the Internet of Medical Things (IoMT) with low-resourced sensor devices. These schemes are often related to the Internet of Things (IoT) systems where resources are always constrained.

The white-box context [5] assumes that an attacker gains full access and control over algorithm execution. Chow *et al.* [6] seminally proposed the implementation of white-box AES. The method of white-boxing a cipher is called the CEJO framework, which relies on look-up tables, random perturbations

D. He et al. (Eds.): BlockSys 2024, CCIS 2264, pp. 118–132, 2025.
https://doi.org/10.1007/978-981-96-1411-0_10

and encodings. Despite subsequent CEJO implementations [7,8], all of them have been broken [9,10] and three generic attacks have been proposed [11,12]. Apart from the CEJO framework, another white-box implementation approach called the self-equivalence framework was introduced in 2020 [13]. Subsequently, Vandersmissen *et al.* proposed the self-equivalence implementation of the ARX cipher SPECK [14]. However, it is not secure enough to protect the key concealed in the encoded affine layers [13,14]. Until 2022, Ranea *et al.* introduced a new white-box implementation scheme (an implicit framework), which relies on self-equivalence encodings and large random affine permutations to build an implicit round function. By implementing white-box cryptographic algorithms, the issue of key security in resource-constrained environments can be effectively addressed.

The secure implementations of block-cipher-based MACs are relatively mature, but they are limited by the length of the message. Several feasible white-box implementations have been proposed to counter key extraction attacks targeting HMAC [15,16]. However, these implementations lack practical significance because anyone can obtain the MAC value of any message using the preprocessed value. Moreover, these implementations cannot withstand code-lifting attacks where adversaries simply copy and run the code of the program without the key extraction. Lv *et al.* [17] introduced a unique white-box KMAC based on the CEJO framework, leveraging mixing bijections and non-linear encodings to transform the original KMAC into a network of encoded look-up tables. Due to the relatively large sizes of its lookup tables and the differences in algebraic operations, the method of white-box KMAC cannot be straightforwardly applied to implement compression functions of MACs. To the best of our knowledge, no formal white-box implementation of MAC based on compression function has been proposed. Therefore, constructing white-box MAC schemes to ensure data integrity and authenticity is crucial in resource-constrained environments.

Contributions. For ensuring data integrity and authenticity in blockchain technology, this paper has the following three main contributions.

- **A generalized method for constructing a white-box MAC implementation.** Given the balance between security and efficiency, we propose a secure scheme initialized by an implicit white-box SPECK implementation (WB-HDBL-MAC). The constructed method can also be applied to other white-box block ciphers.
- **The security analysis of WB-HDBL-MAC.** The utilized large non-linear external encodings of WB-HDBL-MAC resist both algebraic and side-channel analyses [18], including differential computation analysis (DCA) and differential fault analysis (DFA). Combined with hardware/application-binding technology, it can also resist the code-lifting attack.
- **The performance tests of WB-HDBL-MAC.** To verify the performance, the WB-HDBL-MAC scheme is compared with the white-box KMAC implementation. Moreover, based on two versions of the SPECK ciphers (SPECK32/64 and SPECK64/128), we test the performance between WB-

HDBL-MAC and the unprotected HDBL-MAC implementations with five various lengths of messages.

Outline. Section 2 introduces some preliminaries that will be used across this paper. Section 3 introduces an approach to construct implicit white-box implementations of a DBL compression-function-based MAC. We analyze the security of the WB-HDBL-MAC implementation and evaluate its performance in Sects. 4 and 5, respectively. Section 6 concludes this paper.

2   Preliminaries

The vector space consisting of n-bit values is denoted by $\mathbb{F}_2^n$. The symbols Id_n and $\oplus$ denote the identity function and the addition, respectively. Functions that map from $\mathbb{F}_2^n$ to $\mathbb{F}_2^m$ are defined as (n, m)-bit functions. The functions are called n-bit functions if $m = n$. The symbol $\circ$ denotes composition of two functions.

2.1   Encodings and Implicit White-Box Implementation

Definition 1 ([6,19]). *Let F be an (n,m)-bit function, and (I,O) denotes a pair of permutations. The function that encoded F is defined by $\overline{F} - O \circ F \circ I$, where I and O are n-bit input and m-bit output encodings. If $F = O \circ F \circ I$, the pair (I,O) is called a self-equivalence of F. In particular, If I is affine and O is quadratic, the pair (I,O) is called affine-quadratic self-equivalence encodings.*

Definition 2 ([20]). *Let Q be a $(2n, m)$-bit implicit function of F. If for all $x \in \mathbb{F}_2^n$, the (n,m)-bit function $y \mapsto Q(x,y)$ is affine, then the implicit function is quasilinear.*

For the implicit implementation of SPECK, the i-th encoded round function is defined as $\overline{E^{(i)}} = O^{(i)} \circ E^{(i)} \circ I^{(i)} = O^{(i)} \circ AL^{(i)} \circ S \circ I^{(i)}$. The notation S denotes permuted modular addition and $AL^{(i)}$ represents the affine layer containing the i-th round key $k^{(i)}$. The corresponding quasilinear implicit function could be denoted by $Q^{(i)} = T \circ (\mathrm{Id}_n, (AL^{(i)})^{-1}) \circ (I^{(i)}, (O^{(i)})^{-1})$, where T is the quasilinear implicit function of S. And the round encodings are built as

$$
\begin{aligned}
(I^{(i)}, O^{(i)}) &= (A^{(i)} \circ B^{(i-1)} \circ (C^{(i)})^{-1}, C^{(i+1)}) \\
&= (B^{(i-1)} \circ (C^{(i)})^{-1}, C^{(i+1)} \circ (B^{(i)})^{-1}),
\end{aligned}
\tag{1}
$$

where $(A^{(i)}, B^{(i)})$ is a pair of affine-quadratic self-equivalence encodings of $E^{(i)}$, $C^{(i)}$ is a random affine encoding. The consecutive encoded rounds satisfy the cancellation rule as illustrated in Fig. 1. Particularly, $B^{(0)}$ should be a random quadratic permutation. Thus, when using round encodings given by Eq. (1), an implicit implementation of SPECK $\overline{E_k}$ could be represented as:

$$
\begin{aligned}
\overline{E_k} &= \overline{E^{(n_r)}} \circ \overline{E^{(n_r-1)}} \circ \cdots \circ \overline{E^{(1)}} \\
&= (O^{(n_r)} \circ E^{(n_r)} \circ I^{(n_r)}) \circ \cdots \circ (O^{(1)} \circ E^{(1)} \circ I^{(1)}) \\
&= (C^{(n_r+1)} \circ (B^{(n_r)})^{-1}) \circ (E^{(n_r)} \circ E^{(n_r-1)} \circ \cdots \circ E^{(1)}) \circ (B^{(0)} \circ (C^{(1)})^{-1}) \\
&= (C^{(n_r+1)} \circ (B^{(n_r)})^{-1}) \circ E_k \circ (B^{(0)} \circ (C^{(1)})^{-1}) \\
&= O_{ext} \circ E_k \circ I_{ext},
\end{aligned}
\tag{2}
$$

where I_{ext} and O_{ext} are the external encodings.

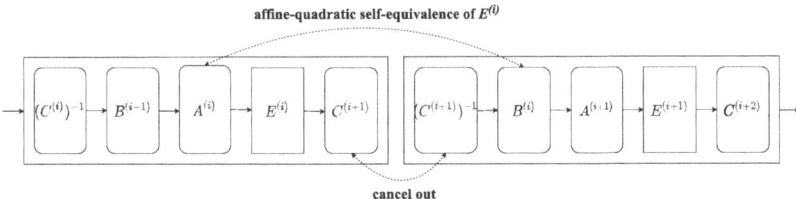

Fig. 1. Cancellation of encodings for two consecutive rounds [20].

2.2   Double-Block-Length Compression Function

Let n be the block size, the compression function is composed of a component function with $n/2n$-bit output is called a single/double-block-length compression function (SBL/DBL-CF). According to the key length, the DBL-CF can be categorized into two groups: one uses an n-bit keyed block cipher (DBL^n), and the other uses a $2n$-bit keyed block cipher (DBL^{2n}). Let F be a compression function composed of a block cipher and m_i be n-bit message blocks. The rate r is widely used as a measurement of efficiency, which is defined as follows:

$$
r - \frac{|m_i|}{(the\ number\ of\ block\text{-}cipher\ calls\ in\ F) \times n}.
$$

Typically a DBL compression function with the rate at $1/2$ has been proposed by Hirose [21] (HDBL-CF). For DBL^n class, Mennink *et al.* [22] proposed the optimally secure compression function (MDBL-CF). However, compared HDBL-CF, the rate of MDBL-CF is $1/3$ and the complexity of resisting preimage attacks is lower. For achieving a small memory size, Naito *et al.* [23] proposed the smallest DBL modes. However, this structure is complex, which makes it difficult to construct a white-box implementation of a compression function. The HDBL-CF described in Definition 3 exhibits advantages in collision security, efficiency, and constructing a white-box implementation.

Definition 3 ([21]). *Let F be a (3n, 2n)-bit compression function such that $(g_i, h_i) = F(g_{i-1}, h_{i-1}, m_i)$, where $g_i, h_i, m_i \in \mathbb{F}_2^n$, c is a non-zero constant. F consists of a n-bit block cipher E as follows.*

$$g_i = E(m_i, g_{i-1}||h_{i-1}) \oplus m_i,$$
$$h_i = E(m_i, g_{i-1}||(h_{i-1} \oplus c)) \oplus m_i.$$

3   White-Box Implementations of MAC

Choosing block cipher algorithms for in-depth study can help avoid potential flaws in compression functions. However, the SBL-CF with the maximum output length is no longer secure against the collision-finding attack. Hence, the DBL-CF using the implicit white-box implementation of block ciphers is considered. Due to the vulnerability to length extension attacks, transforming iterative compression functions based on the Merkle-Damgård construction into a secure MAC is not readily implemented. Additionally, block-cipher-based MACs are restricted by data width, especially with implicit white-box implementations. Therefore, we decided to combine CBC-MAC [24] and HDBL-CF to build an implicit white-box implementation of MAC, as depicted in Fig. 2.

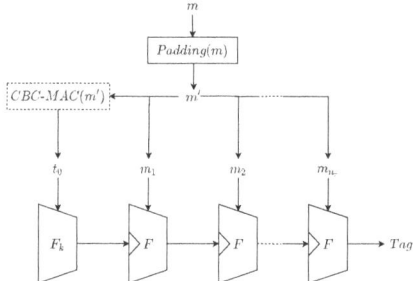

Fig. 2. Scheme of WB-HDBL-MAC implementation.

First, we should preprocess the message m to obtain a value t_0, which uniquely determines the message m. That is

$$CBC\text{-}MAC(Padding(m)) = t_0.$$

The message padding algorithm *Padding* and the algorithm *CBC-MAC* will be described in Sect. 3.1. The precomputed value t_0 will serve as the first block input of the scheme, the secret value k is the key of the WB-HDBL-MAC. The padded message value m' would be divided into multiple blocks and used sequentially as input to the compression function F. To the best of our knowledge, this is the first white-box implementation to construct a compression-function-based MAC relying on the implicit framework.

3.1   Preprocessing

In order to resist the length expansion attack mentioned above, preprocessing the message m into an output with a fixed length is essential. This could prevent an attacker from appending one or more message blocks and resulting correct MAC value. Let n be the block size of SPECK, a message m requires to be padded to a minimum multiple of n for processing. And the padded value m' is divided into a number of n-bit blocks $m_1, m_2, \cdots, m_{n_r}$. The padding rule will refer to the standard document RFC4634 US Secure Hash Algorithms (SHA and HMAC-SHA) [25] and can be described as Algorithm 1.

Algorithm 1. *Padding*

Input: the message m $\{|m| \leq 2^{32} - 1\}$
Output: the padded message m'
   $a \leftarrow (n - 33 - |m|) \bmod n$
   $b \leftarrow binary\ representation\ of\ the\ |m|$
   {use a fixed 32-bit binary to represent the length of the message m}
   $m' \leftarrow m\ ||\ 1\ ||\ 0^a\ ||\ b$

As depicted in Fig. 3, two cases need to be considered for securely implementing CBC-MAC. If a trusted execution environment exists in hardware, the original CBC-MAC algorithm with the original block cipher E_{c_i} would be utilized. The output t_0 of the CBC-MAC algorithm would be generated in a specific hardware within the device. If there is no trusted execution environment, the block cipher E_{c_i} should be replaced by a white-box implementation of the block cipher (i.e. $WB\text{-}E_{c_i}$). The application-binding technology [26] and software obfuscation techniques [27] would be applied to ensure that the program generating the value t_0 can only execute on one specified application.

3.2   White-Box Implementation of DBL Compression Function

Taking into account collision resistance security and structural complexity, the compression function F described in Definition 3 is considered. The core of the WB-HDBL-MAC scheme is the white-box implementation of the first block compression function F_k containing the key. Thus, we restructured the HDBL-CF and obtained the white-box implementation of the function F_k. It can be defined as follows and also be represented in Fig. 4.

$$WB\text{-}E_k(t_0) \oplus t_0 = g_0,$$
$$WB\text{-}E_{k \oplus c'}(t_0) \oplus t_0 = h_0,$$

where the value c' is a vector of length $2n$ containing the non-zero constant c in the first n positions and zero in the last n positions. The key k is hidden in

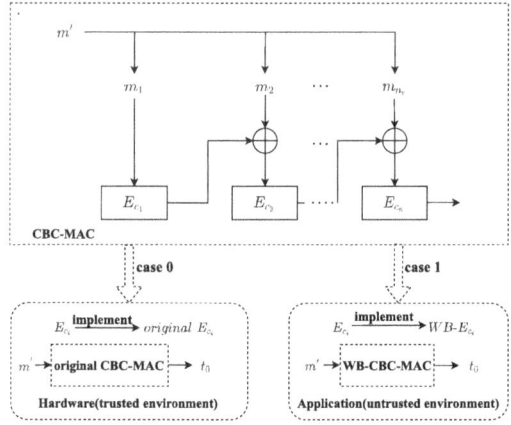

Fig. 3. CBC-MAC algorithm under trusted and untrusted execution environments.

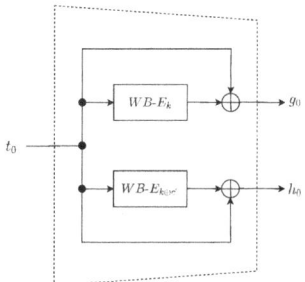

Fig. 4. The white-box implementation of the first block compression function

the quasilinear implicit functions by the implicit white-box implementation of the block ciphers.

Constructing an efficient DBL-CF-based MAC using an ARX cipher is a new attempt. Notably, the block cipher E illustrated in Definition 3 is different from Fig. 4. The former corresponds to the original SPECK implementation with public parameters as keys. That is, the key for the first block cipher in the compression function F is represented by the value $g_{i-1}||h_{i-1}$, while the key for the second block cipher is represented by the value $g_{i-1}||(h_{i-1} \oplus c)$. The latter is the implicit white-box implementation of SPECK as depicted in Sect. 2.1. The round encodings are composed of large random affine permutations and affine-quadratic self-equivalence encodings given by Eq. (1). The encoded round function is described in an implicit function, enabling the calculation of its values by solving sets of linear equations.

The implicit white-box SPECK implementation (i.e. $WB\text{-}E_k$) is not functionally equivalent to the original SPECK implementation (i.e. E_k). It can be further concluded that the WB-HDBL-MAC is not functionally equivalent to the unprotected HDBL-MAC. To maintain the validity of the WB-HDBL-MAC, both communicating parties must use the WB-HDBL-MAC algorithm with the same external encodings. Due to the irreversibility of the first block compression function, extracting the key solely based on obtaining g_0 and h_0 would pose a considerable challenge. Although there is no way to prevent an attacker from appending arbitrary message blocks after obtaining the values g_0 and h_0, it could be verified whether the message is modified. Furthermore, once the key, external encoding, or message is updated, the values g_0 and h_0 will be regenerated on the specific device, resulting in a new MAC value Tag. The overview of the WB-HDBL-MAC algorithm is depicted as Algorithm 2.

Algorithm 2. WB-HDBL-MAC

Input: the message m
Output: the MAC value Tag
   $Tag \leftarrow 0^{2n}$
   $m' \leftarrow Padding(m)$
   $t_0 \leftarrow CBC\text{-}MAC(m')$
   $Partition\ m'\ into\ m_1 \cdots m_{n_r}$
   for $i = 0 : n_r$ **do**
     if $i = 0$ **then**
       $g_0, h_0 \leftarrow F_k(t_0)$
     else
       $g_i, h_i \leftarrow F(g_{i-1}, h_{i-1}, m_i)$
     end if
   end for
   $Tag \leftarrow g_{n_r} || h_{n_r}$

---

4 Security Analysis

In this work, it is proven that the WB-HDBL-MAC is resistant to existential forgery in black-box context. Moreover, we focus on the resistance of the key-recovery attack in the white-box context. The WB-HDBL-MAC can mitigate algebraic, side-channel and code-lifting attacks.

4.1 Existential Forgery Resistnce

In the black-box context, the unforgeability security of the WB-HDBL-MAC under chosen-message attack can be measured by the following experiment.

$$Exp_{WB\text{-}HDBL\text{-}MAC,\mathcal{A}}^{uf\text{-}cma}$$

$$k \xleftarrow{r} \mathbb{F}_2^{2n}$$

$$(m, \sigma) \leftarrow \mathcal{A}^{WB\text{-}HDBL\text{-}MAC_k(\cdot)}$$

$if\ WB\text{-}HDBL\text{-}MAC_k(m) = \sigma\ and\ m\ was\ not\ a\ query\ of\ \mathcal{A}\ to\ its\ oracle$

$then\ return\ 1\ else\ return\ 0$

Let $\mathcal{A}$ be any forger possessing an oracle $WB\text{-}HDBL\text{-}MAC_k(\cdot)$. It can invoke this oracle on any message of its choice, this phase can be seen as its learning stage. And then $\mathcal{A}$ is going to forge an authentication tag of a new message. The unforgeability of a message authentication code would be measured by an advantage function, where

$$\mathbf{Adv}_{WB\text{-}HDBL\text{-}MAC}^{uf\text{-}cma}(\mathcal{A}) = \mathbf{Pr}[Exp_{WB\text{-}HDBL\text{-}MAC,\mathcal{A}}^{uf\text{-}cma}\ return\ 1].$$

To demonstrate the unforgeability of the message authentication code, one cannot only directly prove it by solving $\mathbf{Adv}_{WB\text{-}HDBL\text{-}MAC}^{uf\text{-}cma}(\mathcal{A})$, but also to solve the advantage function $\mathbf{Adv}_{WB\text{-}HDBL\text{-}MAC}^{uf\text{-}cma}(\mathcal{B}_\mathcal{A})$. An adversary $\mathcal{B}_\mathcal{A}$ distinguishes between MAC and rand function. As long as this advantage is negligible, a message authentication code is resistant to forgery.

Theorem 1. *Let CBC-MAC be securely implemented, then the resulting output t_0 satisfies the property of resisting existential forgery. Suppose that compression-function-based MAC is existentially unforgeable, then the WB-HDBL-MAC is resistant to existential forgery.*

Proof. It has been proved that the compression function F specified in Definition 3 behaves like a random function in the iteration. When performing a white-box implementation of the first block compression function, the collision resistance and randomness are not diminished. Thus, the security of the compression-function-based MAC can be reduced to the compression function. The WB-HDBL-MAC can be seen as consisting of CBC-MAC and compression-function-based MAC. Therefore, when CBC-MAC is securely implemented, the WB-HDBL-MAC exhibits resistance to existential forgery. □

4.2 White-Box Security Analysis

Key-Extraction Resistance. Due to the capability of the implicit white-box implementation, our WB-HDBL-MAC implementation mainly tackles the key extraction attacks. It is assumed that the specifications of the underlying compression function and the implicit implementation are public, but the key and the encodings are unknown to an adversary.

Algebraic Attacks. At present, most algebraic white-box attacks target the CEJO framework. It is confirmed that three proposed generic CEJO attacks [11,12,28] are not effective in Ranea et al.'s work [20]. However, several attacks pointed at the implicit framework have proposed by Biryukov et al. at CHES 2023 [29]. Firstly, the setting where one of the external encodings is omitted should be considered. Biryukov *et al.* indicated a feasible degree-2 algebraic attack to recover the key. But in this paper, we use both external encodings and neither is an identity function. Thus, the degree-2 algebraic attack is not efficient. However, Biryukov *et al.* described a developing decomposition method and showed the affine-quadratic encodings could be decomposed and reduced to the affine case. The majority of round subkeys could be recovered by decompositions and inversion methods. Thus, when using affine-quadratic encodings, the key recovery attack time complexity is $\mathcal{O}(N^9)$, where N refers to the word size of the underlying block cipher.

Side-Channel Attacks. Several side-channel attacks (DCA and DFA) have been proposed to break CEJO implementations. These attacks assume the external encodings are the identity functions. The only DFA attack proposed by Amadori et al. [30] successfully resists 8-bit non-trivial external encodings. The existing side-channel attacks usually target an intermediate computation where the output is encoded with small sizes, which depends on a small range of the round key bits. However, the WB-HDBL-MAC implementation would be represented by multiple Boolean polynomials with large inputs and outputs. The intermediate computations are confused by large encodings and rely on the whole round keys. Furthermore, large nonlinear permutations are employed to construct external encodings and neither is an identity function. The input external encodings are used to confuse the real plaintext to resist DCA attacks. The output external encodings are used to confuse the real ciphertext to resist DFA attacks. Thus, current side-channel attacks cannot be applied to the WB-HDBL-MAC implementation.

Code-Lifting Resistance. Typical techniques to mitigate code-lifting are relying on a trusted execution environment in hardware. When there is no trusted environment, the application-binding technology combined with software obfuscation is also used to resist code-lifting attacks. As depicted in Fig. 3, if value t_0 is generated in a trusted execution environment of hardware, the value t_0 could be generated in specific hardware. If there is no trusted environment, the WB-CBC-MAC algorithm is bound to specific application. In other words, the program generating the value t_0 should only be executable on one specific device (application). Thus, the WB-HDBL-MAC implementation will have the capability to be bound to devices or applications, thereby enabling resistance against code-lifting attacks.

5   Experimental Results

The authors [20] provide the open-source codes to generate the implicit white-box implementations of SPECK block cipher (WB-IF-SPECK)[1]. We instantiate the implicit white-box implementations of SPECK32/64 (WB-IF-SPECK32/64) and SPECK64/128 (WB-IF-SPECK64/128) with affine-quadratic self-equivalence encodings, excluding SPECK128/256 due to security-performance trade-offs. Based on these implementations, we developed WB-HDBL-MAC in C code. All experiments have been tested with 11th Gen Intel(R) Core(TM) i7-11800H Processor (2.3 GHz, 40 GB memory) and Ubuntu 20.04.6 LTS operation system. The WB-HDBL-MAC scheme is compared with the only white-box KMAC implementation [17]. The white-box HMAC-SHA256 is not considered due to no practical significance. For each white-box MAC implementation, the basic case with one message block is executed 10,000 times to derive average execution time. To comprehensively compare the performance, each WB-HDBL-MAC and unprotected HDBL-MAC implementation based on two versions of the SPECK cipher (SPECK32/64 and SPECK64/128) are tested 10,000 times with five various lengths of messages.

5.1   Storage Complexity

As depicted in Table 1, the storage space of the WB-HDBL-MAC implementation required is approximately twice that of one WB-IF-SPECK. The reason is that the WB-HDBL-MAC involves two WB-IF-SPECK implementations under different keys. The memory costs of the WB-HDBL-MAC mainly depend on the block size. That is, as the block size increases, the multivariate Boolean polynomials will have a higher number of variables and terms, leading to an expansion in memory allocation. The storage complexity has nothing to do with message content and message length. For the white-box KMAC implementation, the storage space is determined by the size and quantity of the look-up tables used. The unprotected HDBL-MAC, which does not store any tables or the coefficients of the Boolean polynomials, with the block size increase, the storage costs remain nearly unchanged.

Table 1. Performance of the White-box KMAC and the WB-HDBL-MAC

Scheme	Underlying block cipher				Message block sizes (Bytes)	Execution time (ms)	RAM (MB)
	Block cipher	Message block sizes (Bytes)	Encryption time (ms)	RAM (MB)			
White-box KMAC	Null				136	1.10917	109.3
WB-HDBL-MAC	WB-IF-SPECK32/64	4	11.63	5.3	4	25.42	11.2
	WB-IF-SPECK64/128	8	176.84	44.7	8	388.77	90.1

---

[1] https://github.com/ranea/whiteboxarx.

Table 2. Performance of WB-HDBL-MAC and unprotected HDBL-MAC based on SPECK32/64 and SPECK64/128 with five various lengths of messages

Scheme	Block cipher	RAM (MB)	Message length (Bytes)	Execution time (ms)
Unprotected HDBL-MAC	SPECK32/64	1.2	4	0.00060
			8	0.00092
			32	0.0028
			256	0.0209
			4096	0.3270
WB-HDBL-MAC	WB-IF-SPECK32/64	11.2	4	25.42
			8	25.91
			32	26.07
			256	26.14
			4096	26.40
Unprotected HDBL-MAC	SPECK64/128	1.3	8	0.00064
			16	0.00096
			64	0.0031
			512	0.0218
			8192	0.3368
WB-HDBL-MAC	WB-IF-SPECK64/128	90.1	8	388.77
			16	401.60
			64	402.68
			512	405.40
			8192	408.16

5.2   Performance Test

The performance of the WB-HDBL-MAC primarily depends on the time required for solving implicit functions, which is converted from Boolean polynomials. For white-box KMAC, 1088-bit messages will be executed iteratively to process any messages. As the message blocks increase, the time cost rises linearly. The running time is determined by the table look-up operations. Compared with unprotected HDBL-MAC, the results listed in Table 2 indicate that the performance of WB-HDBL-MAC is notably slower than the unprotected HDBL-MAC. However, with larger messages, the performance gap would be gradually narrowing.

6   Conclusion

The message authentication code guarantees that the data is integrity-protected and authenticity-verified in the blockchain system. To address the issue of resource constraints in IoT, we initially introduced a generalized method to construct an efficient white-box MAC based on DBL-CF. The scheme is initialized by an implicit white-box SPECK implementation (WB-HDBL-MAC). Moreover, it is confirmed that the WB-HDBL-MAC is efficient to mitigate side-channel and code-lifting attacks. While the performance of the WB-HDBL-MAC implementation may not be optimal, it can still be acceptable in certain application scenarios where frequent requests for MAC are not necessary. In the future, there are two potential areas for further research. On the one hand, the more secure white-box block cipher could be replaced in the WB-HDBL-MAC rather than implicit white-box SPECK implementation. On the other hand, affine-cubic encodings, quadratic-quadratic encodings, or higher-degree encodings could be found to construct a more secure implicit white-box implementation of MAC.

Acknowledgments. This work was supported by National Key Research and Development Program of China (2024QY2501), National Natural Science Foundation of China (U2336209), Guangdong Basic and Applied Basic Research Foundation (2022A1515140090) and Guangzhou Key Research and Development Program (2023B03J0172).

References

1. Noh, J., Jeon, S., Cho, S.: Distributed blockchain-based message authentication scheme for connected vehicles. Electronics **9**(1), 74 (2020)
2. Wu, Y., Song, L., Liu, L., et al.: IoT data privacy protection scheme based on blockchain. In: IOP Conference Series: Earth and Environmental Science, vol. 769, p. 042034. IOP Publishing (2021)
3. Panasenko, S.: A lightweight blockchain scheme for the internet of things. In: 2023 IEEE 15th International Conference on Computational Intelligence and Communication Networks (CICN), pp. 353–357. IEEE (2023)
4. Panasenko, S.: A lightweight blockchain for the internet of medical things using hash-based message authentication codes. In: 2023 International Wireless Communications and Mobile Computing (IWCMC), pp. 1095–1100. IEEE (2023)
5. Chow, S., Eisen, P., Johnson, H., van Oorschot, P.C.: A white-box DES implementation for DRM applications. In: Feigenbaum, J. (ed.) DRM 2002. LNCS, vol. 2696, pp. 1–15. Springer, Heidelberg (2003). https://doi.org/10.1007/978-3-540-44993-5_1
6. Chow, S., Eisen, P., Johnson, H., Van Oorschot, P.C.: White-box cryptography and an AES implementation. In: Nyberg, K., Heys, H. (eds.) SAC 2002. LNCS, vol. 2595, pp. 250–270. Springer, Heidelberg (2003). https://doi.org/10.1007/3-540-36492-7_17
7. Xiao, Y., Lai, X.: A secure implementation of white-box AES. In: 2009 2nd International Conference on Computer Science and its Applications, pp. 1–6. IEEE (2009)
8. Karroumi, M.: Protecting white-box AES with dual ciphers. In: Rhee, K.-H., Nyang, D.H. (eds.) ICISC 2010. LNCS, vol. 6829, pp. 278–291. Springer, Heidelberg (2011). https://doi.org/10.1007/978-3-642-24209-0_19
9. De Mulder, Y., Roelse, P., Preneel, B.: Cryptanalysis of the Xiao – Lai white-box AES implementation. In: Knudsen, L.R., Wu, H. (eds.) SAC 2012. LNCS, vol. 7707, pp. 34–49. Springer, Heidelberg (2013). https://doi.org/10.1007/978-3-642-35999-6_3
10. Lepoint, T., Rivain, M., De Mulder, Y., Roelse, P., Preneel, B.: Two attacks on a white-box AES implementation. In: Lange, T., Lauter, K., Lisoněk, P. (eds.) SAC 2013. LNCS, vol. 8282, pp. 265–285. Springer, Heidelberg (2014). https://doi.org/10.1007/978-3-662-43414-7_14

11. Michiels, W., Gorissen, P., Hollmann, H.D.L.: Cryptanalysis of a generic class of white-box implementations. In: Avanzi, R.M., Keliher, L., Sica, F. (eds.) SAC 2008. LNCS, vol. 5381, pp. 414–428. Springer, Heidelberg (2009). https://doi.org/10.1007/978-3-642-04159-4_27

12. Derbez, P., Fouque, P.-A., Lambin, B., et al.: On recovering affine encodings in white-box implementations. IACR Cryptol. ePrint Arch., pp. 96 (2019)

13. Ranea, A., Preneel, B.: On self-equivalence encodings in white-box implementations. In: Dunkelman, O., Jacobson, Jr., M.J., O'Flynn, C. (eds.) SAC 2020. LNCS, vol. 12804, pp. 639–669. Springer, Cham (2021). https://doi.org/10.1007/978-3-030-81652-0_25

14. Vandersmissen, J., Ranea, A., Preneel, B.: A white-box speck implementation using self-equivalence encodings. In: Ateniese, G., Venturi, D. (eds.) ACNS 2022. LNCS, vol. 13269, pp. 771–791. Springer, Cham. Springer (2022). https://doi.org/10.1007/978-3-031-09234-3_38

15. Kolegov, D., Oleksov, N., Broslavsky, O.: White-box HMAC: make your cryptography secure to white-box attacks, Moscow, Russia, 17–18 May 2016. Video posted online on 20 May 2016

16. Github Website: HMAC-SHA256 Whitebox. Posted online on 12 April 2017. https://github.com/aguinet/hmac_sha256_whitebox

17. Lu, J., Zhao, Z., Guo, H.: White-box implementation of the KMAC message authentication code. In: Heng, S.-H., Lopez, J. (eds.) ISPEC 2019. LNCS, vol. 11879, pp. 248–270. Springer, Cham (2019). https://doi.org/10.1007/978-3-030-34339-2_14

18. Bock, E.A., Bos, J.W., Brzuska, C., et al.: White-box cryptography: don't forget about grey-box attacks. J. Cryptol. **32**(4), 1095–1143 (2019)

19. Biryukov, A., De Cannière, C., Braeken, A., Preneel, B.: A toolbox for cryptanalysis: linear and affine equivalence algorithms. In: Biham, E. (ed.) EUROCRYPT 2003. LNCS, vol. 2656, pp. 33–50. Springer, Heidelberg (2003). https://doi.org/10.1007/3-540-39200-9_3

20. Ranea, A., Vandersmissen, J., Preneel, B.: Implicit white-box implementations: white-boxing ARX ciphers. In: Dodis, Y., Shrimpton, T. (eds.) CRYPTO 2022, Part I. LNCS, vol. 13507, pp. 33–63. Springer, Cham (2022). https://doi.org/10.1007/978-3-031-15802-5_2

21. Hirose, S.: Some plausible constructions of double-block-length hash functions. In: Robshaw, M. (ed.) FSE 2006. LNCS, vol. 4047, pp. 210–225. Springer, Heidelberg (2006). https://doi.org/10.1007/11799313_14

22. Mennink, B.: Optimal collision security in double block length hashing with single length key. In: Wang, X., Sako, K. (eds.) ASIACRYPT 2012. LNCS, vol. 7658, pp. 526–543. Springer, Heidelberg (2012). https://doi.org/10.1007/978-3-642-34961-4_32

23. Naito, Y., Sasaki, Yu., Sugawara, T.: Double-block-length hash function for minimum memory size. In: Tibouchi, M., Wang, H. (eds.) ASIACRYPT 2021. LNCS, vol. 13092, pp. 376–406. Springer, Cham (2021). https://doi.org/10.1007/978-3-030-92078-4_13

24. Bellare, M., Kilian, J., Rogaway, P.: The security of the cipher block chaining message authentication code. J. Comput. Syst. Sci. **61**(3), 362–399 (2000)

25. Eastlake, D.E., III., Hansen, T.: US secure hash algorithms (SHA and SHA-based HMAC and HKDF). RFC **6234**, 1–127 (2011)

26. Bock, E.A., Amadori, A., Brzuska, C., et al.: On the security goals of white-box cryptography. IACR Trans. Cryptogr. Hardw. Embed. Syst. **2020**, 327–357 (2020)

27. Banescu, S., Pretschner, A.: A tutorial on software obfuscation. Adv. Comput. **108**, 283–353 (2018)
28. Baek, C.H., Cheon, J.H., Hong, H.: White-box AES implementation revisited. J. Commun. Netw. **18**(3), 273–287 (2016)
29. Biryukov, A., Lambin, B., Udovenko, A.: Cryptanalysis of ARX-based white-box implementations. IACR Trans. Cryptogr. Hardw. Embed. Syst. **2023**(3), 97–135 (2023)
30. Amadori, A., Michiels, W., Roelse, P.: A DFA attack on white-box implementations of AES with external encodings. In: Paterson, K.G., Stebila, D. (eds.) SAC 2019. LNCS, vol. 11959, pp. 591–617. Springer, Cham (2020). https://doi.org/10.1007/978-3-030-38471-5_24

A Survey on Blockchain Scalability

Wei Tong[1], Jian Li[1], Lingxiao Yang[2(✉)], Xiyan Huang[3], Xiangshang Gao[1], and Zesong Dong[1]

[1] Hangzhou Institute of Technology, Xidian University, Hangzhou 310000, China
[2] School of Computer Science and Technology, Xidian University, Xi'an 710000, China
lxyang@stu.xidian.edu.cn
[3] College of Electronics and Information Engineering, Tongji University, Shanghai 200000, China

Abstract. As an advanced technology, blockchain is the core of trust establishment, data interaction, and value delivery in a distributed zero-trust environment. However, due to the characteristics of equal autonomy of nodes, multi-party maintenance of data, and closed isolation between chains, the blockchain system faces the problem of impossible triangle. Many researchers have studied blockchain scalability methods. This paper investigates the existing methods from three aspects of the network scalability, throughput scalability, and function scalability. It also compares and summarizes these methods, aiming to direct future research in the scalability optimization of blockchain.

Keywords: Blockchain · performance optimization · network scalability · throughput scalability · function scalability

1 Introduction

The concept of blockchain originated from the publication of "Bitcoin: A Peer-to-Peer Electronic Cash System" by Satoshi Nakamoto in 2008 [1]. Essentially, blockchain is a collective term for the underlying technologies that support Bitcoin, including data structures, networking techniques, consensus algorithms, cryptographic algorithms, smart contracts, and various other computer technologies. With its features of decentralization, transparent storage, and traceability, blockchain has attracted widespread attention and exploration from both academia and industry.

Decentralization, security, and scalability constitute the impossible triangle of distributed blockchain systems [2]. Decentralization refers to having a large number of equally participating nodes in the distributed system's operation and maintenance, with a higher degree of decentralization achieved with more nodes. Security refers to the cost of maintaining the consistency of the distributed system state, which can be measured by the number of blockchain nodes participating in state maintenance, with higher security achieved with

D. He et al. (Eds.): BlockSys 2024, CCIS 2264, pp. 133–146, 2025.
https://doi.org/10.1007/978-981-96-1411-0_11

more nodes. Scalability refers to network scalability, throughput scalability, and function scalability. To maintain decentralization and security, blockchain systems face significant scalability optimization challenges [3]. This paper focuses on researching the scalability of blockchain.

Different from the existing research surveys, this paper analyzes the application requirements connotation of blockchain scalability, and summarizes the existing research from three aspects, including network scalability, throughput scalability, and function scalability. First, in view of the application node size requirements, we explore the underlying blockchain technology that limits the number of nodes and analyze the impact of existing blockchain consensus algorithms on network load and node size. Secondly, for application high-performance requirements, we explore different levels of performance constraints, and analyze the impact of existing blockchain performance scalability solutions on transaction throughput. Finally, in view of the application's frequent interaction requirements, we explore the underlying technologies that hinder functional convergence, and analyze the impact of existing blockchain functional scalability solutions on interoperability and on-chain off-chain interaction.

This paper is organized as follows. In Sect. 2, the explanations of network scalability, throughput scalability, and function scalability of blockchain are presented. Sections 3, 4 and 5 summarize existing researches on network scalability, throughput scalability, and function scalability of blockchain, respectively. Section 6 introduces the differences between this paper with existing surveys, and Sect. 7 concludes this paper.

2   Scalability

In blockchain systems, network scalability refers to the number of nodes the network can support; throughput scalability denotes transaction throughput, or transactions processed per second; and function scalability involves cross-chain interactions, including trust transmission, data exchange, and value transfer between different blockchains.

Network Scalability. The problem of network scalability optimization is manifested in the limitation of the number of participants in the consensus layer consensus protocol. During the consensus process, a large number of messages are transmitted in the network, which can easily cause network congestion. Taking the globally mainstream consortium blockchain platform Hyperledger Fabric v0.6 [4] as an example, the platform's consensus layer uses the Practical Byzantine Fault Tolerance (PBFT) protocol. Tests have shown that under a hundred-megabit fiber network, the capacity of Fabric network does not exceed 20 nodes, the problem of network scalability optimization is severe.

Throughput Scalability. Throughput scalability refers to increasing the number of transactions that blockchain processes per second, which is reflected in

Table 1. Comparison among consensus algorithms for network scalability.

Consensus algorithms	Communication complexity	Network capacity	Leader	Consistency	Application projects
PoW [1]	$O(w)$	∞	many	weak	Bitcoin, Ethereum
PoS [6]	$O(w)$	∞	many	weak	Ethereum, ATOM
DPoS [7]	$\leq O(w)$	∞	many	weak	EOS
PoT [8]	$O(w)$	∞	many	weak	/
RAFT [9]	$O(N)$	≥ 100	single	strong	Fabric, FISCO BCOS
PBFT [10]	$O(N^2)$	≤ 20	single	strong	Fabric, FISCO BCOS
Zyzzyva [11]	$O(N)$ or $O(N^2)$	≥ 100	single	strong	ZyConChain
Tendermint [12]	$O(N^2)$	≤ 20	single	strong	Cosmos
HoneyBadgerBFT [13]	$O(N)$	≥ 100	single	strong	Fabric
Trust-PBFT [14]	$O((N - N^*)/N)$	∞	single	strong	CrowdChain
SG-PBFT [15]	$O(N^2)$	≥ 100	single	strong	/
PBFT-PoW [16]	$O(N^2)$	≤ 20	single	strong	TrueChain, Zilliqa
BFT-DPoS [17]	$O(N^2)$	≤ 20	single	strong	EOS

the limitations of the consensus protocol at the consensus layer and the way nodes execute the consensus protocol at the network layer. Taking the Fabric consortium blockchain platform as an example, the transaction throughput of the Fabric platform does not exceed 2,000 tps [5], the low transaction throughput poses a serious scalability issue.

Function Scalability. Function scalability requires enriching blockchain functions through interacting with external data sources and other blockchains. Taking the Fabric consortium blockchain platform and the FISCO BCOS consortium blockchain platform as examples, the two platforms do not trust each other, and their underlying technologies, including consensus protocols and encryption mechanisms. For blockchain systems with strong internal security measures and heterogeneous underlying technologies, the issue of function scalability is significant.

3   Network Scalability

For blockchain systems, network scalability depends on the complexity of network communication. Currently, blockchain consensus protocols mainly fall into two categories: proof-based consensus protocols and voting-based consensus protocols. The existing consensus protocols are summarized in Table 1.

3.1   Proof-Based Consensus Algorithms

- **Proof of Work (PoW).** PoW is applied in the Bitcoin blockchain proposed by Satoshi Nakamoto [1]. PoW requires all participating nodes in the consensus to independently solve the same mathematical problem, and the node that first solves the problem broadcasts the answer to all nodes in the network. Participating nodes that receive the answer suspend solving the problem and instead verify the answer. If the answer is correct, the answer and the block broadcasted by the winning node are recorded; otherwise, they continue solving the problem. The communication complexity of the PoW consensus protocol is $O(w)$, where w represents the number of winning nodes.

- **Proof of Stake (PoS).** PoS stipulates that only nodes with a certain amount of Ether can become true consensus participants and participate in solving the mathematical problem, and the difficulty of node problem-solving is negatively correlated with the amount of tokens they possess; that is, the more tokens a node owns, the lower the difficulty of problem-solving for that node [6]. As for communication complexity, PoS does not fundamentally optimize it and remains $O(w)$, where w represents the number of winning nodes.
- **Delegated Proof of Stake (DPoS).** DPoS optimizes PoS, further reducing the number of participating nodes and energy consumption [7]. DPoS achieves this by conducting voting among nodes qualified to participate in the consensus, electing the top N nodes with the highest number of votes as consensus participants to solve the problem. DPoS typically sets a fixed number N of consensus participant nodes, with a maximum communication complexity of $O(N)$.

3.2 Voting-Based Consensus Algorithms

Voting-based consensus protocols can be divided into two categories: Byzantine Fault Tolerance (BFT) consensus protocols and non-BFT consensus protocols. BFT can tolerate a certain number of Byzantine faulty nodes in the network.

BFT-Based Consensus Algorithms

- **PBFT.** PBFT is a fundamental and representative Byzantine fault-tolerant consensus protocol [10]. PBFT consists of 5 phases: the *request* phase, where the *client* sends a *request* message to the primary node; then the primary node broadcasts a related $pre-prepare$ message to other participant nodes (with a total of N consensus participant nodes); if the participant nodes accept the $pre-prepare$ message, they verify the message and package the result into *prepare* messages to broadcast to other participant nodes; if a participant node receives $2f(N = 3f + 1)$ identical prepare messages from different nodes, the node broadcasts a *commit* message; if a participant node receives $2f + 1$ *commit* messages from different nodes (including its own), consensus is reached. Finally, each node sends *reply* messages to the *client*, and the PBFT consensus protocol execution concludes. The PBFT consensus protocol requires all consensus participants to frequently broadcast voting messages to achieve consensus, with a communication complexity of $O(N^2)$.
- **Zyzzyva.** Zyzzyva is a Speculative Byzantine Fault Tolerance (SBFT) consensus protocol that utilizes speculation to simplify the design of the PBFT

consensus protocol and reduce communication complexity [11]. Compared to PBFT, Zyzzyva predicts two consensus scenarios. Under normal consensus, the communication complexity of the Zyzzyva consensus protocol is $O(N)$. In the case of faulty consensus, the communication complexity of the Zyzzyva consensus protocol is the same as PBFT, $O(N^2)$. If the *client* receives fewer than $2f + 1$ identical *reply* messages, consensus fails.

- **Tendermint.** Tendermint is an improved BFT algorithm and software, mainly consisting of two parts: the Tendermint Core Engine and the Application Blockchain Interface (ABCI) [12]. The Tendermint Core Engine is responsible for data transmission and consensus execution, while the ABCI serves as a bridge for transferring data between multiple Tendermint Core Engines. The communication complexity of Tendermint is also $O(N^2)$.
- **Honey Badger of BFT (HoneyBadgerBFT).** HoneyBadgerBFT is the first complete asynchronous consensus protocol capable of ensuring liveness without any time assumptions [13]. The core of HoneyBadgerBFT is an Asynchronous Common Subset (ACS) protocol. This protocol uses erasure coding to achieve reliable broadcast, thereby reducing the number of consensus data transmissions. The communication complexity of HoneyBadgerBFT is $O(N)$.

Non-BFT-Based Consensus Algorithms

- **RAFT.** RAFT is a leader-based consensus protocol, meaning it requires the election of a leader to oversee the consensus process [9]. The election of the leader is achieved through voting, and a candidate node that receives more than half of the votes becomes the leader. The communication complexity of the RAFT consensus protocol during the consensus phase is $O(N)$, where N is the number of consensus participant nodes.

3.3 Hybrid Consensus Algorithms

- **PBFT-PoW.** PBFT-PoW consensus protocol is a hybrid protocol combining PBFT and PoW, leveraging the advantages of both consensus protocols [16]. The PBFT-PoW consensus protocol is employed in the TrueChain project, which consists of two chains: slowchain and fastchain. Slowchain is maintained by the PoW consensus protocol and is not responsible for updating the ledger, while fastchain is maintained by the PBFT consensus protocol and is responsible for recording messages. The communication complexity of the PBFT-PoW consensus protocol is $O(N^2)$.
- **BFT-DPoS.** PBFT-DPoS consensus protocol is a hybrid protocol combining BFT and DPoS, leveraging the advantages of both consensus protocols [17]. BFT-DPoS simply concatenates the two protocols to improve block confirmation speed: first, the DPoS protocol is executed to produce blocks, then the BFT protocol quickly confirms the blocks. The communication complexity of the BFT-DPoS consensus protocol is $O(N^2)$.

4   Throughput Scalability

In addition to network scalability, existing high-performance application sce-narios demand higher scalability from blockchain systems, particularly in terms of throughput scalability. Currently, research on throughput scalability focuses partly on on-chain block size increment and parallel processing methods, while another part aims to migrate a large number of blockchain transactions to off-chain execution, storing only the final execution results on-chain to enhance throughput. The existing optimization methods are summarized in Table 2.

Table 2. Comparison among optimization solutions for throughput scalability.

Solution	Methodology	Throughput	Application Project
BIP X [18,19]	on-chain (block size increment)	≤ 28 tps	Bitcoin
DAG [20]	on-chain (DAG)	≤ 100 tps	IOTA
Elastico [21]	on-chain (sharding)	linear improvement	Zilliqa
MDIoTSP [22]	on-chain (sharding)	linear improvement	/
CHChain [23]	on-chain (sharding)	linear improvement	/
Tong et al. [24]	on-chain (sharding)	linear improvement	/
HAC-Bchain [25]	on-chain (sharding)	linear improvement	/
Lightning [26]	off-chain (payment channel)	high	Bitcoin
Liquidity [27]	off-chain (payment channel)	high	Bitcoin
CYCLE [28]	off-chain (payment channel)	high	/
Splicer [29]	off-chain (payment channel)	high	Bitcoin
TrueBit [30]	off-chain (off-chain computation)	high	Ethereum
Ekiden [31]	off-chain (off-chain computation)	high	Cosmos
Amiri et al. [32]	on-chain (sharding, DAG)	/	/

4.1   On-Chain Solutions

On-chain optimization methods aim to enhance the performance of a blockchain by modifying its structure to facilitate faster transaction processing. Block size expansion, Directed Acyclic Graph (DAG) schemes, and blockchain sharding are three such on-chain optimization methods. Let's analyze the performance optimization effects and the technical/application limitations of each of these methods:

Block Size Increment. BIP 102 is a representative block size expansion pro-posal put forward by the Bitcoin community, which increases the block size from the original 1 MB to 2 MB [18]. Through block size expansion, the Bitcoin trans-action throughput increased from the original 3–7 tps to a maximum of 14 tps. After a series of discussions and attempts (BIP 100, BIP 101, BIP 102, BIP 109, etc. [18, 19]), researchers found that the Bitcoin block size cannot be increased indefinitely, as excessively large blocks would result in a significant number of forks, posing serious challenges to system stability.

Structure Modification. DAG is first proposed in IOTA White Paper. In this scheme, except for the first two blocks, each new block generated needs to validate two other blocks, creating a complex graph structure rather than a linear chain structure like Bitcoin. Testing has shown that the peak transaction throughput of the IOTA blockchain can reach 100 tps. Apart from the IOTA blockchain project, other projects such as DagCoin [33], Byteball [34], RaiBlocks [35], and others are also developed based on DAG.

Sharding. Sharding technology was initially applied to distributed databases, aiming to improve data processing performance by independently and parallelly executing data management operations on different shards. In blockchain systems, sharding technology exists in the form of protocols.

– **Ethereum 2.0.** Ethereum 2.0 aimed to expand a single blockchain network into multiple blockchain shard networks, and to scale a single blockchain into multiple chains, thereby achieving parallel processing of blockchain transactions and increasing transaction throughput [36].
– **ELASTICO.** Elastico is a classic blockchain sharding protocol that stores all blockchain transactions on a single blockchain, thereby avoiding atomicity issues with cross-shard transactions [21]. Elastico combines the PoW protocol and the PBFT protocol. Under the assumptions of a small number of shards and infinite block sizes, Elastico can almost linearly increase the throughput of blockchain transactions.

4.2   Off-Chain Solutions

Off-chain optimization methods do not alter the blockchain structure but instead add functionality to enable rapid processing of blockchain transactions off-chain. The main analysis focuses on the performance optimization effects and technical/application limitations of the following off-chain optimization solutions.

Payment Channel

– **Lightning Network.** The Lightning Network is the earliest proposed off-chain payment channel system, aimed at alleviating Bitcoin's difficulty in handling large-scale high-frequency low-value transactions [26]. In this system, two parties create a payment channel and deposit funds into a 2-2 multisig address as collateral. Then, they can conduct high-frequency low-value transactions within the channel by exchanging signed off-chain "commitment transactions".

– **Liquidity Network.** The Liquidity Network aims to address the liquidity and high intermediary fees issues associated with the Lightning Network [27]. It introduces multi-party off-chain transaction hubs where parties do not need to establish channels with each other individually. Instead, they leverage hubs to facilitate instant off-chain payments with lower transaction fees.

Off-Chain Computation

– **TrueBit.** TrueBit utilizes an interactive off-chain verifiable computation technique to migrate computationally intensive tasks, such as machine learning, from on-chain execution to off-chain execution [30]. The computed results are then submitted to the blockchain, while a multi-party economic mechanism based on validators ensures the verifiability of off-chain computations. Users submit smart contract tasks to TrueBit to address the issue of publicly auditing computation results.
– **Ekiden.** Ekiden utilizes Trusted Execution Environment (TEE) to build a secure off-chain computation platform for smart contracts, handling encryption and computation tasks for contract requests. This approach separates contract computation from blockchain consensus, providing efficient computing power while ensuring contract privacy protection [31].

4.3 Hybrid Throughput Optimization Solutions

Amiri et al. proposed a high-performance consortium blockchain model that leverages sharding techniques and a DAG structure to increase blockchain transaction throughput and enhance node resource utilization [32]. This model slices not only the node network but also the block data, and utilizes Byzantine-class consensus protocols to achieve on-chain data storage.

5 Function Scalability

In addition to the single-chain network and performance scalability of blockchain systems, complex application scenarios have raised higher demands for the function scalability of blockchain systems, especially in terms of security and fairness in heterogeneous blockchain cross-chain interactions. Cross-chain interaction solutions for blockchain systems have been proposed to address the function scalability optimization issues in blockchain systems. The existing cross-chain interaction solutions are summarized in Table 3.

5.1   Cross-Chain Interaction

Hash-Time Lock

- **Atomic Cross-Chain Swaps (ACCS).** ACCS is a method for digital asset transactions involving three parties, capable of achieving cross-chain exchange of heterogeneous digital assets [37]. The core idea ACCS is to use hash locks and time locks to facilitate cross-chain transactions while ensuring their atomicity.
- **XClaim.** XClaim is a non-interactive cross-chain atomic interaction protocol that combines hashed time-locked contracts with collateral providers and custodians to enable multi-party participation in cross-homogeneous chain digital asset exchanges [38].

Table 3. Comparison among interoperation solutions for function scalability.

Interoperation solution	Methodology	Ability	Heterogeneity	Application project
ACCS [37]	Hash-Time Lock	asset transfer	✓	Bitcoin, Litecoin
XClaim [38]	Hash-Time Lock	asset transfer	✗	Bitcoin, Polkadot
Jiang et al. [39]	notary	data migration	✗	IOTA
Zhong et al. [40]	notary	data migration	✓	/
Liu et al. [41]	notary	asset migration	✗	/
Sober et al. [42]	notary	data migration	✓	Ethereum
TI-BIoV [43]	notary	data migration	✓	/
Tong et al. [44]	relay	data migration	✓	/
Generic-NFT [45]	relay	asset migration	✓	/
Polkadot [46]	relay	asset transfer	✓	Polkadot
Cosmos [47]	relay	data migration,	✓	Cosmos
Interledger [48]	notary, Hash-Time Lock	asset transfer	✓	Ripple
Hyperservice [49]	notary, delay	data migration, asset transfer	✓	Ethereum
Wang et al. [50]	notary, Hash-Time Lock	asset transfer	✓	/

Notary Mechanism

- **Jiang et al.** Jiang et al. proposed a framework for applying the IOTA blockchain to multi-domain IoT scenarios and designed a distributed cross-chain data interaction method [39]. This method establishes a consortium chain as notaries and utilizes IOTA to construct a blockchain for IoT devices.

– **Sober et al.** Sober et al. designed a voting-based interoperable oracle to facilitate cross-chain interaction, aiming to alleviate the high verification costs and resource intensiveness associated with traditional relay mechanisms [42]. This oracle method utilizes Distributed Key Generation (DKG) protocols to create distributed private keys supporting the Boneh-Lynn-Shacham (BLS)threshold signature algorithm, thereby enabling off-chain aggregation to reduce oracle operation costs.

Relay Mechanism. The function scalability solutions based on relay mechanism are implemented through intermediary nodes, relay routes, or relay chains, with cross-chain transaction verification achieved through a combination of off-chain and on-chain methods. The main analysis focuses on the heterogeneity and technical/application limitations of the following function scalability solutions based on relay mechanism.

– **Polkadot.** Polkadot aims to establish a parallel chain network to connect blockchains [46]. The Polkadot network consists of a relay chain and multiple parachains, with the relay chain serving as the central hub for cross-chain interaction, providing cross-chain communication services to various parachains based on the Cross-Chain Message Passing Protocol (XCMP).
– **Cosmos.** Cosmos is a decentralized network of parallel blockchains designed for multiple applications [47]. In the Cosmos network, the first blockchain is the Cosmos Hub, while other parallel application blockchains are called Zones. Zones conduct cross-chain operations with the Cosmos Hub through the Inter-Blockchain Communication (IBC) protocol. Acting as a relay for cross-chain interactions, the Cosmos Hub connects various Zone blockchains, reducing the resource and communication overhead associated with direct interconnection between application blockchains.

5.2   Hybrid Function Scalability Solutions

Single cross-chain interaction methods struggle to meet the demands of modern collaborative service applications for function expansion of blockchain systems and inter-system interaction. Therefore, hybrid cross-chain interaction methods have emerged. The main analysis focuses on the heterogeneity and technical/application limitations of the following methods.

– **Interledger.** Interledger, proposed by Ripple, is a cross-chain mechanism transmission protocol that enables currency exchange between two different ledgers through trusted third-party notaries [48]. Interledger allows for the existence of superusers, registered users on two separate ledgers, who facilitate the transfer of assets across ledgers.
– **HyperService.** Hyperservice provides an interactive and editable solution for heterogeneous blockchains [49]. Actually, Hyperservice offers a platform that allows developers to build cross-chain applications within a unified programming model. This platform integrates the advantages of notary and relay

mechanisms, abstracts the underlying technologies of cross-chain transactions and smart contract languages, and can dynamically scale blockchain systems.

6   Comparison of Existing Surveys

Kim *et al.* [51] first published a summary of the blockchain scalability schemes. They categorize these schemes into: on-chain, off-chain, side-chain, child-chain and inter-chain. However, both the side-chain and child schemes are offsets of the off-chain schemes, both of which are layer 2 extensions, and the inter-chain schemes have now been summarized as function scalability schemes. In addition, because the public time is too early, the content of the blockchain interoperable scheme they have mastered is limited, and many follow-up work has not been summarized.

Tyagi *et al.* [52] first aims to consensus algorithms, especially PoW, PBFT, and their improved algorithms. It also summarizes some new blockchain scalability approaches, which includes sharding, off-chain, side-chain, and child-chain. However, it lacks a systematic summary of blockchain scalability research schemes, and is only divided according to the emergence of scalability optimization solutions. This kind of summary scheme can only provide the readers with the timing of the research, but can not provide systematic research. In addition, it has the same shortcoming as the previous one, namely its obsolescence.

Unlike the survey papers above, this paper classifies existing blockchain scalability schemes from a higher perspective: (1) Network scalability solutions contains all schemes for extending network node size of blockchain, which are actually diverse consensus algorithms. (2) Throughput scalability solutions include all scalability solutions, such as layer 0, layer 1, and layer 2. (3) Function scalability solutions includes all the ways to achieve function scalability, including interaction with off-chain data sources, hash time lock schemes, notary schemes, side chain/relay schemes, and blockchain-to-blockchain schemes.

7   Conclusion

This paper briefly describes the current development status of blockchain and existing blockchain projects, and analyzes blockchain systems from three aspects: network scalability, performance scalability, and function system scalability. It provides a detailed analysis of these aspects based on different implementation principles, comparing the theories and pros and cons of various methods. The limitations of current research on blockchain system scalability are analyzed, and the main research contents are summarized. This paper presents a systematic overview of blockchain scalability research and classifies the existing work and analyzes its advantages and disadvantages, which hopes to provide impetus for its research.

Acknowledgments. This work is supported in part by China Postdoctoral Science Foundation (Certificate Number: 2023M742741), in part by National Natural Science Foundation of China under Grant No. 62172141, in part by Major Research Plan of the National Natural Science Foundation of China under Grant No. 92267204, in part by "Pioneer" and "Leading Goose" R&D Program of Zhejiang (Program No. 2023C04038), in part by Natural Science Foundation of Henan under Grant No. 222300420004, in part by the Technology Innovation Leading Program of Shaanxi (No. 2022KXJ-093, 2023KXJ-033), in part by the Innovation Capability Support Program of Shaanxi (No. 2023-CX-TD-02), in part by the National Natural Science Foundation of China (No. 62220106004), and in part by Proof of Concept Foundation of Xidian University Hangzhou Institute of Technology under Grant No. 20107230024.

References

1. Nakamoto, S.: Bitcoin: a peer-to-peer electronic cash system (2008)
2. Gilbert, S., Lynch, N.: Brewer's conjecture and the feasibility of consistent, available, partition-tolerant web services. ACM SIGACT News **33**(2), 51–59 (2002)
3. Xie, J., Yu, F.R., Huang, T., et al.: A survey on the scalability of blockchain systems. IEEE Network **33**(5), 166–173 (2019)
4. Androulaki, E., Barger, A., Bortnikov, V., et al.: Hyperledger fabric: a distributed operating system for permissioned blockchains. In: Proceedings of the Thirteenth EuroSys Conference, pp. 1–15 (2018)
5. Sanka, A.I., Cheung, R.C.: A systematic review of blockchain scalability: issues, solutions, analysis and future research. J. Netw. Comput. Appl. **195**, 103232 (2021)
6. King, S., Nadal, S.: PPCoin: peer-to-peer crypto-currency with proof-of-stake. Self-published paper, August, vol. 19, no. 1 (2012)
7. Larimer, D.: Delegated proof-of-stake (DPoS). Bitshare Whitepaper **81**, 85 (2014)
8. Ye, J., Kang, X., Liang, Y., et al.: A trust-centric privacy-preserving blockchain for dynamic spectrum management in IoT networks. IEEE Internet Things J. **9**(15), 13 263–13 278 (2022)
9. Ongaro, D., Ousterhout, J.: In search of an understandable consensus algorithm. In: 2014 USENIX Annual Technical Conference (USENIX ATC 2014), pp. 305–319 (2014)
10. Castro, M., Liskov, B., et al.: Practical byzantine fault tolerance. OsDI **99**(1999), 173–186 (1999)
11. Kotla, R., Alvisi, L., Dahlin, M., et al.: Zyzzyva: speculative byzantine fault tolerance. In: Proceedings of Twenty-First ACM SIGOPS Symposium on Operating Systems Principles, pp. 45–58 (2007)
12. Buchman, E.: Tendermint: byzantine fault tolerance in the age of blockchains. Ph.D. dissertation, University of Guelph (2016)
13. Miller, A., Xia, Y., Croman, K., et al.: The honey badger of BFT protocols. In: Proceedings of the 2016 ACM SIGSAC Conference on Computer and Communications Security, pp. 31–42 (2016)
14. Tong, W., Dong, X., Zheng, J.: Trust-PBFT: a PeerTrust-based practical byzantine consensus algorithm. In: 2019 International Conference on Networking and Network Applications (NaNA), pp. 344–349. IEEE (2019)
15. Xu, G., Bai, H., Xing, J., et al.: SG-PBFT: a secure and highly efficient distributed blockchain PBFT consensus algorithm for intelligent Internet of vehicles. J. Parallel Distrib. Comput. **164**, 1–11 (2022)

16. Zhang, E., Liu, Y., Sharma, A., et al.: TrueChain: highly performant decentralized public ledger. arXiv preprint arXiv:1805.01457 (2018)
17. Xu, B., Luthra, D., Cole, Z., et al.: EOS: an architectural, performance, and economic analysis, vol. 11, no. 2019, p. 41 (2018). Retrieved June
18. Garzik, J.: Block size increase to 2MB. Bitcoin Improvement Proposal, vol. 102 (2015)
19. Andresen, G.: BIP 109: two million byte size limit with sigop and sighash limits (2016)
20. Williams, T.C., Bach, C.C., Matthiesen, N.B., et al.: Directed acyclic graphs: a tool for causal studies in pediatrics. Pediatr. Res. **84**(4), 487–493 (2018)
21. Luu, L., Narayanan, V., Zheng, C., et al.: A secure sharding protocol for open blockchains. In: Proceedings of the 2016 ACM SIGSAC Conference on Computer and Communications Security, pp. 17–30 (2016)
22. Tong, W., Dong, X., Shen, Y., et al.: A hierarchical sharding protocol for multi-domain IoT blockchains. In: ICC 2019-2019 IEEE International Conference on Communications (ICC), pp. 1–6. IEEE (2019)
23. Tong, W., Dong, X., Shen, Y., Zhang, Y., Jiang, X., Tian, W.: CHChain: secure and parallel crowdsourcing driven by hybrid blockchain. Futur. Gener. Comput. Syst. **131**, 279–291 (2022)
24. Tong, W., Dong, X., Shen, Y., et al.: A blockchain-driven data exchange model in multi-domain IoT with controllability and parallelity. Futur. Gener. Comput. Syst. **135**, 85–94 (2022)
25. Joni, S.A., Rahat, R., Tasnin, N.: HAC-Bchain: a secure and scalable blockchain-shard based e-voting system. In: IEEE Technology & Engineering Management Conference-Asia Pacific (TEMSCON-ASPAC), pp. 1–6. IEEE (2023)
26. Poon, J., Dryja, T.: The bitcoin lightning network: scalable off-chain instant payments (2016)
27. BLOCKSTREAM, Liquid network (2022). https://liquid.net
28. Hong, Z., Guo, S., Zhang, R., et al.: CYCLE: sustainable off-chain payment channel network with asynchronous rebalancing. In: 2022 52nd Annual IEEE/IFIP International Conference on Dependable Systems and Networks (DSN), pp. 41–53. IEEE (2022)
29. Yang, L., Dong, X., Gao, S., et al.: Optimal hub placement and deadlock-free routing for payment channel network scalability. In: 2023 IEEE 43rd International Conference on Distributed Computing Systems (ICDCS), pp. 692–702. IEEE (2023)
30. Teutsch, J., Reitwießner, C.: A scalable verification solution for blockchains. In: Aspects of Computation and Automata Theory with Applications, pp. 377–424. World Scientific (2024)
31. Cheng, R., Zhang, F., Kos, J.: Ekiden: a platform for confidentiality-preserving, trustworthy, and performant smart contracts. In: IEEE European Symposium on Security and Privacy (EuroS&P), pp. 185–200. IEEE (2019)
32. Amiri, M.J., Agrawal, D., El Abbadi, A.: On sharding permissioned blockchains. In: 2019 IEEE International Conference on Blockchain (Blockchain), pp. 282–285. IEEE (2019)
33. Lerner, S.D.: DagCoin: a cryptocurrency without blocks (2015)
34. Churyumov, A.: Byteball: a decentralized system for storage and transfer of value (2016). https://byteball.org/Byteball.pdf
35. LeMahieu, C.: Raiblocks: a feeless distributed cryptocurrency network (2017). https://raiblocks.net/media/RaiBlocks_Whitepaper__English.pdf
36. Buterin, V.: Ethereum 2.0 mauve paper. In: Ethereum Developer Conference, vol. 2 (2016)

37. Herlihy, M.: Atomic cross-chain swaps. In: Proceedings of the 2018 ACM Symposium on Principles of Distributed Computing, pp. 245–254 (2018)

38. Zamyatin, A., Harz, D., Lind, J.: XClaim: trustless, interoperable, cryptocurrency-backed assets. In: IEEE Symposium on Security and Privacy (SP), pp. 193–210. IEEE (2019)

39. Jiang, Y., Wang, C., Huang, Y., et al.: A cross-chain solution to integration of IoT tangle for data access management. In: 2018 IEEE International Conference on Internet of Things (iThings) and IEEE Green Computing and Communications (GreenCom) and IEEE Cyber, Physical and Social Computing (CPSCom) and IEEE Smart Data (SmartData), pp. 1035–1041. IEEE (2018)

40. Zhong, X., Liu, Y., Xie, K., et al.: A local electricity and carbon trading method for multi-energy microgrids considering cross-chain interaction. Sensors **22**(18), 6935 (2022)

41. Liu, Y., Shan, G., Liu, Y., et al.: Blockchain bridges critical national infrastructures: e-healthcare data migration perspective. IEEE Access **10**, 28 509–28 519 (2022)

42. Sober, M., Scaffino, G., Spanring, C., et al.: A voting-based blockchain interoperability oracle. In: 2021 IEEE International Conference on Blockchain (Blockchain), pp. 160–169. IEEE (2021)

43. Tong, W., Dong, X., Zhang, Y., et al.: TI-BIoV: traffic information interaction for blockchain-based IoV with trust and incentive. IEEE Internet Things J. (2023)

44. Tong, W., Shen, C., Dong, Z., et al.: Interoperability solution for blockchain-based internet of vehicles driven by multiple oracles. In: 2023 IEEE 26th International Conference on Intelligent Transportation Systems (ITSC), pp. 196–202. IEEE (2023)

45. Yang, L., Dong, X., Zhang, Y., et al.: Generic-NFT: a generic non-fungible token architecture for flexible value transfer in Web3. Authorea Preprints (2023)

46. Wood, G.: Polkadot: vision for a heterogeneous multi-chain framework. White Paper **21**(2327), 4662 (2016)

47. Kwon, J., Buchman, E.: Cosmos whitepaper. A Netw. Distrib. Ledgers **27**, 1–32 (2019)

48. Armknecht, F., Karame, G.O., Mandal, A., et al.: Ripple: overview and outlook. In: Conti, M., Schunter, M., Askoxylakis, I. (eds.) Trust and Trustworthy Computing: 8th International Conference, TRUST 2015, Heraklion, Greece, 24–26 August 2015, Proceedings 8, vol. 9229, pp. 163–180. Springer, Cham (2015). https://doi.org/10.1007/978-3-319-22846-4_10

49. Liu, Z., Xiang, Y., Shi, J., et al.: HyperService: interoperability and programmability across heterogeneous blockchains. In: Proceedings of the 2019 ACM SIGSAC Conference on Computer and Communications Security, pp. 549–566 (2019)

50. Wang, G., Nixon, M.: InterTrust: towards an efficient blockchain interoperability architecture with trusted services. In: 2021 IEEE International Conference on Blockchain (Blockchain), pp. 150–159. IEEE (2021)

51. Kim, S., Kwon, Y., Cho, S.: A survey of scalability solutions on blockchain. In: 2018 International Conference on Information and Communication Technology Convergence (ICTC), pp. 1204–1207. IEEE (2018)

52. Tyagi, S., Kathuria, M.: Study on blockchain scalability solutions. In: Proceedings of the 2021 Thirteenth International Conference on Contemporary Computing, pp. 394–401 (2021)

Supply Chain Financing Model Embedded with "Full-Process" Blockchain

Ying Fang[1], Haifeng Guo[2(✉)], Yuyun Jie[2], Yong Wang[3], Biliang Wang[2], and Yuwei He[2]

[1] YiBin Vocational and Technical College, Yibin 6441001, China
[2] School of Finance, Southwestern University of Finance and Economics, Chengdu 610000, China
guohf@swufe.edu.cn
[3] Xinjiang Zhongtai Group, Wulumuqi 830026, China

Abstract. Supply chain finance is a crucial pathway to solve the problems of difficult and expensive financing for small and medium-sized enterprises (SMEs). However, due to credibility issues, supply chain finance faces development bottlenecks. Blockchain technology can help overcome the credibility challenges in supply chain finance. Nevertheless, problems such as internal coordination and hindered credit transfer still exist when blockchain technology is integrated with supply chain finance. This paper attempts to construct a blockchain-based supply chain finance model with "full process embedding." The model is based on a dual-chain architecture, consisting of the enterprise information chain and the transaction information chain. The dual-chain architecture separates user privacy information from transaction information. This model can leverage blockchain technology to break through the key challenges in the trust mechanism of supply chain finance and solve the trust issues among various parties. In engineering project management, leveraging the "end-to-end integration" supply chain finance model with blockchain can offer more efficient, transparent, and secure solutions for supply chain finance.

Keywords: Blockchain · Supply chain finance · Full process embedding · Trust issues

1 Introduction

In recent years, China's supply chain finance market has experienced rapid growth, with banks and other financial institutions providing loans, settlement, and asset management services to weaker enterprises based on core enterprises' commercial credit. Supply chain finance alleviates the problems of difficult and expensive financing for SMEs and satisfies the comprehensive needs of modern industrial chains (Zhu et al., 2019). However, frictions persist in the deep integration process between the financial supply side and the real industrial chain, severely hindering the expansion of supply chain finance. The biggest dilemma in traditional supply chain finance is the issue of credibility. Due to difficulties in confirming the ownership of goods and creditor's rights, lack of data authenticity, and information barriers, the commercial credit of core enterprises is challenging to circulate at multiple levels, and supply chain finance faces industry barriers in the process of rising to the industry level. The urgency to solve the credibility issue is becoming prominent.

In the process of engineering project management, various financial and reputational issues may arise, which can significantly impact the smooth progress and ultimate completion of the project. Insufficient funds are a common problem that can occur due to inaccurate budgeting, cost overruns, or improper allocation of funds. This can result in project delays, inadequate supply of materials, or inability to pay suppliers and contractors, thereby affecting the quality and progress of the project. Also, reputation issues may arise, such as poor creditworthiness of contractors or suppliers, non-compliance with contractual obligations, or failure to deliver work on time. This can lead to a breakdown in project partnerships, legal disputes, or compromised project quality. Therefore, adequate monitoring and management of cash flow and partner reputation are crucial in engineering project management to ensure that the project proceeds as planned and achieves success.

With the advent of the Fourth Industrial Revolution, the depth and breadth of the application of cutting-edge technologies such as artificial intelligence, big data, and blockchain in various fields are constantly advancing. Blockchain, as an underlying technology, can achieve the visibility and controllability of the entire supply chain logistics and capital flow, the authenticity and transparency of information flow, and the identification of business flow, breaking through the credibility challenges of supply chain finance and improving the efficiency of industry-finance integration (Du et al., 2020). Therefore, the combination of blockchain and supply chain finance scenarios has emerged, and embedding blockchain technology into the supply chain system has shown unique advantages (Sun et al., 2021). However, there are also bottlenecks in the blockchain process driving the healthy development of supply chain finance. Previous blockchain systems mostly adopted single-chain structures to ensure data security and privacy. However, this approach has problems such as difficult data management and limiting the security and interactivity of data sharing in supply chain finance.

This paper adopts blockchain technology to construct a "full process embedding" supply chain finance model. The model constructs two chains: the supply chain enterprise information chain and the supply chain transaction information chain. The dual-chain architecture separately stores enterprise information and transaction data on the blockchain, ensuring the authenticity, integrity, privacy of information, and openness of transactions. This model can link enterprise nodes and various relevant information systems, enabling blockchain technology to play its role truly. First, asymmetric digital signature technology and public-private keys ensure the security of enterprise-related transaction data. Second, the blockchain structure enables information data traceability and immutability, reducing financial institutions' loan risks and increasing their willingness to lend. Third, the shared ledger and consensus mechanism complete the verification and confirmation of each node, realizing the decomposition and transfer of important enterprise credit on the chain and achieving credit reconstruction (Zheng et al., 2022). Fourth, smart contract technology enables automatic contract execution, simplifying supply chain finance business processes, improving supply chain finance efficiency, and reducing transaction costs (Cong and He, 2019). This model helps release the potential of China's vast supply chain finance market and meets the market's diverse financing needs.

The rest of the paper is organized as follows. Section 2 presents the related works. In Sect. 3, we introduce the "Whole process embedded" supply chain finance model. Finally, we offer concluding remarks in Sect. 4.

2 Related Works

2.1 Supply Chain Finance

Supply chain finance refers to a financing model in which a core enterprise is connected with upstream and downstream SMEs, continuously processing funds and information to improve the efficiency of capital utilization (Caniato et al., 2019). It is also a financial service that revolves around the core enterprise, managing the capital flow, logistics, and information flow of upstream and downstream SMEs, transforming the uncontrollable risks of individual enterprises into the controllable risks of the entire supply chain, and minimizing risks through the multi-dimensional acquisition of various types of information (see Fig. 1).

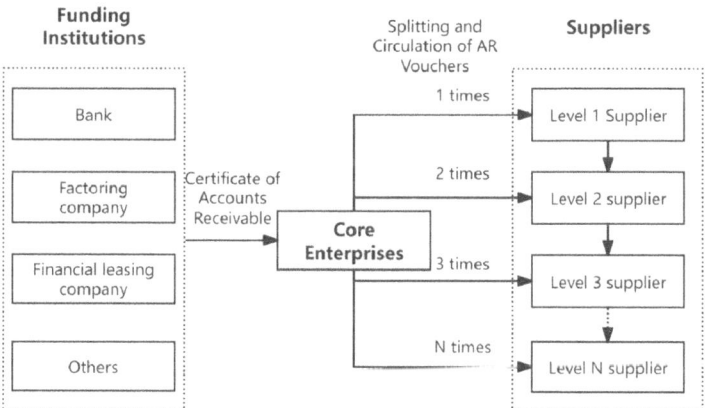

Fig. 1. Traditional Supply Chain Finance Chain

As shown in Fig. 1, supply chain finance involves numerous participants, including core enterprises, upstream and downstream enterprises, third-party logistics companies, and others. By leveraging the characteristic of having multiple participants, banks provide core enterprises with services such as loans and fund management for their upstream and downstream partners. This has facilitated the establishment of an ecosystem wherein banks collaborate and mutually benefit with enterprises along the supply chain (Ioannou and Demirel, 2022).

Supply chain finance encompasses six primary business models, with their specific descriptions and main service offerings detailed in Table 1.

Table 1. Business models of supply chain finance

Business model	Descriptions	Main service
Accounts Receivable Pledge	Enterprises sign contracts with banks or financial institutions to obtain short-term loan financing using accounts receivable as collateral	Short-term loan financing
Warehouse Receipt Factoring	Based on warehouse receipts issued by storage providers as financing guarantees, financial institutions provide financing services secured by pledged warehouse receipts	Financing services
Inventory Pledge Factoring	Enterprises pledge proprietary raw materials or product inventories to banks, which grant short-term working capital loans by taking possession or monitoring the pledged collateral	short-term working capital loan services
Factoring Business	Includes direct factoring, reverse factoring, factoring pools, and bill factoring, mainly resolving accounts receivable financing issues	Debt financing services
Order Financing	Enterprises obtain financing based on product orders from creditworthy buyers, organize production, and immediately repay loans upon receiving payments	Order financing services

However, traditional supply chain finance faces the following primary challenges. Firstly, there are difficulties in establishing and controlling the rights to collateral and accounts receivable, lack of data authenticity and diversity, delayed risk identification, and information asymmetry. Secondly, there is an inability to ensure the authenticity of information and data provided by enterprises. Thirdly, both pre-lending and post-lending risks are relatively difficult to control. These issues are major concerns for financial institutions and serve as stumbling blocks hindering the further development of supply chain finance. These challenges manifest a core difficulty: resolving the issue of trust.

2.2   The Integration of Blockchain Technology and Supply Chain Finance

Blockchain technology is an emerging data processing method that ensures data security and reliability through a decentralized approach (Brau, 2002). The fundamental characteristics of blockchain can effectively address the trust issue in supply chain finance (Jiang et al., 2022). Blockchain enables data to be openly transparent among all parties, forming a complete, smooth, and immutable information flow throughout the supply chain (Omran, 2016). This ensures that all parties can promptly identify issues arising during the operation of the supply chain system and develop targeted solutions, ultimately enhancing the overall efficiency of supply chain management (see Fig. 2).

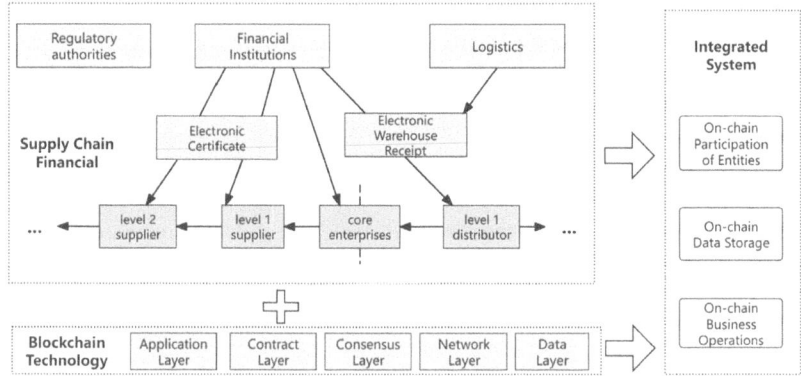

Fig. 2. The integration of blockchain technology and supply chain finance

Supply chain finance involves multiple parties, including core enterprises, upstream and downstream SMEs, financial institutions, and others, necessitating a reliable new technology to connect data across parties and build a trusted ecosystem for supply chain finance. The network protocols, encryption algorithms, and other elements of blockchain technology can establish diversified data-sharing mechanisms that adapt to multiple scenarios. While ensuring the compliant and authorized use of enterprise data with limited disclosure, this promotes cross-party data connectivity. In a blockchain system, all nodes jointly provide network services, enabling information sharing and collective maintenance without the need for third-party intermediaries. In supply chain finance, suppliers and distributors can transition from traditional one-to-one business models to team-based collaborative modes, thereby enhancing supply chain transparency and enabling the rapid sharing of accounts payable and related transaction data. Therefore, applying blockchain technology to the supply chain finance system can mitigate the information silos of traditional supply chain finance, forming a trusted supply chain network with end-to-end information fluidity.

However, the process of integrating blockchain with supply chain finance encounters challenges. This model may be constrained by limitations in funding, industrial foundations, and blockchain technology maturity. Simultaneously, use cases are typically confined to specific groups, making industry-wide scaling and large-scale application difficult. Numerous companies may be involved at the industry level, with some being competitors. Sharing information through blockchain technology could lead to trade secrets' leakage, undermining core interests. Therefore, blockchain-based supply chain finance models must effectively manage data and protect business confidentiality. However, the single-chain blockchain architecture previously adopted cannot ensure data security.

Integrating blockchain with supply chain finance in engineering project management can bring many advantages, such as increased transparency, traceability, and efficiency. For example, blockchain can enable real-time tracking of project materials, streamline payment processes, and enhance trust among project stakeholders. However, in addressing the aforementioned challenges, ensuring that the adopted blockchain solution provides robust data security measures to protect sensitive project information is important.

This paper proposes a supply chain finance model with "full-process embedding" based on a dual-chain architecture. This model can effectively guarantee data security and enhance supply chain finance efficiency.

3 "Whole Process Embedded" Supply Chain Finance Model

We constructed a supply chain finance model with "full-process embedding" based on a dual-chain architecture and formulated a standard identification resolution system to support it. Through this model, we bridge the interconnectivity between enterprise nodes and various related information systems, enabling blockchain technology to truly play its role.

For core enterprises and their upstream and downstream partners, transactions between them involve a large amount of private data, including supplier and distributor names, locations, products, prices, logistics, and settlement methods. The integration of blockchain technology and supply chain finance can overcome the issue of insufficient credit mechanisms in traditional supply chain finance. However, most previous blockchain systems adopted a single-chain structure, packaging data into block structures through the blockchain system to ensure data security and privacy. This approach presents difficulties in data management, and trade secret information cannot be specially protected, greatly limiting the security and interactivity of data sharing in supply chain finance.

To address the above problems, we propose a blockchain-based "full-process embedding" supply chain finance model with a dual-chain architecture (as illustrated in Fig. 3). This dual-chain architecture comprises the enterprise information chain and the transaction information chain. The enterprise information chain employs a Merkle tree structure for storage, aimed at recording and storing user information of upstream and downstream enterprises in the supply chain. This ensures the authenticity and integrity of the information and the privacy of individual enterprise information for participating entities.

The transaction information chain utilizes a Merkle Patricia tree structure to record and store all supply chain transaction data. This chain guarantees the authenticity and completeness of transaction outcomes, enabling trusted multi-party data sharing. Key-value lookups facilitate easy querying and tracking of transaction results, thereby enhancing account management and data retrieval efficiency.

The dual-chain architecture offers the following advantages. It segregates user privacy information from supply chain transaction information, striking a balance between the openness and security of transaction data and the privacy of enterprise information. Meanwhile, it ensures that any blockchain node can query supply chain transaction data without needing to access other enterprises' private information, adaptively enabling resource matching. This model significantly enhances the credibility of supply chain management and the overall system efficiency.

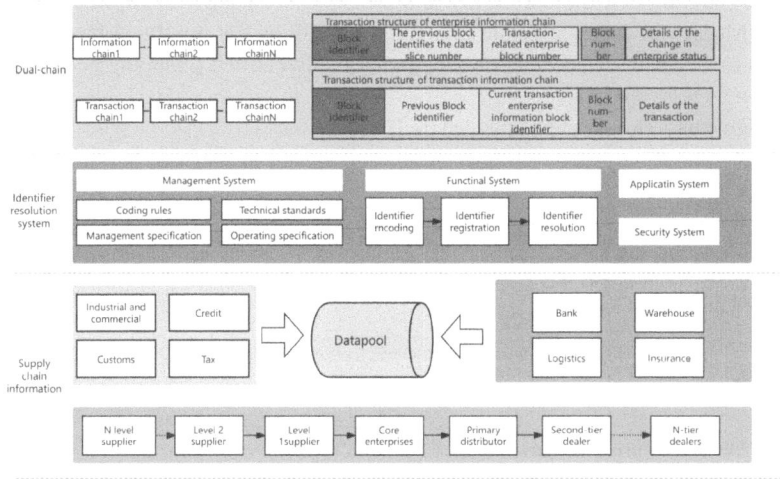

Fig. 3. The supply chain finance model of "Whole process embedding"

Integrating blockchain technology in construction project management can provide a more reliable and efficient solution for supply chain financing. By recording information about each stage of the construction project and the relevant parties on the blockchain, traceability, and transparency can be achieved throughout the supply chain management. This resolves trust issues between construction companies and suppliers and also enhances the efficiency of the entire supply chain.

Through blockchain technology, construction project progress and quality data can be uploaded and shared in real-time. All parties involved in the supply chain can monitor the progress and quality of the project, enabling early warning and problem-solving. This method of information sharing improves collaboration and decision-making efficiency in project management, reducing information asymmetry and delays.

4   Conclusions

With the advancement of blockchain technology, the trust issues in traditional supply chain finance can be resolved. Blockchain is essentially a distributed database that ensures data security. Integrating blockchain technology in construction project management can provide a more trustworthy, efficient, and transparent solution for supply chain financing. It also enhances the effectiveness of project management and the level of quality control. Simultaneously, blockchain technology can generate trust without relying on a trusted third party, making it applicable to traditional supply chain finance where the credit environment is imperfect. However, there are concerns such as information leakage when integrating blockchain with supply chain finance. Therefore, this paper innovatively proposes a supply chain finance model with "full-process embedding" based on a dual-chain architecture. This model segregates user privacy information from supply chain transaction data, ensuring data security and interactivity during sharing. By adopting this model, the credibility and efficiency of supply chain finance can be enhanced. Moreover, it can alleviate financing difficulties for small and medium-sized enterprises to a certain extent, meeting the market's diversified financing needs.

Acknowledgments. This paper is supported by The Key Research and Development Program of Science & Technology Department of Sichuan Province (2024YFHZ0161).

Disclosure of Interests. The authors have no competing interests to declare that are relevant to the content of this article.

References

Brau, J.C.: Do banks price owner–manager agency costs? an examination of small business borrowing. J. Small Bus. Manage. **40**, 273–286 (2002)

Caniato, F., Henke, M., Zsidisin, G.A.: Supply chain finance: historical foundations, current research, future developments. Elsevier, pp. 99–104 (2019)

Cong, L.W., He, Z.: Blockchain disruption and smart contracts. Rev. Fin. Stud. **32**, 1754–1797 (2019)

Du, M., Chen, Q., Xiao, J., Yang, H., Ma, X.: Supply chain finance innovation using blockchain. IEEE Trans. Eng. Manage. **67**, 1045–1058 (2020)

Ioannou, I., Demirel, G.: Blockchain and supply chain finance: a critical literature review at the intersection of operations, finance and law. J. Banking Financ. Technol. **6**, 83–107 (2022)

Jiang, R., et al.: A trust transitivity model of small and medium-sized manufacturing enterprises under blockchain-based supply chain finance. Int. J. Prod. Econ. **247**, 108469 (2022)

Omran, Y.: Inclusive supply chain finance approach: Integrated supply chain finance solution with digitalization. White paper, Fraunhofer IML (2016)

Sun, R., He, D., Su, H.: Evolutionary game analysis of blockchain technology preventing supply chain financial risks. J Theor. Appl. El Comm. **16**, 2824–2842 (2021)

Zheng, K., et al.: Blockchain technology for enterprise credit information sharing in supply chain finance. J. Innov. Knowl. **7**, 100256 (2022)

Zhu, Y., Zhou, L., Xie, C., Wang, G.-J., Nguyen, T.V.: Forecasting SMEs' credit risk in supply chain finance with an enhanced hybrid ensemble machine learning approach. Int. J. Prod. Econ. **211**, 22–33 (2019)

Blockchain Performance Optimization

ReCon: Faster Smart Contract Vulnerability Detection by Reusable Symbolic Execution Tree

Huanze Chen and Peilin Zheng[(✉)]

School of Software Engineering, Sun Yat-Sen University, Zhuhai 519000, China
{chenhz8,zhengpl3}@mail2.sysu.edu.cn

Abstract. Smart contracts are being applied widely in several fields. Meanwhile, attacks against smart contracts have been occurring constantly, causing serious financial loss, which reflects the importance of research on smart contract vulnerability detection. Currently, academics and industry have proposed several vulnerability detection tools based on symbolic execution. However, once a new vulnerability pattern is found, previous tools need to repeatedly do path exploration on the same contracts to detect the new bug, and the redundant exploration costs a lot of time. Hence, the efficiency is limited by such an "explore-and-detect" method. To address this issue, we propose ReCon, a new "explore-then-detect" framework that decouples path exploration and vulnerability detection for smart contracts. ReCon preserves the results of previous symbolic execution and then reuses them to accelerate the detection of new vulnerabilities. Firstly, we propose an extraction method for the symbolic execution tree of smart contracts. Secondly, we propose a vulnerability detection method based on the extracted symbolic trees to detect new bugs. Finally, we evaluate ReCon on two datasets, SmartBugs and Top-10 real-world contracts. The results show that using reusable symbolic trees, ReCon can save 54.9% of time on SmartBugs and 89.6% of time on Top-10 real-world contracts.

Keywords: Smart contract · Symbolic execution · Vulnerability detection

1 Introduction

Smart contracts on the blockchain have been applied in several fields. Unfortunately, attacks on smart contracts cause severe financial loss. According to the report by SlowMist [11], the total loss due to smart contract vulnerability has exceeded $28 billion. Therefore, vulnerability detection for smart contracts has become a hot research topic.

There are various vulnerability detection tools for smart contracts, such as Mythril [5], Oyente [1], etc. And their key technical solutions encompass a wide range, including symbolic execution, fuzz testing, static analysis, etc. Symbolic

D. He et al. (Eds.): BlockSys 2024, CCIS 2264, pp. 157–170, 2025.
https://doi.org/10.1007/978-981-96-1411-0_13

execution can traverse the execution space of the smart contract to obtain the precise execution path. Hence, it is vital and has been widely used to detect vulnerabilities in smart contracts.

Explore-and-detect. As for smart contracts, current symbolic detection tools usually detect vulnerabilities while exploring the execution paths symbolically. In this paper, this is called the "explore-and-detect" method. For traditional codes (e.g. Java), this detection method works well. The reason is that the defect patterns for traditional codes are not always changed, e.g., array overflow. Therefore, their defects can be detected only once. However, new vulnerability patterns are constantly being found in smart contracts. Once there is a new vulnerability, the symbolic execution tasks of previous contracts need to be repeated. During the repeated symbolic execution, the path exploration is repeatedly done, which costs lots of time.

Explore-then-detect. To address the above problem, we need a new detection tool that supports the reuse of previous symbolic execution results for vulnerability detection when new patterns are found. In this paper, we propose ReCon, a new "explore-then-detect" framework. Its main idea is to preserve the exploration results of previous symbolic execution and then reuse the results in the detection of new vulnerabilities. In this way, the exploration only needs to be done once. Hence, the future detection of new vulnerabilities can be accelerated.

Based on this main idea, we propose the following methods:

S1: Symbolic Tree Extraction Method for Smart Contracts is proposed to extract the necessary symbolic tree information. When a new state is executed, ReCon will generate a node to record the symbolic execution results and insert it into the symbolic tree. After the symbolic execution steps, a symbolic tree will be constructed. Finally, ReCon stores the tree as a formatted file with the other global information.

S2: Vulnerability Detection Method based on Pre-extracted Symbolic Tree is introduced to reuse the previously extracted results. Instead of finishing the symbolic execution task instruction by instruction, ReCon will take the pre-extracted symbolic tree as input. With the help of the symbolic tree, ReCon can know the executed path in advance and finish the execution and detection task efficiently.

Details about challenges and solutions will be discussed in Sect. 4 and Sect. 5. The main contributions of this paper are as follows:

- We propose ReCon, a new vulnerability detection framework that could do faster symbolic execution when detecting a new vulnerability.
- We design a symbolic tree extraction method for smart contracts to generate the reusable symbolic tree.
- We design a vulnerability detection method based on the pre-extracted symbolic tree to achieve efficiency and consistency.

– We will publish reusable symbolic data to help further research on smart contracts.

The rest of the paper is organized as follows: Sect. 2 presents the background of smart contracts and symbolic execution. In Sect. 3, we present the related work of smart contract vulnerability detection tools based on symbolic execution. In Sect. 4, we discuss the goals and challenges of ReCon and describe the whole framework. In Sect. 5, we demonstrate detailed solutions for challenges. Section 6 introduces the implementation and evaluation of our work. Finally, we conclude the paper Sect. 7.

2   Background

Smart Contract. Smart contract [23] is a piece of code driven by the blockchain that handles complex businesses and financial transactions. Ethereum [25] is one of the largest blockchain that supports smart contracts. Ethereum Virtual Machine (EVM) is proposed to execute smart contracts. Given the contract operation code, EVM will execute each contract instruction in order.

Symbolic Execution. Symbolic execution [24] is a traditional technique of program analysis. It uses symbolic values as inputs for the program, obtains the potential path of the program, and solves the constraint set of the path according to the Satisfiability Modulo Theories. Finally, it will obtain the input values of the reachable paths, i.e., the concrete inputs that trigger the vulnerabilities.

Vulnerability Detection. Symbolic execution is a commonly used analysis technique in smart contract vulnerability detection. There are several tools based on symbolic execution, e.g., Oyente [1], Mythril [5], Maian [2], etc. Using symbolic execution to explore the reachable paths, these tools can detect the patterns of vulnerabilities during the exploration.

3   Related Work

Oyente [1] is the first proposed contract vulnerability detection tool using symbolic execution techniques and detects four types of contract vulnerabilities. Maian [2] used inter-procedural symbolic analysis and concrete value verifier to analyze trace flow information, such as cash flow. Torres et al. [3] proposed the HoneyBadger, which utilized symbolic execution and heuristics to detect honeypot contracts. State et al. [4] proposed the Osiris tool, which focused on refining the detection of integer vulnerabilities using symbolic execution and taint analysis. Mythril [5] is another security analysis tool for EVM bytecode. It detected security vulnerabilities in smart contracts built for Ethereum, Hedera, Quorum, Vechain, Roostock, Tron and other EVM-compatible blockchains. Zhang et al. [6] developed Mpro based on Mythril. Mpro optimized the pruning process of symbolic execution in Mythril using static analysis to address the inefficiency with depth-n vulnerabilities. Empirical studies [8–10] have evaluated the validity of the above symbolic execution tools, showing these tools can hardly achieve high efficiency of symbolic execution in smart contracts.

In summary, the existing symbolic execution studies on smart contracts are usually based on the "explore-and-detect" method. In other words, the above studies do not focus on reusing the results of symbolic execution. Towards new proposed vulnerabilities, repeated path exploration costs time and limits efficiency. Therefore, it is needed to design a new method to attack this problem.

4   Overview

4.1   Goals

We design ReCon with the following goals:

Faster Detection of New Vulnerabilities. ReCon should optimize the symbolic execution process to achieve faster detection. When there is a new vulnerability, instead of doing symbolic execution repeatedly on previous contracts, it should reuse the previous symbolic execution tree to guide the detection task, skipping unnecessary steps to improve the efficiency of detection.

Consistency of Results. By reusing the symbolic execution tree, we achieve faster detection. In the meanwhile, we need to ensure the consistency of results. This consistency refers to the consistency of the vulnerability detection results and the consistency of the executed symbolic execution tree paths. Only when this consistency is guaranteed can the improvement of efficiency be convincing.

4.2   Challenges

Facing the above goals, we design ReCon. Before implementing this framework, two major technical challenges should be addressed first.

Firstly, in previous studies, vulnerability detection and symbolic execution tasks are coupled in one process. Hence, it is difficult to extract and store results in this coupled process. For data extraction, we need to consider how to implement the data extraction and what part of the symbolic execution data should be extracted to complete the vulnerability detection task. For data storage, we need to consider the storage format of the symbolic execution so that it is reusable and easy to read.

Secondly, in the original tools, symbolic execution is performed sequentially by instruction. When we have reusable symbolic execution data, the execution of vulnerability detection and symbolic execution tasks need to be guided by these intermediate results, thus making it possible to skip some of the steps to improve overall efficiency.

4.3   Framework

We propose ReCon, a "explore-then-detect" framework for smart contracts as follows. First, as for the exploration, ReCon is designed to pre-execute the smart contract, record the edges of the symbolic execution tree, and output the explored tree in a formatted file. Second, as for the detection, ReCon takes the intermediate data file as input, using the information of the symbolic tree to guide the process of symbolic execution and vulnerability detection. In this way, when a new vulnerability is proposed, ReCon can skip unnecessary constraint solving steps and finally generate the corresponding vulnerability detection report.

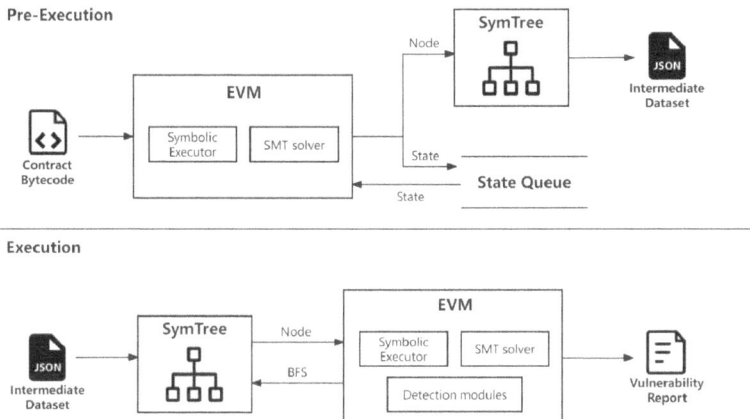

Fig. 1. The two-phase architecture of vulnerability detection framework

In short, ReCon is designed as a two-phase framework, as shown in Fig. 1. As shown in the upper part of Fig. 1, the exploration is done in the "Pre-Execution" phase. As shown in the lower part of Fig. 1, the detection is done in the "Execution" phase.

The roles in ReCon are explained as follows:

Contract Bytecode. The bytecode of the contract to be detected which is a long string format.

Intermediate Dataset. The formatted file extracted in the pre-execution phase. It contains the symbolic tree and global information of the contract.

EVM. The runtime machine for Ethereum smart contracts. There are three modules in it. The symbolic executor is in charge of the symbolic execution task. SMT solver is used when a constraint set needs to be solved. Detection modules contain detailed rules for vulnerability detection.

SymTree. SymTree is the executed symbolic tree extracted in the pre-execution phase which will guide ReCon in the execution phase.

Vulnerability Report. The report of detected vulnerabilities, which contains the location of vulnerabilities, the bug type, etc.

In this paper, the symbolic executor and detection modules are implemented with the reference of Mythril [5] and the SMT solver is constructed based on the Z3 solver.

Based on the above framework, we propose the detailed solutions of ReCon in the next section.

5 Detailed Solutions

5.1 Symbolic Tree Extraction for Smart Contracts

To address **C1**, we propose a symbolic tree extraction method for smart contracts, as shown in Algorithm 1.

ReCon takes the contract bytecode as input. And then, the symbolic executor in EVM will continuously take out the old state from the queue for execution, generate new states, and push them back to the queue again until the end of symbolic execution. In Line 11, when EVM finishes executing a state, ReCon will generate a corresponding node and insert it into the symbolic execution tree. At the end of execution in Line 27, ReCon will extract the symbolic execution tree into a JSON-type file and output it. The structure of each node is shown in Fig. 2a. The "Pc" represents the value of the program counter (instruction pointer), which is the index value of the EVM instruction. The "Op" represents the operation corresponding to the node. The "Children" array contains the child nodes. The final generated data file is a JSON-type file shown in Fig. 2b. It contains the "creationCode" and "runtimeCode" of the contract. The "FailIndex" array records the index of the WorldState whose result of constraint solving is not SAT. The "SymTree" records the information of the whole symbol execution tree, which is the vital information in the execution phase.

```
1 type SymTreeNode struct
       {
2     Pc  int
3     Op  string
4     Children []*
          SymTreeNode
5 }
```

(a) Symbolic node

```
1 type ContractObj struct
       {
2     CreationCode string
3     RuntimeCode  string
4     FailIndex []int
5     SymTree *SymTreeNode
6 }
```

(b) JSON object

Fig. 2. The structure of the node and JSON object

Algorithm 1: Pseudocode of symbolic tree extraction

---

1 **for** $i \in TransactionCount$ **do**
2   **for** $WorldState \in EVM.OpenStates$ **do**
3   /* **Constraint Solving** */
4   **if** $SOLVE(WorldState) == SAT$ **then**
5 | queue ← GlobalState ← WorldState
6   **end**
7   **end**
8   **for** $state \leftarrow queue$ **do**
9   /* **Symbolic Execution and vulnerability detection** */
10   newStates = INSTRUCTION(state)
11   /* **Extract the symbolic results as a node** */
12   node = NEWNODE(state)
13   SymTree ← node
14   **if** $newStates.length > 1$ **then**
15   tmpStates = [ ]
16   **for** $newState \in newStates$ **do**
17   /* **Constraint Solving** */
18   **if** $SOLVE(newState) == SAT$ **then**
19 | tmpStates ← newState
20   **end**
21   **end**
22   newStates = tmpStates
23   **end**
24   queue ← newStates
25   **end**
26 **end**
27 JSON-type File ← SymTree

5.2 Vulnerability Detection Based on Pre-extracted Symbolic Tree

In this subsection, we propose a vulnerability detection method based on the pre-extracted symbolic tree. The pseudocode is shown in Algorithm 2.

ReCon will take the corresponding JSON file of the previously extracted tree as input. Then, EVM will traverse the nodes in the tree using the Breath-First-Search (BFS) policy. After that, it will finish the symbolic execution task and the vulnerability detection task based on the node information. In this process, the SMT solver is mainly used for constraint solving in vulnerability detection.

The reason ReCon uses the BFS policy to traverse the tree is that the execution phase needs to keep the same execution order as the pre-execution phase. The state in the pre-execution phase is stored in a queue structure, which conforms to the first-in-first-out principle. Hence, the whole symbolic execution tree is also executed according to the BFS policy during the pre-execution phase.

After traversing the whole tree, EVM will output the final vulnerability detection report. Since the whole process is guided by the symbolic execution tree extracted in the pre-execution phase, the constraint solving steps in symbolic

---

Algorithm 2: Pseudocode of detection on pre-extracted symbolic tree

---
Input: Symbolic Tree JSON File
1 $SymTree \leftarrow JSON\ File$
2 state = INITIALIZE()
3 MAP(state, SymTree.headNode)
4 /* **BFS search** */
5 **for** $node \in SymTree$ **do**
6 | state = map.Search(node)
7 | /* **Symbolic Execution and vulnerability detection** */
8 | newStates = INSTRUCTION(state)
9 | **for** $childNode \in node.Children$ **do**
10 | | childState = GetState(childNode.Pc)
11 | | MAP(childState, childNode)
12 | **end**
13 **end**

---

execution will be skipped. In this way, ReCon shortens the time of the whole detection process.

Furthermore, consistency of results in ReCon is guaranteed. The optimized symbolic execution is run according to the symbolic execution tree information, i.e., EVM is guaranteed to execute the same part of the symbolic execution tree every time. Moreover, we replace "timeout" with "rlimit" as a solver parameter to ensure the consistency of vulnerability detection. The "timeout" is often used as a parameter of the SMT solver to complete the constraint solving task. It limits the total time for constraint solving. However, we found that even if we set the same timeout for the solver and solve the same constraints set on one machine, the results of constraint solving will be different when the CPU computing power fluctuates. The "rlimit" is computed in terms of the resources consumed in the solving process, thus ensuring that the same constraints can be solved as the same result in different environments compared to timeout.

6   Implementation and Evaluation

In this section, we first introduce the implementation of ReCon, the datasets used, and the experiment setup. Then, we will focus the experimental evaluation of ReCon on the following research questions.

- RQ1: Do the constraint solving steps in symbolic execution consume most of the time?
- RQ2: How efficient is our detection framework based on the reusable symbolic execution tree?
- RQ3: Are the results in our detection framework consistent with the original tools?

Implementation. Before implementing ReCon, we need an existing vulnerability detection tool as a base to optimize its symbolic execution. In this way, it can generate reusable symbolic trees and output vulnerability detection reports with intermediate results as input. In this paper, ReCon is implemented on Go-Mythril, which is a tool that we have constructed for symbolic execution. Go-Mythril is a Golang version of Mythril and has similar vulnerability detection capabilities as Mythril. We implemented the core ideas of ReCon on Go-Mythril, and the validity will be evaluated in Sect. 6.2.

Datasets. We generated corresponding reusable symbol execution results for two smart contract datasets, SmartBugs [12] and Top-10 most triggered contracts, and compared the difference in efficiency between the original tool and the optimized tool. The former dataset SmartBugs is the most commonly used labeled dataset in the field of smart contract vulnerability detection, which contains 142 contracts in 10 categories. SmartBugs has been used by the abovementioned vulnerability detection tools for their evaluation, which proves its authority in the field of vulnerability detection. The latter dataset is the top 10 most triggered contracts on Ethereum, and this dataset allows us to verify the efficiency of ReCon in the real world.

Experiment Setup. We ran all our experiments on one server which is equipped with an Intel(R) Xeon(R) Gold 5218R CPU (20 CPU cores) and 440 GB of RAM. For the parameters of the framework, we set the maximum execution time per contract to half an hour and replaced the timeout parameter of SMT solver with the "rlimit" parameter.

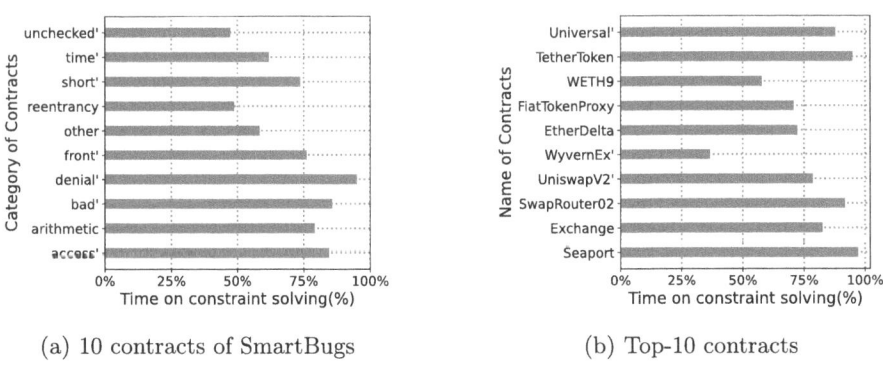

(a) 10 contracts of SmartBugs   (b) Top-10 contracts

Fig. 3. The cost of constraint solving (RQ1)

6.1 RQ1: Cost of Constraint Solving

As mentioned in Sect. 4, we use the pre-extracted symbolic execution data to guide the symbolic execution process to skip the unnecessary constraint solving steps, which finally improves the efficiency of vulnerability detection. In order to investigate the exact cost of time in constraint solving, we ran experiments on SmartBugs and Top-10 contracts to calculate the time proportion of the two constraint solving steps in Algorithm 1. For SmartBugs, we randomly selected one contract from each of the 10 categories of contracts for execution. The relevant parameters of the detection tools are: rlimit = 1,000,000, transactionCount = 2.

The result of SmartBugs is shown in Fig. 3a. 8 out of 10 contracts spent more than 50% of the time on constraint solving steps. Among these 10 contracts, the highest proportion of time is 95.03%, and the lowest is 47.35%. In the meanwhile, note that each of these 10 contracts finished their detection within 40 s. When more complex contracts are encountered, the time proportion of constraint solving may be larger. The result of Top-10 contracts is shown in Fig. 3b. The time proportion varies from 36.72% to 97.25%. And there are 9 contracts whose time proportion on constraint solving is more than 50%. The above data shows that the constraint solving task is time-consuming in the symbolic execution process. Each time the same contract is detected, these tasks need to be performed repeatedly, which can be omitted.

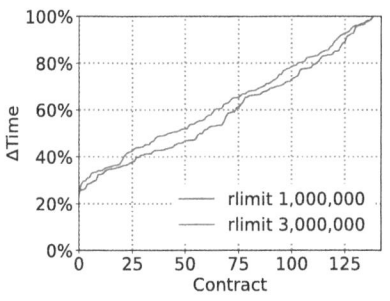
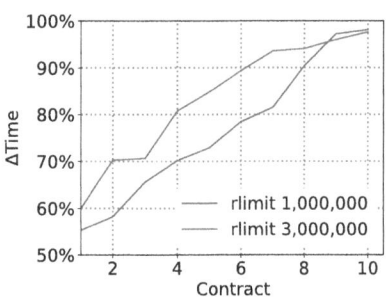

(a) The time saved on SmartBugs   (b) The time saved on Top-10 contracts

Fig. 4. The time saved by ReCon (RQ2)

6.2   RQ2: Improvement of Symbolic Execution

We answer the RQ2 by performing comparison experiments on two datasets, SmartBugs and Top-10 real-world contracts, respectively, in order to evaluate the efficiency of ReCon. For each dataset, we ran the original detection method first. After the reusable symbolic execution results were constructed, we ran our optimized method and finally compared whether the execution results were correct, as well as the detection time. The relevant parameters of the detection tools are: rlimit = 1,000,000 & 3,000,000, transactionCount = 2.

Results on SmartBugs are shown in Fig. 4a. We divided the experiment into two groups, rlimit 1,000,000 and rlimit 3,000,000, and calculated the time saved for each contract in SmartBugs. Eventually, we sorted the results in each group in ascending order. The results illustrate that the acceleration of the contract's detection varies widely depending on its contents. The lowest is 23.3%, and the highest is 99.4%. Results on Top-10 real-world contracts are shown in Fig. 4b and Table 1. For rlimit = 1,000,000, the saved time proportion varies from 60.0% to 97.6%. For rlimit = 3,000,000, it varies from 55.2% to 98.1%. We can observe that contracts with obvious acceleration also have a larger time proportion for their original constraint solving tasks. For example, when rlimit=1,000,000, Seaport [14], which saved 97.6% time, spent 97.25% detection time on its original constraint solving tasks mentioned in Sect. 6.1.

Table 1. Performance of ReCon on Top-10 Real-world Contracts (RQ2)

ContractName	Time (s)					
	rlimit = 1,000,000			rlimit = 3,000,000		
	Original	ReCon	ΔTime	Original	ReCon	ΔTime
Universal' [13]	573.55	60.93	89.4%	1567.91	655.51	58.2%
Seaport [14]	639.08	15.38	97.6%	1800.09	34.28	98.1%
SwapRouter02 [15]	1800.09	115.06	93.6%	1800.04	487.52	72.9%
WyvernEx' [16]	1800	71.98	96.0%	1800.08	618.67	65.6%
UniswapV2' [17]	1676.28	322.96	80.7%	1800.09	173.1	90.4%
Exchange [18]	235.63	35.78	84.8%	1122.33	207.33	81.5%
FiatTokenProxy [19]	34.01	9.98	70.7%	42.92	12.82	70.1%
WETH9 [20]	146.26	58.57	60.0%	217.79	97.49	55.2%
EtherDelta [21]	287.42	85.44	70.3%	1269.08	273.88	78.4%
TetherToken [22]	642.28	38.05	94.1%	1800.09	50.53	97.2%

Based on the above results, we can find that the efficiency of ReCon is obvious, especially in some contracts with more branches. For them, the detection time could be reduced from half an hour to half a minute.

6.3 RQ3: Consistency of Results

While improving the detection efficiency, we also need to ensure the consistency of the results, i.e., the consistency of the vulnerability results and the consistency of the execution part of the symbolic tree. We collected data on the number of states and the number of vulnerabilities in both datasets for analysis when running the experiment(rlimit = 1,000,000) in Sect. 6.2, in order to answer the RQ3.

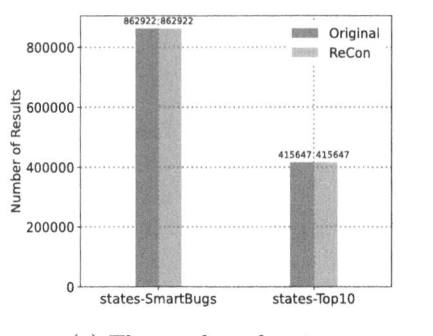

(a) The number of states

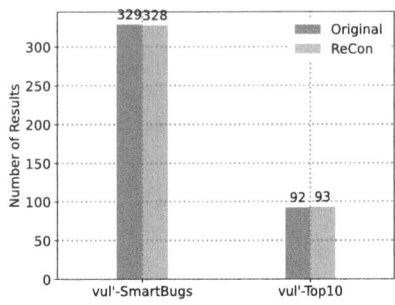

(b) The number of vulnerabilities

Fig. 5. The detection results of the framework (RQ3)

Results are shown in Fig. 5a and Fig. 5b. The states in both ReCon and the original tool are equal, indicating the consistency of the execution of symbolic trees. The numbers of vulnerabilities of both are similar. However, some of the vulnerability patterns use some random data structures leading to unequal situations, which will be further investigated in our future work. Overall, the similar numbers indicate the consistency of the vulnerability detection results.

7 Conclusion

In this paper, we propose ReCon, a new symbolic execution framework for smart contracts, using reusable symbolic execution results to improve the detection efficiency of new proposed vulnerabilities. ReCon proposes a symbolic tree extraction method for smart contracts. It also proposes a vulnerability detection method based on the pre-extracted symbolic tree. Experimental results on SmartBugs and Top-10 real-world contracts show that, after pre-execution, ReCon can save 54.9% of time on SmartBugs and 89.6% of time on Top-10 real-world contracts.

Acknowledgment. This research is supported by the National Natural Science Foundation of China (62302538), China Postdoctoral Science Foundation Grand (2023M734010).

References

1. Luu, L., Chu, D.-H., Olickel, H., Saxena, P., Hobor, A.: Making smart contracts smarter. In: Proceedings of the ACM SIGSAC Conference on Computer and Communications Security, pp. 254–269 (2016)
2. Nikolić, I., et al.: Finding the greedy, prodigal, and suicidal contracts at scale. In: Proceedings of the 34th Annual Computer Security Applications Conference (2018)

3. Torres, C.F., Steichen, M., et al.: The art of the scam: demystifying honeypots in ethereum smart contracts. In: 28th USENIX Security Symposium, pp. 1591–1607 (2019)
4. Torres, C.F., Schutte, J., State, R.: Osiris: hunting for integer bugs in ethereum smart contracts. In: Proceedings of the 34th Annual Computer Security Applications Conference, pp. 664–676 (2018)
5. Mueller, B.: Smashing ethereum smart contracts for fun and real profit. In: 9th Annual HITB Security Conference, vol. 54 (2018)
6. Zhang, W., Banescu, S., Pasos, L., Stewart, S., Ganesh, V.: MPro: combining static and symbolic analysis for scalable testing of smart contract. In: IEEE 30th International Symposium on Software Reliability Engineering, pp. 456–462 (2019)
7. Zheng, P., Zheng, Z., Luo, X.: Park: accelerating smart contract vulnerability detection via parallel-fork symbolic execution. In: Proceedings of the 31st ACM SIGSOFT International Symposium on Software Testing and Analysis (2022)
8. Durieux, T., et al.: Empirical review of automated analysis tools on 47,587 ethereum smart contracts. In: Proceedings of the ACM/IEEE 42nd International Conference on Software Engineering (2020)
9. Ghaleb, A., Pattabiraman, K.: How effective are smart contract analysis tools? Evaluating smart contract static analysis tools using bug injection. In: Proceedings of the 29th ACM SIGSOFT International Symposium on Software Testing and Analysis (2020)
10. Perez, D., Livshits, B.: Smart contract vulnerabilities: vulnerable does not imply exploited. In: 30th USENIX Security Symposium (2021)
11. SlowMist. Hacked Event (2021). https://hacked.slowmist.io/en/
12. Ferreira, J.F., et al.: SmartBugs: a framework to analyze solidity smart contracts. In: Proceedings of the 35th IEEE/ACM International Conference on Automated Software Engineering (2020)
13. Ethereum. Contract (2023). https://etherscan.io/address/0xef1c6e67703c7bd7107 eed8303fbe6ec2554bf6b
14. Ethereum. Contract (2023). https://etherscan.io/address/0x00000000006c3852 cbef3e08e8df289169ede581
15. Ethereum. Contract (2023). https://etherscan.io/address/0x68b3465833fb72a70 ecdf485e0e4c7bd8665fc45
16. Ethereum. Contract (2023). https://etherscan.io/address/0x7be8076f4ea4a4ad 08075c2508e481d6c946d12b
17. Ethereum. Contract (2023). https://etherscan.io/address/0x7a250d5630b4cf 539739df2c5dacb4c659f2488d
18. Ethereum. Contract (2023). https://etherscan.io/address/0x2a0c0dbecc7e4d658f 48e01e3fa353f44050c20
19. Ethereum. Contract (2023). https://etherscan.io/address/0xa0b86991c6218b36 c1d19d4a2e9eb0ce3606eb48
20. Ethereum. Contract (2023). https://etherscan.io/address/0xc02aaa39b223fe 8d0a0e5c4f27ead9083c756cc2
21. Ethereum. Contract (2023). https://etherscan.io/address/0x8d12a197cb00d4747 a1fe03395095ce2a5cc6819
22. Ethereum. Contract (2023). https://etherscan.io/address/0xdac17f958d2ee523a 2206206994597c13d831ec7
23. Szabo, N.: The idea of smart contracts. Nick Szabo's Papers Concise Tutorials **6**(1), 199 (1997)

24. Cadar, C., Sen, K.: Symbolic execution for software testing: three decades later. Commun. ACM **56**(2), 82–90 (2013)
25. Wood, G.: Ethereum: a secure decentralised generalised transaction ledger. Ethereum Project Yellow Paper **151**, 1–32 (2014)

SVD-SESDG: Smart Contract Vulnerability Detection Technology via Symbol Execution and State Variable Dependency Graph

Cong Tan, Jiahao Wu, Zhao Liu, and Sujuan Qin[✉]

State Key Laboratory of Networking and Switching Technology,
Beijing University of Posts and Telecommunications, Beijing 100876, China
{mandu33,wjh_bianca,qsujuan}@bupt.edu.cn

Abstract. Symbolic execution is a critical technique for detecting vulnerabilities in smart contracts on the blockchain. Existing tools struggle with high false positive rates and often fail to identify multi-function trigger vulnerabilities. To address these challenges, we introduce SVD-SESDG, which constructs a dependency graph for smart contract state variables to identify and analyze critical paths linked to potential vulnerabilities. By focusing on these paths and using actual state values to solve path constraints, SVD-SESDG enhances both efficiency and detection of complex vulnerabilities. Our experiments on an open-source dataset, targeting four types of vulnerabilities, demonstrate that SVD-SESDG significantly outperforms existing tools (Oyente, Mythril, TeEther) in reducing false positives and improving accuracy.

Keywords: Ethereum · Smart Contracts · State Variable Dependency Graph · Symbol Execution · Vulnerability Analysis

1 Introduction

Ethereum [1], launched in 2015 by Vitalik Buterin, is a decentralized open-source blockchain [2] platform that has significantly impacted the world of digital assets and decentralized applications (dApps), provides a robust framework for developers to create and deploy smart contracts and dApps on its blockchain. Smart contracts, an essential concept in Ethereum, are self-executing contracts with terms written directly into code [3]. They are stored and replicated on the blockchain network to ensure transparency, verifiability, and immutability. Once the specified conditions are met, smart contracts automatically execute agreed actions without intermediaries. However, their complexity brings new challenges in terms of security vulnerabilities. It is crucial to pay attention to the security of smart contracts on Ethereum as any breach could lead to significant financial losses and undermine trust in the ecosystem [4].

To detect smart contract vulnerabilities, researchers have proposed various analytical methods such as symbolic execution, formal verification, and fuzzing. The most widely used is symbolic execution [5], which abstracts program input into symbolic variables to simulate program execution while exploring all possible paths using constraint solvers. However, using symbolic execution to detect smart contract vulnerabilities also has the following problems: symbolic execution makes it difficult to cover all possible paths in a smart contract, leading to a path explosion problem during analysis. In addition, symbol execution may produce false positives and false negatives, and additional verification is required to improve the accuracy of detection.

To tackle the challenges in smart contract vulnerability detection, we've developed SVD-SESDG, a groundbreaking tool that combines data flow and control flow analysis. It constructs a detailed dependency graph of state variables from assembly code, allowing for the accurate identification of execution paths linked to potential vulnerabilities. SVD-SESDG filters and consolidates critical paths related to vulnerabilities, addressing the challenge of path explosion by identifying critical contract slices and building a critical path. This method traces the change path of source state variables, merging it with the critical path to uncover vulnerabilities from multi-function interactions. By pinpointing feasible vulnerabilities and disregarding those that are theoretically possible but impractical to trigger, SVD-SESDG markedly reduces false positives during symbolic execution and significantly improves the accuracy of vulnerability detection.

The rest of this paper is organized as follows. In Sect. 2, we cover the background of smart contracts and the related work of symbolic execution tools. Section 3 mainly describes the implementation details of SVD-SESDG. In Sect. 4, we performed experimental evaluations on SVD-SESDG and other symbolic execution tools based on the open-source dataset. Finally, we conclude this paper in Sect. 5.

2   Background and Related Work

2.1   Smart Contracts and Vulnerabilities

Szabo initially proposed smart contracts in 1997, defining them as a collection of commitments specified in digital form, and protocols through which contract participants can enforce those commitments. Solidity [6] is a high-level language used for writing smart contracts with a syntax similar to JavaScript. On the Ethereum platform, smart contracts written in Solidity can be compiled into bytecode and executed on the Ethereum virtual machine EVM [7].

After being deployed on Ethereum, the smart contract will get a unique address identifier and establish a smart contract account. The account includes the executable code, contract address, private status variables, and ETH balance [8]. Smart contracts cannot be changed once deployed. Any vulnerability in its code could be exploited maliciously. There are multiple security vulnerabilities in the design and implementation of smart contracts that could lead to the loss of assets or other security issues.

We focus on four types of vulnerabilities including reentrancy vulnerability, integer overflow vulnerability, timestamp dependency vulnerability, and access control vulnerability [9]: **Reentrancy Vulnerability** Reentrancy vulnerability occurs when a smart contract calls an external contract and can occur if the external contract changes the state of the original contract while processing the call, and the original contract relies on those states in subsequent operations. **Integer Overflow Vulnerability** Integer overflow vulnerability occurs when smart contracts perform numerical calculations, especially when the results are outside the range of integers that the contract programming language can represent. The attacker could exploit this vulnerability to change the logic of the contract. **Timestamp Dependency Vulnerability** The timestamp dependency vulnerability is related to the contract code's handling and dependence on the timestamp value. The attacker may attempt to exploit a contract's time dependence to perform a replay attack, advance or delay certain operations, or bypass time-based security checks in a contract by manipulating timestamps [10]. **Access Control Vulnerability** Access control vulnerability occurs when smart contracts fail to properly enforce or verify user permissions. The attacker could exploit this vulnerability to perform unauthorized actions, such as modifying contract status, withdrawing funds, or breaking contract logic.

2.2   Symbol Execution and Related Work

Symbolic execution is a widely used technique for analyzing smart contracts, simulating execution with symbolic values to uncover security vulnerabilities. It transforms inputs into symbolic variables, representing a range of potential inputs, and as the execution proceeds, each conditional branch forges two paths: one for true and another for false. This process yields path constraints. Symbolic execution employs Z3 solver [11] to identify specific symbolic values that meet all constraints, signifying the existence of an input that directs the program down a particular path. Z3 solver is a high-performance, open-source solver developed by Microsoft Research, which is designed to verify complex mathematical logic in software and hardware systems. Z3 slover supports a wide range of logical and arithmetic tasks, such as linear arithmetic operations and bit vectors. However, symbolic execution can encounter path explosion, limiting its practical coverage. There are many symbolic execution tools designed to analyze and detect vulnerabilities in smart contracts.

Oycnte [12] specializes in Ethereum smart contract analysis, using contract bytecode and Ethereum's global state to identify security issues and provide symbolic paths to these issues. It leverages the Z3 solver for constraint solving and features a modular design with key components like CFGBuilder and Explorer. However, it may overlook critical violations and produce false positives. Mythril [13] is renowned for its security analysis of Ethereum contracts. It simulates contract execution in a dedicated virtual machine, initializing states and exploring transaction outcomes to assess vulnerability reachability. Capable of detecting a range of vulnerabilities, Mythril's analysis can be slowed by the expansive state space of complex contracts. TeEther [14] reconstructs the CFG from bytecode, pinpoint key and state-changing instructions, and generates exploit transactions based on constraint satisfaction. Yet, its symbolic execution approach may face path explosion and complex constraint-solving obstacles. Osiris [15] is based on a single path vulnerability detection, the state variable is treated as a symbolic value, resulting in a relatively high false positive rate. It does not support the detection of multi-function vulnerabilities. And sCompile [16] uses random function combinations to execute symbols but will cause the problem of path explosion.

The above tools do not take into account the impact of state variables [17] which are based on the storage of vulnerability detection. Existing Symbolic execution detection tools may inadvertently trigger vulnerability conditions that would not occur in practice, resulting in false positives. In addition, state variables can lead to multi-function trigger vulnerabilities. Misinterpreting a state variable as an actual value rather than a symbolic value during symbolic execution can result in false positives. Unauthorized access to a state variable could allow other functions to change its value and potentially exploit the vulnerability.

3   Method

To solve the problem of false positives and false negatives caused by the state variables in the smart contract, we propose SVD-SESDG, a smart contract vulnerability detection method based on the state variable dependency graph and symbol execution.

3.1   Detection Process

To build the state variable dependency graph, based on the dependency graph, the critical path is combined with symbolic execution to detect vulnerabilities. SVD-SESDG is divided into four detection processes, as Fig. 1 shows:

1. **Construction of the Control Flow Graph(CFG)**
   The assembly code is sliced according to the control flow transfer instructions, and then the jump target is obtained by simulating execution, adding edges directly to the slice in CFG.
2. **Construction of the State Variable Dependency Graph(SVDG)**
   According to the characteristics of the assembly code, the state variables are identified, and then the data dependencies and control dependencies are constructed, and the dependencies are merged for analysis.
3. **Construction of Critical Combined Paths**
   To avoid path explosion, the key slices are first found in the contract and the critical path is constructed. Then, according to the SVDG, the change path of the state variable is tracked and combined with the critical path to form the critical combined path.
4. **Vulnerability Analysis and Detection**
   Establish a vulnerability pattern based on the vulnerability principle and find the critical path related to the pattern. Establish constraints for jumps in the combined path where the critical path is located, and then use Z3 solver to solve the constraints and generate a vulnerability report.

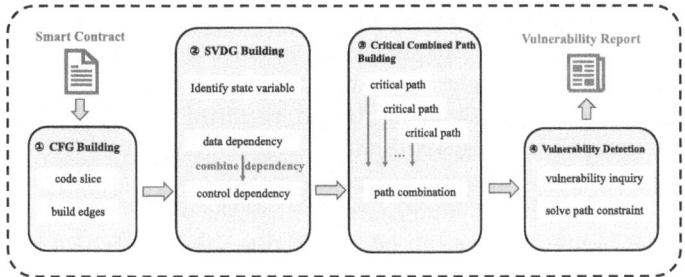

Fig. 1. The Structure of the SVD-SESDG

3.2   Construct the Control Flow Graph

Control flow graph (CFG) describes the execution path of a program [1]. We need to create CFG for EVM bytecode. Firstly, it is necessary to identify the control flow transfer instructions [18], such as JUMP, as shown in Table 1. According to the above instructions and their operands, the bytecode is segmented to obtain the basic block of CFG, and the edges in the CFG graph are constructed according to the jump relationship.

Table 1. Control Flow Transfer Opcodes

Command	Operand	Function
JUMP	s1	Jump to address s1
JUMPI	s1,s2	Jump to s1 if s2 is non-zero
JUMPDEST	–	Mark a valid jump destination
STOP	–	Halt the program and clear the stack
RETURN	s1,s2	Stop execution and return data from memory
REVERT	s1,s2	Stop execution, revert state, and return data

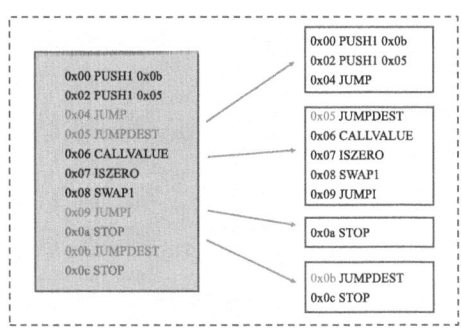

Fig. 2. Opcodes Slicing

Figure 2 illustrates the process of slicing assembly code. Control flow transfer instructions JUMP, JUMPI, JUMPDEST, and STOP are identified, and the code is partitioned accordingly, with JUMPDEST indicating a slice's start and JUMP, JUMPI, and STOP signaling its end, resulting in four slices.

After slicing opcodes, edges are added between slices to reflect jump relationships. Assembly code jump can be divided into direct jump and indirect jump. Indirect jumps do not immediately follow the JUMP or JUMPI opcode, and identifying indirect jumps can be challenging. SVD-SESDG addresses indirect jumps by simulating assembly execution, monitoring stack transitions to pinpoint jump targets, and setting constraints for symbolic execution.

Figure 3-a illustrates the changes in the stack during the execution of the assembly code. Before the JUMP is executed, the stack elements are 0x05 and 0x0b, where 0x05 is the top element and is the operand of the JUMP, the destination jump address. Therefore, the jump target for the first slice is the slice starting at address 0x05. The elements before executing JUMPI are 0x0b and ISZERO (CALLVALUE), where 0x0b indicates the jump target and ISZERO (CALLVALUE) is the jump condition. Since JUMPI is a conditional jump, the second slice has two subsequent slices: 0x0a and 0x0b. If the jump condition is met, it will jump to 0x0b slice; Otherwise, it continues to execute downward. After adding edges for all slices, the CFG is shown in Fig. 3-b.

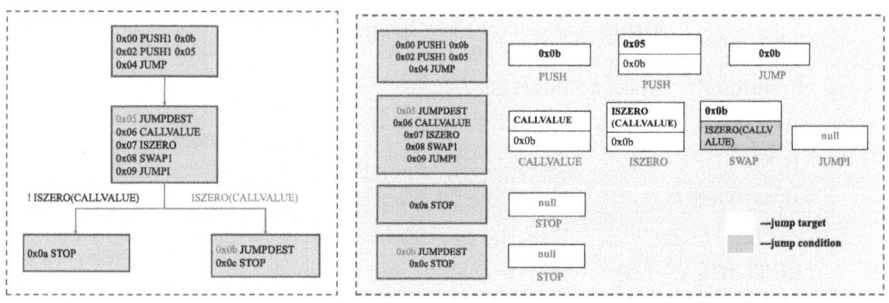

(a) Simulation of Stack Changes   (b) Control Flow Graph

Fig. 3. Simulation of Stack Changes and Control Flow Graph

3.3   Construct the State Variable Dependency Graph

This section describes how to construct the State Variable Dependency Graph. Dependencies include control dependencies and data dependencies. Control dependency means that in the control flow graph, if the execution path of subsequent slices is completely determined by the previous slice, the subsequent slice control depends on the previous slice. Data dependency means that one slice uses variable a and another slice defines variable a, so the slice data that uses the variable depends on the slice that defines the variable. Vulnerability detection for smart contracts needs to reflect dependencies at the slice level. As with all slices, there may be multiple use of state variables, so there are multiple data dependencies.

A slice can contain many opcodes, and for a slice-level control flow diagram, it is difficult to accurately extract this relationship. Therefore, we decided to extract a dependency graph for state variables, which includes the control and data dependencies of state variables.

State Variable Identification. Building a state variable dependency graph starts with pinpointing state variables within the assembly code, which needs to be analyzed according to the storage structure of the assembly. State variables, permanently stored on the blockchain, are manipulated via SSTORE and SLOAD commands. By tracking these commands and their execution context, state variables can be identified through operand addresses.

EVM has a minimum storage unit size of 32 bytes, yet smart contracts feature various types with shorter lengths (e.g., uint8, uint16, int128, address). EVM permits multiple variables to share a single storage unit. As Fig. 4 shows, an uint128 'a' and a 1-byte 'b' combine for a 17-byte storage in one address, while the "c" of 32 bytes requires a full storage unit. Similarly, 'd' and 'e' fit into one address. For shared variables like 'a' and 'b', assembly code employs a consistent opcode pattern. The process for 'b' is detailed in the following code block, involving division to ignore low-order bits, data retrieval, division for high-order values, and an AND operation to extract 'b'. We use the address and offset to locate the variable.

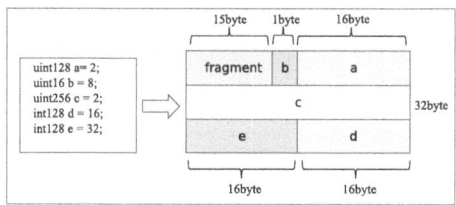

Fig. 4. Storage Structure of State Variables

SVD-SESDG simulates the stack to get the address and offset of the variable to identify the state variable. In the process of simulation execution, the stack state before the execution of SSTORE and SLOAD opcode is obtained, and the top element of the stack is the address of the state variable. If the simulation execution needs to execute DIV opcode, the offset of the second element before the execution of DIV opcode is obtained. If there is no DIV opcode, the variable is shown to be exclusive to an address space, and the offset is set to 0. Iterate through all SLOAD and SSTORE and their associated DIV opcodes in the assembly code, record the stack state, and thus identify all state variables. The operations on the variable are also recorded when the variable is identified, as well as which slice it came from, and finally, the state variable is identified by a quadruple (address, offset, operation, slice).

```
PUSH1 10
PUSH1 00
SLOAD
SWAP1
PUSH2 0100
EXP
SWAP1
DIV
PUSH2 ffff
AND
```

Table 2. Signed and Unsigned Number Calculation Operation Codes

Opcode	Operand Type	Operand	Function
ADD	signed/unsigned	a,b	a+b
SUB	signed/unsigned	a,b	a-b
MUL	signed/unsigned	a,b	a*b
DIV	unsigned	a,b	unsigned a/b
SDIV	signed	a,b	signed a/b
MOD	unsigned	a,b	unsigned a%b
SMOD	signed	a,b	signed a%b
LT	unsigned	a,b	if a<b, return 1; else return 0
GT	unsigned	a,b	if a>b, return 1; else return 0
SLT	signed	a,b	if a<b, return 1; else return 0
SGT	signed	a,b	if a>b, return 1; else return 0
SIGNEXTEND	signed	i,x	sign-extend x from i8+7

We also need to identify the type and length of the initial state variable. After reading the state variable, the operation can be performed to get the length. Types include address (20 bytes), signed number, and unsigned number. To determine the type based on the opcodes, Table 2 shows the opcodes for calculating signed and unsigned numbers.

Data Dependency. Data dependence needs to obtain the definition and usage relationship of state variables. The operation code SSTORE is used to store data as the definition of state variables, and SLOAD uses state variables. Iterate over all state variables looking for pairs of SSTOREs and SLOADs to build data dependencies. The process of calculating the data dependency graph is shown in Algorithm 1. To quickly find the same variables, we use a hash scheme to put the same variables into the same bucket. The address and offset are used as keys and then divided into two arrays according to the opcode type, with the opcode SSTORE stored in the first array and the opcode SLOAD stored in the second array. The dependency graph G is represented by the adjacency matrix, and the horizontal and vertical coordinates are represented by the state variable and slice number. Traverse the two arrays in the bucket, marking the corresponding position in G as 1.

Algorithm 1. Construct the Data Dependency Graph

1: **Input:** State Variable Quadruple $V = \{(address, offset, opcode, slice)\}$
2: **Output:** Data Dependency Graph G
3: **Begin**
4: **for** $v \in V$ **do**
5:     **if** $v.opcode ==$ SSTORE **then**
6:         insert v.slice into the first array of the H[(v.address, v.offset)]
7:     **else**
8:         insert v.slice into the second array of the H[(v.address, v.offset)]
9:     **end if**
10: **end for**
11: **for** key,value in H **do**
12:     **for** $i \in$ the first array of $H[(key)]$ **do**
13:         **for** $j \in$ the second array of $H[(key)]$ **do**
14:             $G[(key.address, key.offset, i)][(key.address, key.offset, j)] \leftarrow 1$
15:         **end for**
16:     **end for**
17: **end for**
18: **End**

Control Dependency. Figure 5 shows how to build control dependency. We first add the entry node En, exit node Ex, and connection node St to the CFG to create the AugCFG. AugCFG's post dominator tree [19] is then built, where the parent dominates the child backward. Consider a pair of nodes A and B such that: (1)$<A, B>$ are an edge in AugCFG; (2) In the post dominator tree, B is not the ancestor of A. In a post dominator tree, all nodes passed from the most recent common ancestor of A and B to node B depend on A. For example, for nodes 2 and 5, the closest common ancestor is "Ex", and the nodes that pass from "Ex" to node 5 include nodes 5 and 6, both of which depend on the control of node 2. The information about the control dependency is stored in the adjacency matrix, which is ultimately used to build the SVDG.

State Variable Dependency Graph. The state variable dependency graph (SVDG) is formed by combining data and control dependencies. Algorithm 2 demonstrates the process of merging data and control dependencies into the SVDG. The SVDG is represented by an adjacency matrix. It is initially populated with the data dependency graph, and as the control dependency graph

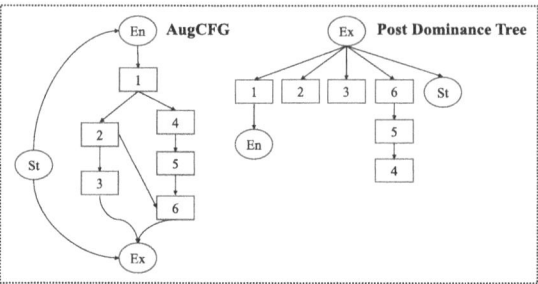

Fig. 5. Calculation of Control Dependencies

G_c is traversed, a value of 1 indicates a control dependency between variables. To differentiate between the two types of dependencies, a value of 2 is assigned in the corresponding location of the dependency graph G.

Algorithm 2. Construct the State Variable Dependency Graph

1: **Input:** Data dependency graph G_d and control dependency graph G_c
2: **Output:** State variable dependency graph G
3: **Begin**
4: Initialize G with G_d
5: **for** x in the number of rows of G_c **do**
6:     **for** y in the number of columns of G_c **do**
7:         **if** $G_c[x][y] == 1$ **then**
8:             $G[x][y] \leftarrow 2$
9:         **end if**
10:     **end for**
11: **end for**
12: **End**

3.4 Construction of Critical Combined Paths

Single Path Construction. The SVDG contains multiple slices to trace the execution path in the CFG. Find the shard that contains the definition of the state variable in the graph, and then start from the definition slice and perform the forward depth-first search in CFG to collect all possible sets of slices to get the forward slice set. At the same time, a backward depth-first search from the definition slice yields a backward slice set. The complete execution path associated with the state variable is the result of merging the forward slice set and the backward slice set. For critical path identification, the approach is similar but only needs to focus on constructing a backward-slicing set, as the vulnerability ends at the critical instruction and does not extend further forward.

Critical Combined Path Construction. To deal with multi-function trigger vulnerabilities, a combined path is proposed. Combine the state variable dependency path and the critical path according to the SVDG. The combination situation is divided into two kinds. One is to combine the path from the parameters of the critical instruction, and the other is to combine the path according to the control dependency conditions of the critical slice.

In the first case, state variables are identified from key instruction parameters, and then paths are combined according to the dependency graph. The combined path is stored on a stack. First, the critical path is pressed into the stack, and then the key instruction parameter contains the state variable. If not, there is no need to combine the paths. If a state variable is included, the dependency of the variable needs to be queried from the dependency graph. If there is a dependency, the dependency path of the variable is pushed into the path combination stack until all the dependency paths are pushed into the stack. The order of putting into the stack is the critical path, the dependency path of the state variable, and the order of bouncing the stack is exactly in line with the execution order.

The algorithm steps of the second case are roughly the same as those of the first case, both of which store paths by way of stack. The critical path is first pushed into the stack, and then the dependent path is pushed into the stack according to the dependency graph. The difference is to query the position of the state variable, the former from the critical instruction parameter query, the latter from the critical instruction parameter combination path query.

3.5   Vulnerability Analysis and Detection

This paper detects reentrancy vulnerabilities, access control vulnerabilities, timestamp dependency vulnerabilities, and integer overflow vulnerabilities. These vulnerabilities can all be affected by state variables. Even if these vulnerabilities are triggered by multiple functions, they can be detected based on critical combined paths. This paper performs symbolic execution and vulnerability detection on critical combined paths. Firstly, it is necessary to study the vulnerability, analyze the vulnerability pattern, and then summarize the detection method. Then, during symbolic execution, state variables affect the flow of program execution, so they cannot simply be treated as symbolic values. Instead, state variables are used as real values to form path constraints to ensure the feasibility of the path.

4   Evaluation

4.1   Dataset

We collected a smart contract source code dataset from published literature and the Awesome-Buggy-ERC20-Tokens [20] project, obtaining a total of 51,039 contracts. After removing duplicates and blank contracts, there were a total of 18,134 contracts. Among them, 8,523 contracts contained vulnerabilities, including 2,392 with reentrancy vulnerabilities, 1,596 with unrestricted operation vulnerabilities, 3,419 non-vulnerability integer overflows, and 1,116 timestamp dependency vulnerabilities. There were 8,691 contracts without vulnerabilities, with the data distribution shown in Table 3.

Table 3. Distribution of Vulnerabilities in the Dataset

Sample Type	Number of Samples (count)
Non-vulnerable Contract	9608
Reentrancy Vulnerabilities	2392
Access Control Vulnerabilities	1596
Integer Overflow Vulnerabilities	3419
Timestamp Dependency Vulnerabilities	1116

4.2   Experimental Environment

The CPU configuration used for the experiments was an Intel Xeon E5-1620 CPU with a clock speed of 3.50 GHz and 16G of memory. The programming language was Python, and the main integrated development environment was PyCharm.

4.3   Experiment Results

The Influence of State Variable Dependency Paths & Compare with Other Symbolic Execution Tools. To verify the effectiveness of symbolic execution using state variable dependency paths, the SVD-SESDG method was compared with existing tools, including Oyente, Mythril, and TeEther. Oyente and Mythril support the detection of reentrancy vulnerability, integer overflow vulnerability, and timestamp dependency vulnerability. Mythril and TeEther support the detection of access control vulnerability. The dataset was divided into 4 subsets according to the vulnerability type, and the accuracy rate, false positive rate, and false negative rate were taken as evaluation indicators. The results were shown in Table 4. The results showed that both Oyente and Mythril had false positive rates of more than 20%. In contrast, SVD-SESDG has consistently had a false positive rate of less than 10%. Compared to Oyente and Mythril, SVD-SESDG achieved an average reduction in false positive rates of 80% and 76%, respectively, making significant progress.

Regarding reentrancy, integer overflow, and timestamp dependence vulnerabilities, Oyente and Mythril had accuracy rates below 82%, with an average of 78.53% and 80.20%, respectively, an improvement of 14% and 12%, whereas SVD-SESDG's accuracy rate was below 88%, with an average of 89.80%. Comparing SVD-SESDG to Oyente and Mythril, the average false negative rate was

5.1% and 9.6% lower, respectively. With an average false positive rate of 6.62%, SVD-SESDG outperformed Oyente and Mythril by 81% and 79%, respectively.

While SVD-SESDG was quite effective in lowering the false positive rate of vulnerability detection, its capacity to lower the false negative rate was just mediocre. This is caused by timeouts in symbolic execution, which prevent accessibility in determining the vulnerability path, making it impossible to report the vulnerability. The analysis shows that timeouts occur when path constraints are too complex or cannot be resolved, causing symbol execution to exceed predefined time limits. When there are more complex constraints or unsolvable constraints in the path, the Z3 solver cannot finish the solution normally, resulting in the entire symbol execution time exceeding the set time, which may lead to missing declarations. This problem stems from a fundamental problem in symbolic execution itself, which cannot be solved by optimization.

Regarding access control vulnerability, TeEther has a lower false positive rate than SVD-SESDG. TeEther is based on a strict definition of vulnerabilities and thus has a lower false positive rate compared to SVD-SESDG, which identifies vulnerability patterns and then uses symbolic execution to determine path feasibility. However, TeEther has a high false negative rate of 20.43%. The high false negative rate is partly due to timeouts during the path combination process, which results in not extracting paths containing vulnerabilities.

Table 4. Results of Different Symbolic Execution Tools for 4 Vulnerabilities

Vulnerability	Tool	Accuracy (%)	False Negative Rate (%)	False Positive Rate (%)
Reentrancy Vulnerability	SVD-SESDG	**90.89**	**14.71**	**5.35**
	Oyente	79.32	14.97	33.72
	Mythril	81.43	15.06	30.34
Access Control Vulnerability	SVD-SESDG	**88.77**	**15.57**	**7.74**
	Mythril	79.36	18.45	21.15
	TeEther	85.25	20.43	6.32
Integer Overflow Vulnerability	SVD-SESDG	**88.47**	**15.84**	**8.85**
	Oyente	75.54	16.59	40.37
	Mythril	77.92	17.77	35.75
Timestamp Dependency Vulnerability	SVD-SESDG	**90.03**	**17.31**	**5.66**
	Oyente	80.74	19.35	30.32
	Mythril	81.26	20.02	28.58

The Influence of Critical Combined Paths on Multi-function Vulnerabilities. To investigate this issue, multi-function trigger vulnerabilities were manually screened from an open-source dataset, combined with non-vulnerable contracts to form a new dataset, and tested using the proposed solution. Of the 8,523 vulnerable smart contracts, there were 546 multi-function trigger vulnerabilities. Multi-function trigger vulnerability can be classified as access control vulnerability in essence, but for the sake of comparison, this paper statistics the distribution of multi-function trigger vulnerability in all vulnerabilities.

As shown in Table 5, the proposed scheme has a very good effect on the detection of multi-function trigger vulnerability. The accuracy of all kinds of vulnerabilities is high. The average is 90.95%, and it has a good performance in reducing false negatives and false positives. The average is 11.82% and 4.51%, respectively. These detection results prove the effectiveness of critical combined path construction based on SVDG, which can support the detection of multi-function trigger vulnerability.

Table 5. Evaluation Metrics for Four Multi-function Trigger Vulnerabilities

Vulnerability	Accuracy	FNR	FPR
Reentrancy Vulnerability	91.89%	12.55%	4.25%
Access Control Vulnerability	90.25%	11.35%	90.25%
Integer Overflow Vulnerability	91.71%	10.79%	4.71%
Timestamp Dependency Vulnerability	89.96%	12.57%	3.73%

In summary, the proposed solution, SVD-SESDG, is superior to existing symbolic execution tools in detecting various types of vulnerabilities. It improves the detection effect of symbol execution by tracking state variables in the CFG and merging critical combined paths.

5   Conclusion

To solve the problem of multi-function trigger vulnerability and missing reports in symbolic execution, a smart contract vulnerability detection scheme based on the state variable dependency graph named SVD-SESDG has been designed. A smart contract dataset was collected from a publicly available vulnerability database, and a comprehensive experiment was conducted to demonstrate the effectiveness of SVD-SESDG with an accuracy that exceeds existing symbolic execution tools, reducing false positive and false negative rates. However, due to the complexity of the constraints or the unsolvable constraints, the symbol execution may time out, resulting in false negatives. In order to solve this problem, we consider combining deep learning to detect whether there are vulnerabilities in a certain path.

Acknowledgments. This work is supported by the National Key R&D Program of China under Grant 2021YFB2700400.

References

1. He, D., Wu, R., Li, X., Chan, S., Guizani, M.: Detection of vulnerabilities of blockchain smart contracts. IEEE Internet Things J. (2023)
2. Conti, M., Kumar, E.S., Lal, C., Ruj, S.: A survey on security and privacy issues of bitcoin. IEEE Commun. Surv. Tutorials **20**(4), 3416–3452 (2018)
3. Hu, T., Li, J., Storhaug, A., Li, B.: Why smart contracts reported as vulnerable were not exploited? Authorea Preprints (2023)
4. Munir, S., Taha, W.: Pre-deployment analysis of smart contracts–a survey. arXiv preprint arXiv:2301.06079 (2023)
5. Wang, Y., Sheng, S., Wang, Y.: A systematic literature review on smart contract vulnerability detection by symbolic execution. In: Chen, J., Wen, B., Chen, T. (eds.) Blockchain and Trustworthy Systems, BlockSys 2023. CCIS, vol. 1896, pp. 226–241. Springer, Singapore (2023). https://doi.org/10.1007/978-981-99-8101-4_16
6. Dannen, C., Dannen, C.: Solidity programming. In: Introducing Ethereum and Solidity: Foundations of Cryptocurrency and Blockchain Programming for Beginners, pp. 69–88 (2017)
7. He, L., Zhao, X., Wang, Y.: Parse: efficient detection of smart contract vulnerabilities via parallel and simplified symbolic execution. In: Proceedings of the 2024 IEEE/ACM 46th International Conference on Software Engineering: Companion Proceedings, pp. 272–273 (2024)
8. Ethereum: a secure decentralised generalised transaction ledger (2019)
9. Wei, Z., Sun, J., Zhang, Z., Zhang, X., Li, M., Zhu, L.: A comparative evaluation of automated analysis tools for solidity smart contracts. arXiv preprint arXiv:2310.20212 (2023)
10. Qian, P., et al.: Demystifying random number in ethereum smart contract: taxonomy, vulnerability identification, and attack detection. IEEE Trans. Softw. Eng. (2023)
11. Z3Prover. A theorem prover from microsoft research: Z3 (2008). https://github.com/Z3Prover/z3
12. Luu, L., Chu, D.-H., Olickel, H., Saxena, P., Hobor, A.: Making smart contracts smarter. In: Proceedings of the 2016 ACM SIGSAC Conference on Computer and Communications Security, pp. 254–269 (2016)
13. ConsenSys. Mythril-security analysis tool for EVM bytecode (2021). https://github.com/ConsenSys/mythril
14. Krupp, J., Rossow, C.: {teEther}: gnawing at ethereum to automatically exploit smart contracts. In: 27th USENIX Security Symposium (USENIX Security 2018), pp. 1317–1333 (2018)
15. Torres, C.F., Schütte, J., State, R.: Osiris: hunting for integer bugs in ethereum smart contracts. In: Proceedings of the 34th Annual Computer Security Applications Conference, pp. 664–676 (2018)
16. Chang, J., Gao, B., Xiao, H., Sun, J., Cai, Y., Yang, Z.: sCompile: critical path identification and analysis for smart contracts. In: International Conference on Formal Engineering Methods (ICFEM 2019), Shenzhen, China, pp. 5–9 (2019)
17. Perez, D., Livshits, B.: Smart contract vulnerabilities: vulnerable does not imply exploited. In: 30th USENIX Security Symposium (USENIX Security 2021), pp. 1325–1341 (2021)
18. Chen, T., et al.: A large-scale empirical study on control flow identification of smart contracts. In: 2019 ACM/IEEE International Symposium on Empirical Software Engineering and Measurement (ESEM), pp. 1–11. IEEE (2019)

19. Gupta, R.: Generalized dominators and post-dominators. In: Proceedings of the 19th ACM SIGPLAN-SIGACT Symposium on Principles of Programming Languages, pp. 246–257 (1992)
20. SEC-BIT. A collection of vulnerabilities in erc20 smart contracts with tokens affected (2019). https://github.com/sec-bit/awesome-buggy-erc20-tokens

Dual-View Aware Smart Contract Vulnerability Detection for Ethereum

Jiacheng Yao[1,2], Maolin Wang[1,2], Wanqi Chen[1,2], Chengxiang Jin[1,2], Jiajun Zhou[1,2]([✉]), Shanqing Yu[1,2], and Qi Xuan[1,2]

[1] Institute of Cyberspace Security, Zhejiang University of Technology, Hangzhou 310023, China
jjzhou@zjut.edu.cn
[2] Binjiang Institute of Artificial Intelligence, ZJUT, Hangzhou 310056, China

Abstract. The wide application of Ethereum technology has brought technological innovation to traditional industries. As one of Ethereum's core applications, smart contracts utilize diverse contract codes to meet various functional needs and have gained widespread use. However, the non-tamperability of smart contracts, coupled with vulnerabilities caused by natural flaws or human errors, has brought unprecedented challenges to blockchain security. Therefore, in order to ensure the healthy development of blockchain technology and the stability of the blockchain community, it is particularly important to study the vulnerability detection techniques for smart contracts. In this paper, we propose a **D**ual-view Aware Smart Contract **V**ulnerability **Det**ection Framework named DVDet. The framework initially converts the source code and bytecode of smart contracts into weighted graphs and control flow sequences, capturing potential risk features from these two perspectives and integrating them for analysis, ultimately achieving effective contract vulnerability detection. Comprehensive experiments on the Ethereum dataset show that our method outperforms others in detecting vulnerabilities.

Keywords: Smart Contract · Vulnerability Detection · Ethereum

1 Introduction

Ethereum [1] is the first blockchain platform to achieve Turing completeness, enabling a variety of functional applications through smart contracts. Smart contracts [2], one of Ethereum's core technologies, define the rules and conditions of contracts in the form of programming code on the blockchain, enabling automatic contract execution. These contracts can automatically handle various tasks such as asset transfers, voting execution, and digital asset management without relying on third-party trust mechanisms. However, smart contracts also pose potential risks due to vulnerabilities that may lead to stolen funds, abnormal contract behavior, or data leaks, causing financial losses and trust crises for users [3]. For example, incidents like TheDao event and the Poly Network attack were triggered by smart contract vulnerabilities, leading to significant financial losses. Since 2016, the number of blockchain security incidents has been increasing annually, with a significant proportion caused by smart contract vulnerabilities. These incidents not only jeopardize the property safety of users but also intensify public skepticism about the security of blockchain platforms, prompting ongoing research into smart contract security.

Existing methods for detecting vulnerabilities in smart contracts include static analysis, dynamic analysis, symbolic execution, fuzz testing, and deep learning-based approaches. However, each of them has its limitations. For instance, static analysis cannot capture the dynamic behaviors of contracts, while dynamic analysis might not cover all execution paths. Symbolic execution and fuzz testing are affected by the path explosion problem, and in terms of accuracy, existing methods often result in false positives or false negatives. Moreover, certain detection techniques may only be applicable to specific types of vulnerabilities and lack effective means to detect new or complex vulnerabilities.

To address these issues, we propose a **D**ual-view Aware Smart Contract **V**ulnerability **Det**ection Framework (DVDet), which focuses on both source code and bytecode to detect vulnerabilities in smart contracts. For source code view, it constructs an augmented contract code graph and feed it to a improved graph neural network model to capture the inherent logical semantics within the code. For bytecode view, it constructs a control flow sequence and enhances the sequence model to extract thorough sequence features. Finally, it integrates the features from both views to achieve effective detection for smart contract vulnerabilities. The main contributions of this paper can be summarized as follows:

- We propose a unique Dual-view Aware Smart Contract Vulnerability Detection Framework, which combines features from both the source code and bytecode of smart contracts for vulnerability detection.
- We propose a data augmentation method for abstract syntax trees by quantifying node importance to further assign edge weights, ultimately converting the augmented abstract syntax tree into a weighted smart contract graph.
- We propose the HyperAGRU model, which integrates attention mechanisms into GRU units. This not only enhances the ability to capture local features of control flow sequences but also effectively highlights the crucial information inherent in the control flow.
- Extensive experiments on real-world datasets demonstrate that our DVDet outperforms existing models for smart contract vulnerability detection.

2   Related Work

2.1   Traditional Vulnerability Detection Methods

Traditional vulnerability detection usually relies on analyzing the underlying logic of the contract.

First, static analysis detects vulnerabilities by analyzing source code syntax, semantics, and data flow. This method can identify issues like reentrancy attacks, overflows, and uninitialized variables, but it is weak to detect complex vulnerabilities. Feist et al. [4] detect vulnerabilities by converting Ethereum smart contract code into an intermediate representation. Schneidewind et al. [5] perform reachability analysis based on EVM bytecode to detect potential vulnerabilities. Second, dynamic analysis detects vulnerabilities by simulating different transactions and operations during actual contract execution. It can capture dynamic information during program runtime, such as memory usage, but requires more resources and time. Azzopardi et al. [6] use dynamic event automata to monitor the control flow and data flow events of contracts. Wustholz et al. [7] propose a lightweight gray-box fuzz testing tool mainly used to detect common vulnerability types. Third, symbolic execution explores contract paths through symbolic variables to discover potential vulnerabilities. It excels at uncovering subtle errors and complex issues but is susceptible to path explosion and has limited capabilities in handling complex data structures. Veloso et al. [8] combine the advantages of static analysis and symbolic execution to simulate contract execution paths under different input conditions. Finally, fuzz testing observes contract behavior by randomly generating inputs to find anomalies. It can discover uncommon boundary cases and anomalies but may generate a large number of invalid inputs, leading to false positives. Nguyen et al. [9] improve testing efficiency using an adaptive fuzzing approach. Jiang et al. [10] generate valid test inputs based on smart contract ABI specifications and monitor the EVM to detect vulnerabilities.

2.2 Deep Learning-Based Detection Methods

In recent years, deep learning has shown great potential in the field of vulnerability detection. Well-trained deep learning models can learn complex program structures and syntax rules, thereby achieving high accuracy and detection effectiveness. In the realm of vulnerability detection, deep learning methods can address the shortcomings of traditional detection methods. For instance, Ashizawa et al. [11] propose the Eth2Vec, utilizing neural networks to learn susceptible features from EVM bytecode and detecting vulnerabilities by comparing the similarity between target EVM bytecode and vulnerable bytecode. Wang et al. [12] design the automated vulnerability detection tool ContractWard, which is capable of detecting five types of vulnerabilities, including timestamp vulnerabilities, reentrancy vulnerabilities, arithmetic overflow, call stack vulnerabilities, and transaction order defects. Furthermore, Liu et al. [13] model smart contract graphs for vulnerability detection. Liang et al. [14] proposed PonziGuard, which detects Ponzi contracts by combining control flow, data flow, and execution behavior information in contract behavior running graphs.

Although smart contract vulnerability detection methods based on deep learning demonstrate significant advantages, they still face some challenges and limitations. One of them is the high dependence on high-quality labeled data, which is often difficult to obtain in practice. Besides, existing methods typically start vulnerability detection from one view of source code auditing or bytecode analysis, failing to fully utilize comprehensive information from both aspects.

3   Dataset

During data collection, we analyze multiple smart contract vulnerability datasets and find that the type labels for vulnerabilities are scarce. Additionally, these datasets often do not fully cover different contract versions. For example, reentrancy vulnerabilities are mostly found in versions above 0.8, but current datasets largely do not include contracts from version 0.7 and above. To address this, we have collected and integrated several smart contract datasets from the open-source community to alleviate the issue of insufficient version coverage in existing datasets, which helps in training models to better detect and adapt to new and more complex vulnerability scenarios.

3.1   Data Collection

We collect training datasets of smart contracts from Github. Initially, by merging multiple open-source datasets and removing duplicates, we obtain 53,000 smart contracts. Subsequently, we clean the data, including eliminating whitespace, comments, and code not conforming to the structure of Solidity's syntax, to obtain 35,000 smart contract datasets suitable for research. To further obtain vulnerability labels for the dataset, we employ a voting tool to review each piece of code, selecting 10,000 smart contracts for the training set. Positive samples in the training set are derived from the 35,000 contracts confirmed to contain vulnerabilities through voting, while negative samples are randomly selected from smart contracts confirmed to be normal. The distribution of contract versions and corresponding vulnerabilities in the training set is illustrated in Fig. 1. For the testing set, positive samples are obtained from the *smartbugs-curated*[1] dataset, while the number of negative samples matches that of positive samples, selected from normal smart contracts.

3.2   Label Generation

To ensure the accuracy and fairness of vulnerability labeling, we employ five voting tools to annotate smart contract vulnerabilities. These tools cover a variety of detection techniques, thus avoiding bias in the voting process towards any particular detection type, including Slither [4], Mythril [15], Oyente [16], Osiris [17], Securify [18]. The voting tools combine two static analysis tools and three symbolic execution tools. The utilization of diverse tools facilitates the acquisition of more comprehensive and precise labels, thereby improving the model's performance and generalization capabilities.

4   Methodology

In this section, we propose a dual-view aware smart contract vulnerability detection framework (DVDet), which captures and fuses potential risk features from both the source code and bytecode of smart contracts to achieve effective detection. The overall framework is illustrated in Fig. 2.

---

[1] https://github.com/smartbugs/smartbugs-curated.

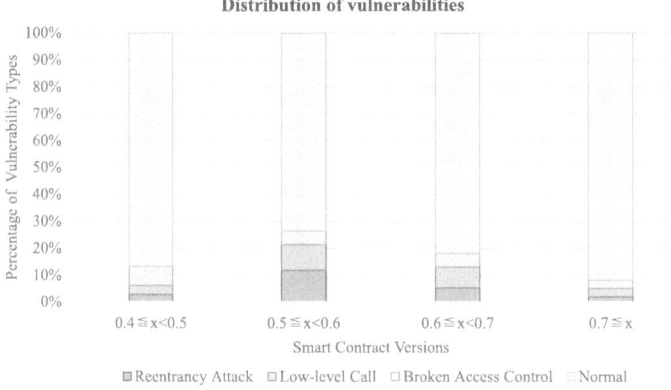

Fig. 1. Distribution of vulnerabilities in different versions of contracts.

4.1 Source-Code Aware Channel

This view aims to perceive potential vulnerabilities by analyzing features of smart contract source code. Specifically, we first convert smart contract source code into abstract syntax trees. Then, we design data augmentation strategies to further transform them into weighted smart contract code graphs. Finally, we utilize edge-aware graph attention networks to learn node features.

Augmented Smart Contract Graph Generation. Abstract Syntax Tree (AST) is a tree-like data structure used to represent the code structure in programming languages. By analyzing the syntax and semantic structure of the code, AST converts the code into a tree representation, where each node represents a syntactic unit of the code, such as expressions, statements, or function definitions, and these nodes are interconnected via parent-child relationships.

In this paper, we utilize the third-party tool *solc-typed-ast*[2] to obtain normalized AST, and obtain vectorized representations of AST nodes via CodeBert [19], as illustrated in Fig. 3. When processing AST, we focus on extracting key information from the nodes to improve the efficiency and accuracy of the analysis. For instance, the *ContractDefinition* node may contain information that is irrelevant for detection purposes. Hence, we retain only crucial fields such as *name*, *kind*, *abstract*, and *fullyImplemented*. Here, *name* represents the contract name, *kind* is used to distinguish whether the contract is of contract, library, or interface, *abstract* indicates whether it is an abstract contract, and *fullyImplemented* being True indicates that the contract has implemented at least one function. This approach not only optimizes the data structure but also ensures that the vulnerability detection can focus on the most critical information.

---

[2] https://github.com/Consensys/solc-typed-ast.

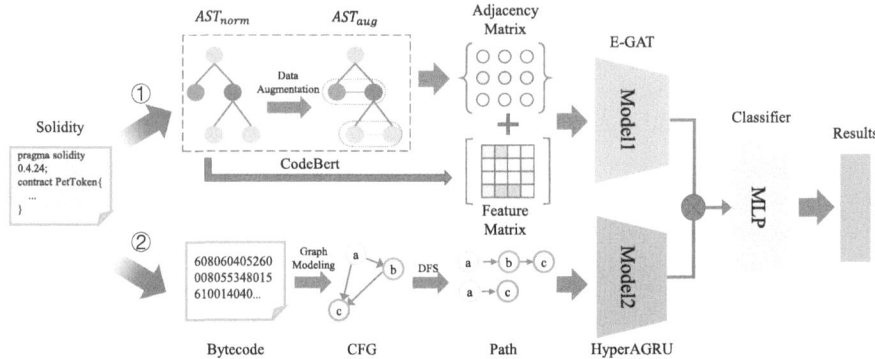

Fig. 2. Dual-view aware smart contract vulnerability detection framework.

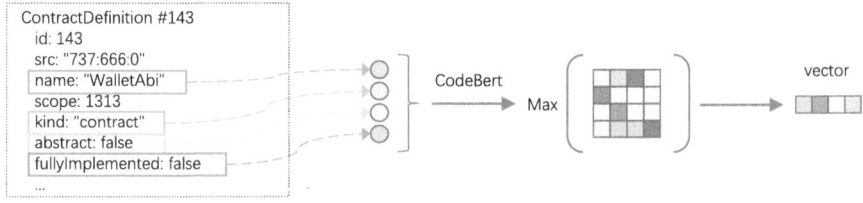

Fig. 3. Illustration of encoding AST nodes using CodeBert.

After the source code is transformed to AST, there still exist numerous irrelevant nodes about vulnerability, which may be considered as noise and not favorable for detection. To address this issue, we propose a data augmentation method for AST, which quantifies the importance of different types of nodes to enhance the representation. Figure 4 takes reentrancy vulnerability as an example to illustrate the augmentation process. On one hand, this type of vulnerability can only be triggered during execution by invoking *call.value()*. On the other hand, the emergence of the vulnerability is not only related to the function caller but also to variable constraints in the context, such as certain variables triggering an *if-else* branch, leading to the execution of vulnerable code. Therefore, in vulnerability detection, the *if-else* blocks are more critical relative to the *call.value()* node. By enhancing the edge features between *if-else* and *call.value()*, the influence of important neighboring nodes can be increased, allowing the neural network to focus more on crucial information during the aggregation process.

During the augmentation process, we first decompose the vulnerable contract into four types of nodes, including core nodes, secondary core nodes, auxiliary nodes, and peripheral nodes. Taking reentrancy vulnerability as an example, its core node is *call.value()*, which directly originates the vulnerability. Sub-core nodes include variables *require, if, msg.sender*, and *balance*, which are relevant to the syntax structure of the core node. Auxiliary nodes represent statements or code blocks like *if-else, while, do-while, for*, as well as nodes within the current

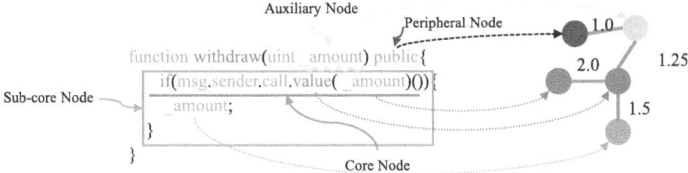

Fig. 4. An example of constructing weighted contract graph of reentry vulnerability.

function that are identical to the core and sub-core nodes. Peripheral nodes have minimal direct logical relationship with the core nodes and hence exert low influence on the vulnerability. In summary, we assign different levels of importance to these four types of nodes, denoted as $S = \{2,\ 1.5,\ 1.25,\ 1\}$.

Then, we transform the AST to a smart contract graph $G_{ast} = (V, E, \mathbf{X})$, where V represents the set of nodes in the AST, E represents the set of edges formed by data flow or control flow, and $\mathbf{X}$ represents the feature matrix of nodes. According to the definitions of node types mentioned above, we assign different importance weights to the edges between different node pairs as follows:

$$S_{ij} = \min\left(S_i, S_j\right) \tag{1}$$

where S_i and S_j represent the importance of nodes v_i and v_j respectively, and S_{ij} denotes the importance weight of the edge. As a result, we transform the AST to a weighted smart contract graph $\hat{G}_{ast} = (V, E, \mathbf{X}, S)$.

Edge-Aware Attention Network. The Graph Attention Network (GAT) [20] is a prevalent graph deep learning model utilized for aggregating high-quality domain features by employing attention mechanisms. However, GAT overlooks the significance of edge features within the graph. Therefore, we propose an Edge-aware Attention Network (E-GAT). Firstly, based on the obtained $\hat{G}_{ast}$, we regard the edge importance S_{ij} as edge features, which will participate in the subsequent computation of the attention:

$$e_{ij}^{(l)} - \text{LeakyReLU}\left(\mathbf{a}^\top \left(\mathbf{W}_h \mathbf{X}_i^{(l)} + \mathbf{W}_h \mathbf{X}_j^{(l)}\right) \cdot S_{ij}\right)$$
$$\hat{\mathbf{X}}_i^{(l+1)} = \sigma\left(\sum_{j \in \mathcal{N}_i} \text{Softmax}\left(e_{ij}^{(l)}\right) \cdot \mathbf{W}_h \mathbf{X}_j^{(l)}\right) \tag{2}$$

where $\mathbf{a}$ is the learnable attention projection vector, $\mathbf{W}_h$ is the learnable weight matrix for nodes and edges respectively, $\mathcal{N}_i$ is the neighbor set of node v_i, and σ is the activation function. By aggregating the node pairs and then multiplying with the edge features, we obtain the attention coefficients e_{ij}.

With the introduction of attention weights, we can selectively aggregate neighborhood information to the target node, thereby obtaining unique and refined node representations.

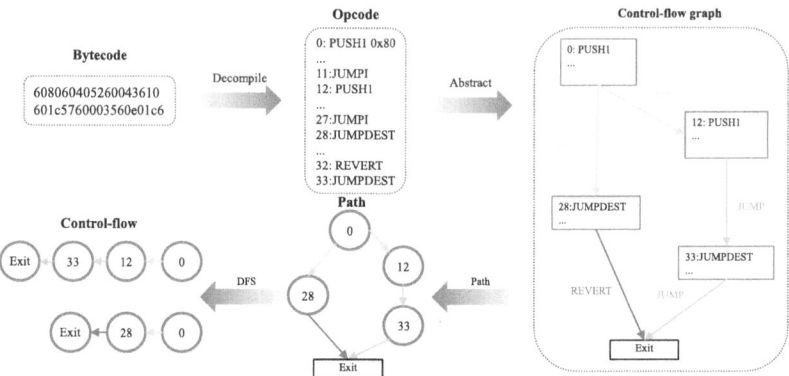

Fig. 5. Illustration of control flow generation.

4.2   Bytecode Aware Channel

This view aims to analyze the bytecode features of smart contracts. Specifically, we first decompile the bytecode of smart contracts into opcodes. Then, according to jump instructions, we further transform them into a control flow graph. Subsequently, we utilize path-searching algorithms to obtain the control flow. Finally, we design sequence models HyperAGRU to learn the representations.

Control Flow Generation. Opcodes are fundamental instructions in Ethereum, which are obtained by decompiling bytecode and enable smart contracts to access memory and interact with others. These opcodes involve accessing and modifying data [21] in the stack, memory, and storage devices.

We utilize these opcodes to construct the Control Flow Graph (CFG) of the contract, which is crucial for understanding the program structure and dynamics.

In the CFG, each node represents a sequence of consecutive opcodes, known as a basic block, while edges represent the jumps between basic blocks.

Additionally, the CFG can eliminate inactive code, reducing interference during the detection process, and providing a more detailed depiction of the data flow sequence during program execution. Hence, we derive all potential and crucial paths that may be traversed during program execution from the CFG.

Specifically, we acquire multiple control flows through the depth-first search algorithm, which is illustrated in Fig. 5.

HyperAGRU. After obtaining the control flow data, we use sequence models to learn the feature representation of the control flow. Considering that traditional GRUs still face the problem of losing long-term dependencies when processing long sequences, we propose the HyperAGRU model. By incorporating an attention mechanism into the GRU, this model can not only capture local patterns within the control flow but also dynamically assign weights to each operation

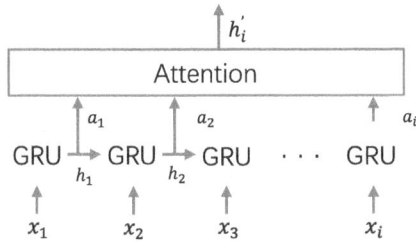

Fig. 6. The framework of the HyperAGRU.

block in different contexts. This approach highlights those instructions and jumps that are crucial for security assessment.

As depicted in Fig. 6, each element in the sequence is associated with an attention weight, indicating its contribution to the final aggregation.

Multiplying each element of the sequence by its respective attention weight and summing the products yields the final representation. Initially, the intermediate representation is computed using the GRU block, shown as follows:

$$
\begin{aligned}
z_t &= \sigma \left(W_z \cdot [h_{t-1}, x_t] + b_z \right) & \tilde{h}_t &= \tanh \left(W_h \cdot [r_t \odot h_{t-1}, x_t] + b_h \right) \\
r_t &= \sigma \left(W_r \cdot [h_{t-1}, x_t] + b_r \right) & h_t &= (1 - z_t) \odot h_{t-1} + z_t \odot \tilde{h}_t
\end{aligned}
\tag{3}
$$

where z_t is the update gate to control the weight of the previous and current elements, r_t is the reset gate to control the influence of the previous element, $\tilde{h}_t$ is the candidate hidden state, and $\odot$ denotes element-wise product. Finally, we obtain the intermediate representation h_t for each element.

Utilizing an attention mechanism for h_t, we efficiently capture the local importance of the sequence and integrate this information into the final representation:

$$
a_t = \mathrm{Softmax} \left(u^\top \cdot h_t \right)
$$

$$
\hat{h}_t = \sum_{t=1}^{L} a_t \cdot h_t
\tag{4}
$$

where u is the learnable attention parameter, L is the length of the sequence, and $\hat{h}_t$ is the final contract representation for the downstream dual-view fusing.

4.3 Dual-View Vulnerability Detection

After obtaining the outputs $\hat{X}$ and $\hat{h}$ from the two views, we aggregate them and employ a MLP as a classifier to generate the predicted values:

$$
p_i = \mathrm{Softmax} \left(W(\hat{X}_i \parallel \hat{h}_i) + b \right)
\tag{5}
$$

where $\|$ denotes the concatenation operation. Then, the loss function $\mathcal{L}$ adopts the cross-entropy loss function, shown as follows:

$$\mathcal{L} = -\sum_i \boldsymbol{y}_i \cdot \log(\boldsymbol{p}_i) \tag{6}$$

Notably, the function can be used for both binary and multi-class classification.

5   Experiments

5.1   Parameter Settings

In this paper, we select three categories of methods for comparison, including sequential neural networks (LSTM [22] and GRU [23]), graph neural network (GCN [24], GIN [25], GraphSAGE [26] and GAT [20]), and traditional static analysis method (Conkas [8]). For LSTM and GRU, we set up a two-layer structure with a fixed input dimension of 350 dimensions. As for GNN, we adopt a three-layer structure with an input dimension of 768 dimensions. To ensure the reliability of the results, all experiments are subjected to three-fold cross-validation on the dataset. Regarding parameter optimization, we employ the Adam optimizer with an initial learning rate of 0.01. Additionally, to adjust the learning rate to improve training effectiveness, we utilize a cosine annealing strategy. A uniform dropout rate of 0.5 is set during the experiments to alleviate the risk of overfitting. We employ two commonly used evaluation metrics: Accuracy and Recall.

5.2   Evaluation on Vulnerability Detection

We evaluate the effectiveness of our method through experiments on detecting the existence and types of vulnerabilities in smart contracts. The former determines the presence of vulnerabilities, while the latter identifies the specific types of vulnerabilities.

Table 1 reports the results of all methods, from which we can derive the follow conclusion:

- Sequence models underperform in vulnerability detection because converting source code into opcode sequences can result in the loss of information related to the source code, such as variable names, which can adversely affect detection performance. Additionally, these sequence models struggle with the forgetting issue when dealing with long sequences. In contrast, our method not only incorporates attention within the bytecode-aware view to enhance the model's capacity for handling sequence data but also includes a source code-aware view to model critical information within the code, thereby achieving better detection performance.

Table 1. Accuracy of smart contract vulnerability detection. The bolding indicates the best result.

Model		LSTM	GRU	GCN	GIN	SAGE	GAT	Conkas	DVDet
Acc (%)	Type	65.35	72.54	80.07	79.99	78.47	81.62	61.97	**84.50**
	Existence	71.46	84.25	86.04	87.83	87.95	89.00	78.48	**90.74**

Table 2. Performance of ablation experiments for different views. The bolding indicates the best results.

Methods		Type						Existence
		ReEn		LoWc		AcCl		
SC	BT	Acc	Recall	Acc	Recall	Acc	Recall	Acc
GAT	–	84.05	73.91	81.21	80.55	78.59	66.66	81.31
E-GAT	–	85.51	80.63	82.52	87.62	78.61	74.75	82.25
–	GRU	78.21	75.12	78.39	79.33	79.53	76.33	78.71
–	HyperAGRU	79.96	74.22	78.41	79.62	80.37	77.85	79.58
GAT	HyperAGRU	84.09	78.86	82.47	80.55	80.22	84.09	82.26
E-GAT	GRU	87.44	79.59	82.45	86.42	**80.78**	75.00	83.55
DVDet		**88.73**	**82.60**	**84.50**	**88.66**	80.28	**87.44**	**84.50**

- GNN-based methods perform better than sequence models because by converting source code into graphs, they can effectively capture the complex logical relationships within the source code. However, GNN-based approaches are highly dependent on effective graph construction strategies and the expressive power of initial features. In contrast, our method, by augmenting the code graph, further strengthens the semantic associations between code elements, thus achieving better detection results.
- The Conkas tool performs poorly in both tasks. As a static analysis tool, it tends to miss vulnerabilities that are only triggered under specific conditions. Moreover, Conkas struggles to handle highly abstract or novel programming constructs, which may introduce vulnerabilities that are difficult to detect.

5.3   Ablation Experiment

To evaluate the effectiveness of our dual-view framework and our improved models, we perform a series of ablation studies, as shown in Table 2. Specifically, SC indicates source code view, and BT indicates the bytecode view.

We can derive the following conclusions:

- From the source code view, our E-GAT outperforms GAT, indicating that our data augmentation strategy designed for contract code graphs effectively strengthens the associations between code elements, aiding in the enhancement of vulnerability detection;

Table 3. Efficiency of Smart Contract Vulnerability Detection.

Methods	Slither	Securify	Oyente	Osiris	Mythril	DVDet
Unit Detection Time(s)	2.09	59.17	4.51	21.16	31.64	**0.14**
Total Detection Time(s)	409.64	10058.92	816.31	4147.36	6201.44	**27.17**

- From the bytecode view, our HyperAGRU generally outperforms GRU, demonstrating that incorporating attention mechanisms into sequence encoding can effectively capture the rich semantic information of the code flow, thereby enhancing vulnerability detection;
- By comparing DVDet with E-GAT+SC (or HyperAGRU+BT), it is evident that there is a complementary effect between the two perspectives within the DVDet framework.

5.4 Efficiency Experiment

To evaluate the efficiency of our method in vulnerability detection, we conduct efficiency analysis experiments. The results, as shown in Table 3, indicate that tools based on symbolic execution, such as Securify, Osiris, and Mythril, have a large time consumption on vulnerability detection. Slither and Oyente demonstrate faster detection speeds. Our DVDet framework exhibits exceptionally high efficiency in vulnerability detection, achieving an order of magnitude advantage over some existing detection tools.

6 Conclusion

Smart contract vulnerabilities have caused serious damage to the ecosystem of the Ethereum platform. Existing methods typically adopt a single view when designing algorithms for vulnerability detection, focusing solely on either the source code perspective or the bytecode perspective. In this paper, to address the issue of one-sided views in existing methods, we propose a smart contract vulnerability detection method that incorporates dual-view fusion.

Extensive experiments demonstrate that our framework achieves outstanding detection performance, indicating that the dual view can acquire more comprehensive information for vulnerability detection. In addition, compared with other traditional detection methods, the deep learning-based method also demonstrates significantly higher detection efficiency, offering a new perspective for subsequent smart contract vulnerability detection.

Acknowledgments. This work was supported by the China Postdoctoral Science Foundation under Grant Number 2024M762912, by the Postdoctoral Science Preferential Funding of Zhejiang Province of China under Grant ZJ2024060, by the Key R&D Program of Zhejiang under Grant 2022C01018, by the National Natural Science Foundation of China under Grant U21B2001.

References

1. Wood, G., et al.: Ethereum: a secure decentralised generalised transaction ledger. Ethereum Project Yellow Paper **151**(2014), 1–32 (2014)
2. Zheng, Z., et al.: An overview on smart contracts: challenges, advances and platforms. Futur. Gener. Comput. Syst. **105**, 475–491 (2020)
3. Mense, A., Flatscher, M.: Security vulnerabilities in ethereum smart contracts. In: Proceedings of the 20th International Conference on Information Integration and Web-Based Applications & Services, pp. 375–380 (2018)
4. Feist, J., Grieco, G., Groce, A.: Slither: a static analysis framework for smart contracts. In: 2019 IEEE/ACM 2nd International Workshop on Emerging Trends in Software Engineering for Blockchain (WETSEB), pp. 8–15. IEEE (2019)
5. Schneidewind, C., Grishchenko, I., Scherer, M., Maffei, M.: eThor: practical and provably sound static analysis of ethereum smart contracts. In: Proceedings of the 2020 ACM SIGSAC Conference on Computer and Communications Security, pp. 621–640 (2020)
6. Azzopardi, S., Ellul, J., Pace, G.J.: Monitoring smart contracts: ContractLarva and open challenges beyond. In: Colombo, C., Leucker, M. (eds.) Runtime Verification: 18th International Conference, RV 2018, Limassol, Cyprus, 10–13 November 2018, Proceedings 18, pp. 113–137. Springer, Cham (2018). https://doi.org/10.1007/978-3-030-03769-7_8
7. Wüstholz, V., Christakis, M.: Harvey: a greybox fuzzer for smart contracts. In: Proceedings of the 28th ACM Joint Meeting on European Software Engineering Conference and Symposium on the Foundations of Software Engineering, pp. 1398–1409 (2020)
8. Veloso, N.: Conkas: a modular and static analysis tool for ethereum bytecode (2021)
9. Nguyen, T.D., Pham, L.H., Sun, J., Lin, Y., Minh, Q.T.: sFuzz: an efficient adaptive fuzzer for solidity smart contracts. In: Proceedings of the ACM/IEEE 42nd International Conference on Software Engineering, pp. 778–788 (2020)
10. Jiang, B., Liu, Y., Chan, W.K.: ContractFuzzer: fuzzing smart contracts for vulnerability detection. In: Proceedings of the 33rd ACM/IEEE International Conference on Automated Software Engineering, pp. 259–269 (2018)
11. Ashizawa, N., Yanai, N., Cruz, J.P., Okamura, S.: Eth2Vec: learning contract-wide code representations for vulnerability detection on ethereum smart contracts. In: Proceedings of the 3rd ACM International Symposium on Blockchain and Secure Critical Infrastructure, pp. 47–59 (2021)
12. Wang, W., Song, J., Xu, G., Li, Y., Wang, H., Su, C.: ContractWard: automated vulnerability detection models for ethereum smart contracts. IEEE Trans. Netw. Sci. Eng. **8**(2), 1133–1144 (2020)
13. Liu, Z., Qian, P., Wang, X., Zhu, L., He, Q., Ji, S.: Smart contract vulnerability detection: from pure neural network to interpretable graph feature and expert pattern fusion. arXiv preprint arXiv:2106.09282 (2021)
14. Liang, R., et al.: PonziGuard: detecting Ponzi schemes on ethereum with contract runtime behavior graph (CRBG). In: Proceedings of the 46th IEEE/ACM International Conference on Software Engineering, pp. 1–12 (2024)
15. Sharma, N., Sharma, S.: A survey of mythril, a smart contract security analysis tool for EVM bytecode. Indian J. Nat. Sci. **13**, 75 (2022)
16. Luu, L., Chu, D.H., Olickel, H., Saxena, P., Hobor, A.: Making smart contracts smarter. In: Proceedings of the 2016 ACM SIGSAC Conference on Computer and Communications Security, pp. 254–269 (2016)

17. Torres, C.F., Schütte, J., State, R.: Osiris: hunting for integer bugs in ethereum smart contracts. In: Proceedings of the 34th Annual Computer Security Applications Conference, pp. 664–676 (2018)
18. Tsankov, P., Dan, A., Drachsler-Cohen, D., Gervais, A., Buenzli, F., Vechev, M.: Securify: practical security analysis of smart contracts. In: Proceedings of the 2018 ACM SIGSAC Conference on Computer and Communications Security, pp. 67–82 (2018)
19. Feng, Z., et al.: CodeBERT: a pre-trained model for programming and natural languages. In: Findings of the Association for Computational Linguistics: EMNLP 2020, pp. 1536–1547 (2020)
20. Velickovic, P., et al.: Graph attention networks. stat. **1050**(20), 10–48550 (2017)
21. Krupp, J., Rossow, C.: {teEther}: gnawing at ethereum to automatically exploit smart contracts. In: 27th USENIX Security Symposium (USENIX Security 2018), pp. 1317–1333 (2018)
22. Gers, F.: Long short-term memory in recurrent neural networks. Ph.D. thesis, Verlag nicht ermittelbar (2001)
23. Cho, K., et al.: Learning phrase representations using RNN encoder-decoder for statistical machine translation. arXiv preprint arXiv:1406.1078 (2014)
24. Kipf, T.N., Welling, M.: Semi-supervised classification with graph convolutional networks. arXiv preprint arXiv:1609.02907 (2016)
25. Xu, K., Hu, W., Leskovec, J., Jegelka, S.: How powerful are graph neural networks? arXiv preprint arXiv:1810.00826 (2018)
26. Hamilton, W., Ying, Z., Leskovec, J.: Inductive representation learning on large graphs. In: Advances in Neural Information Processing Systems, vol. 30 (2017)

Blockchain Layered Sharding Algorithm Based On Transaction Characteristics

Changsong Yang[1,3,5], Yixiong Tang[1,5], Yong Ding[1,2,3(✉)], Yujue Wang[4], and Hai Liang[1,5]

[1] Guangxi Key Laboratory of Cryptography and Information Security, Guilin University of Electronic Technology, Guilin 541004, China
[2] Institute of Cyberspace Technology, HKCT Institute for Higher Education, Hong Kong 999077, China
[3] Guangxi Key Laboratory of Digital Infrastructure, Guangxi Zhuang Autonomous Region Information Center, Nanning, China
stone_dingy@126.com
[4] Hangzhou Innovation Institute of Beihang University, Hangzhou, China
[5] Guangxi Engineering Research Center of Industrial Internet Security and Blockchain, Guilin University of Electronic Technology, Guilin, China

Abstract. To address the challenges of high cross-shard transaction ratios and delays in cross-shard transaction verification encountered in optimizing blockchain performance through sharding technology, this paper proposes a blockchain layered sharding algorithm. Based on the long-term accumulated transaction data in the blockchain, this method predicts and optimizes the shard distribution of transactions by analyzing the transaction characteristics between accounts, thereby reducing the number of transactions that need to be conducted between different shards. A blockchain transaction sharding algorithm (OSABTC) was designed to optimize conventional shards (i-shard) and bridge shards (b-shard) in layered sharding through transaction characteristics. By reducing the cross-shard transaction ratio and increasing the proportion of bridge shard transactions, the problem of high cross-shard transaction ratios in transaction sharding was effectively resolved. Experimental comparisons show that, compared with the Random Sharding Algorithm (RSA), the OSABTC algorithm can reduced the cross-shard transaction ratio and increased the bridge shard transaction ratio, while transaction latency was reduced. These results demonstrate the effectiveness of the OSABTC algorithm in significantly enhancing the performance and efficiency of blockchain systems.

Keywords: Transaction fragmentation · Transaction characteristics · Hierarchical fragmentation · Transaction delay · Bridge shards

1 Introduction

Blockchain technology, a decentralized distributed ledger technology, has shown tremendous potential in various fields such as finance, supply chain management,

D. He et al. (Eds.): BlockSys 2024, CCIS 2264, pp. 201–214, 2025.
https://doi.org/10.1007/978-981-96-1411-0_16

and digital identity verification. It has driven the development of cryptocurrencies like Bitcoin and Ethereum through its secure, transparent, and immutable transaction recording mechanisms, while the use of smart contracts has further expanded its range of applications [1–3]. However, as applications become more widespread and complex, performance bottlenecks such as slow transaction processing speeds, limited throughput, and high latency have become major obstacles to its large-scale deployment [4–6].

To address these challenges, sharding technology has been proposed, which improves system throughput and concurrent processing capabilities by dividing the blockchain network into multiple shards that can process transactions in parallel [7,8]. However, the complexity of handling cross-shard transactions brings new challenges [9–11]. Despite sharding technology's use in projects like Monoxide, Ethereum 2.0, and Zilliqa, the challenge of cross-shard transactions persists due to inadequate consideration of transaction characteristics.

The pyramid scheme first introduces the concept of hierarchical sharding, which belongs to the partial sharding system [12,13], effectively processing cross-shard transactions by using b-shards to connect multiple i-shards handling and storing transactions [14,15]. Although Pyramid has made progress in handling cross-shard transactions, its static sharding configuration method limits the system's flexibility and security [16,17].

1.1   Main Contributions

To address the issue of an exceptionally high ratio of cross-shard transactions in Pyramid's static sharding scheme [16], this paper proposes a dynamic sharding strategy based on node reputation and transaction patterns, as well as a layered blockchain sharding algorithm based on transaction characteristics.

The main contributions of this paper are summarized as follows:

(1) This paper develops a layered sharding model for blockchain systems by analyzing the long-term accumulation characteristics of transaction data.
(2) On the basis of Pyramid's static sharding scheme, this paper designs a blockchain transaction sharding algorithm-optimized shard allocation based on transaction characteristics (OSABTC). The algorithm divides shards into two types: i-shards for processing internal transactions independently, and b-shards for managing cross-shard transactions. The goal is to minimize cross-shard transactions by effectively selecting and utilizing i-shards and b-shards.
(3) Experimental results demonstrate that OSABTC reduces cross-shard transactions by 10% compared to the traditional RSA algorithm, and by optimizing bridge shards, it increases bridge shard transactions by 40% and reduces transaction latency by 30%.

2   Related Works

Sharding, a technique for improving performance by dividing large datasets into manageable parts [18], is widely used in blockchain to enhance processing capability. It involves splitting nodes into smaller groups or shards for parallel transaction processing, greatly boosting blockchain performance. The evolution of blockchain sharding has seen three stages, as depicted in Fig. 1.

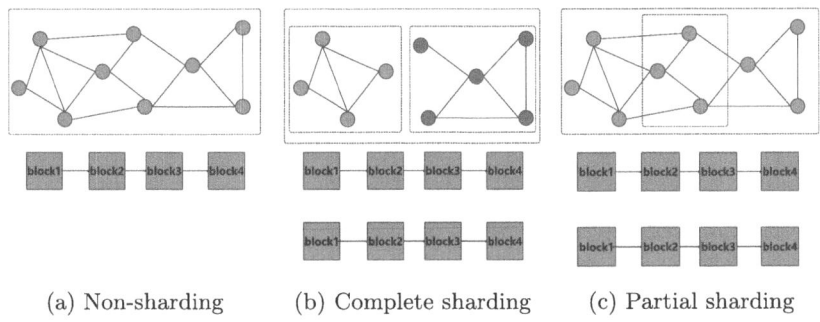

(a) Non-sharding   (b) Complete sharding   (c) Partial sharding

Fig. 1. Development Stages of Blockchain Sharding

2.1   Non-sharded Systems

Notable non-sharded systems like Bitcoin and Ethereum require all nodes to maintain a distributed ledger, enhancing trust and decentralization [19]. However, this necessitates each node to validate and store all transactions and broadcast each consensus message network-wide, leading to scalability issues [20].

2.2   Fully Sharded Systems

Kokoris-Kogias et al. [21] proposed a sharding protocol OmniLedger to manage identities, utilizing ByzCoin's sliding window mechanism to select eligible nodes for the next epoch. A core innovation of OmniLedger is the introduction of the Atomix protocol, a client-driven, two-phase cross-shard transaction processing protocol. It effectively ensures the atomicity of transactions, thereby enabling cross-shard transactions to be executed correctly and without errors.

Wang et al. [22] introduced a sharding protocol Monoxide, which uses an asynchronous Proof of Work (POW) consensus to reduce communication costs. Despite its probabilistic finality requiring longer wait times for cross-shard transactions, Monoxide uses a fixed shard configuration tied to node addresses and the Chu-ko-nu mining algorithm. This allows simultaneous mining across multiple shards, diluting the power of malicious nodes and enhancing system security.

2.3   Partial Sharding Systems

Most sharding schemes treat all validators as homogeneous, overlooking the differences in hardware and network capabilities among nodes. In practice, some nodes are more active than others, which may make a shard more vulnerable to attacks. To address this issue, Huang et al. [23] proposed a reputation-based sharding protocol called Repchain, which encourages participation from high-capability nodes. This protocol assesses nodes' reputations based on their contributions to consensus, assigns nodes to shards according to their reputation, and ensures a balanced quality of nodes within each shard. High-reputation nodes act as leaders, coordinating consensus and rapidly accumulating reputation points, thus providing a positive incentive.

Zhang et al. [24] proposed the CycLedger, a sharding protocol that uses reputation scores to incentivize nodes' honesty, akin to RepChain [23]. CycLedger rewards nodes based on the proximity of their votes to the final consensus, encouraging nodes with more resources to earn more and behave honestly. Unlike RepChain, CycLedger strengthens security with a node assignment scheme using Verifiable Random Functions (VRF) and has a monitoring set to supervise shard leaders, replacing them if necessary. The protocol classifies nodes into four types: arbitration committee, shard leaders, monitoring set members, and non-critical nodes, with only the first three playing active roles in transaction management.

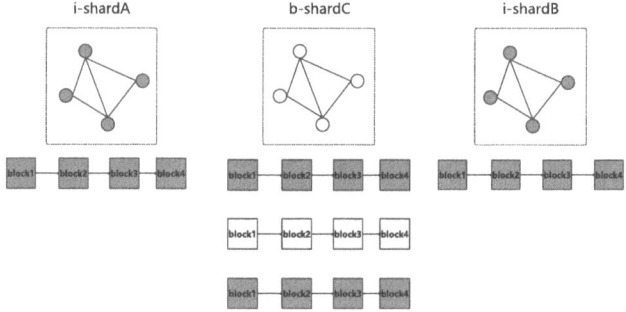

Fig. 2. Pyramid i-shardA and b-shard fragment structure and fragment block content

Hong et al. [16] proposed the Pyramid framework, a hierarchical sharding model with two layers. Nodes, identified via POW, belong to either i-shards or b-shards. I-shards handle intra-shard transactions using PBFT consensus, while b-shards connect i-shards and store their states to validate cross-shard transactions. For complex cross-shard transactions, a splitting mechanism similar to Omnileger's [21] is used, decomposing transactions for processing, as depicted in Fig. 2.

3   System Model

In the blockchain system, the set of accounts is represented by $Ac = \{ac_1, ac_2, \ldots, ac_n\}$, and the set of transactions is represented by $Tx = \{tx_1, tx_2, \ldots, tx_k\}$, where *amount* represents the monetary amount in the transaction. The blockchain has stored transaction data accumulated over many years. The goal of transaction sharding is to efficiently distribute historical data to different shards from the perspective of storage optimization. Data sharding rules are based on a series of transaction sharding strategies. The account-based sharding model first extracts account information from historical transactions, then assigns accounts to corresponding shards based on the account, and maps transactions to the corresponding working shard based on the account address. As depicted in Fig. 3, The OSABTC system mainly consists of the following parts:

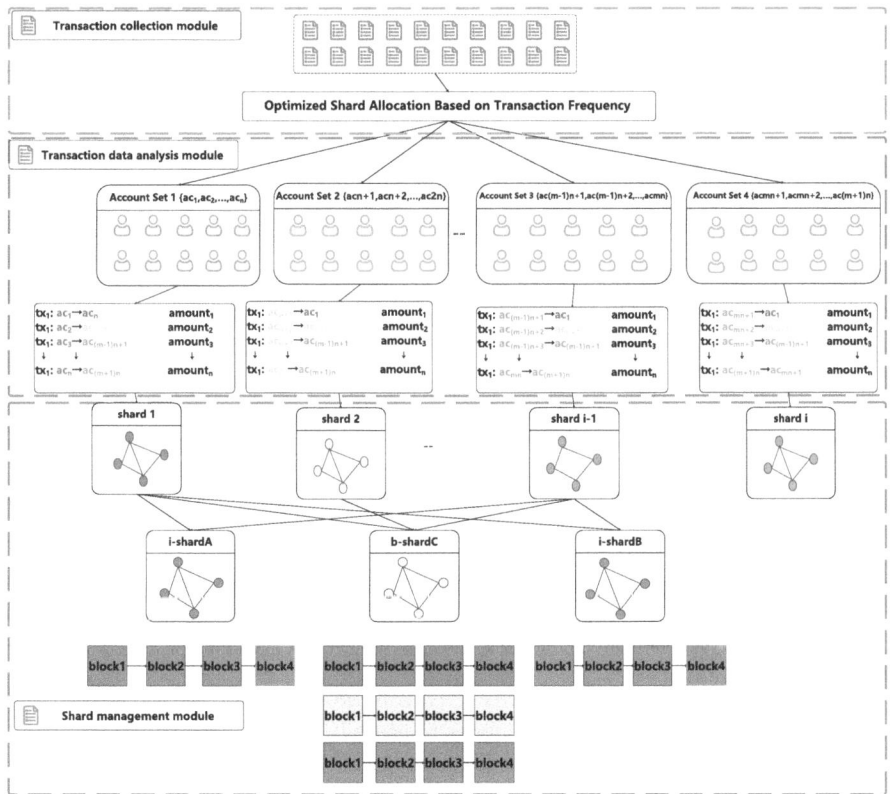

Fig. 3. Transaction fragmentation model

Transaction Collection Module:
Transaction Collection Module monitors the blockchain, capturing all transactions and immediately obtaining the latest data. Each transaction is analyzed

for key features such as amount, accounts involved, and timestamp. Transactions are then classified and labeled by type, frequency, and associated accounts, aiding in the optimization of sharding strategies and transaction handling.

Transaction Data Analysis Module: The Transaction Data Analysis Module scrutinizes transaction data to identify key traits like frequency, amount, and timing, thereby understanding account relationships. This insight helps group related accounts into the same shard, reducing cross-shard transactions. Further, by studying transaction patterns and account links, it develops optimized sharding strategies like account sharding, hierarchical sharding, and shard bridging, boosting sharding management efficiency.

Sharding Management Module: The Sharding Management Module strategically allocates accounts to shards based on account activity and transaction characteristics, creating b-shards for efficient cross-shard processing. It continuously adjusts shard assignments using real-time transaction data and network load, dynamically optimize performance and stability, and reduce transaction latency to improve cross-shard transaction efficiency.

4   OSABTC Scheme

4.1   Transaction Feature Segmentation Algorithm

To address the issues of shard transaction congestion and the aggregation of malicious nodes, the algorithm proposed in this section allocates nodes to multiple shards rationally by considering the transaction frequency and reputation value of nodes. This achieves load balancing and ensures that the reputation value of each shard meets a certain standard. The core idea of the Algorithm 1 is to use a transaction graph to reflect the transaction relationships and activity levels between nodes, and to reflect the quality and reliability of nodes through their reputation values. The algorithm implements the rational distribution of nodes through the following steps:

Constructing the Transaction Graph: The transaction graph is constructed using data from the transaction data analysis module. In this graph $G(V, E)$, nodes V symbolize transaction entities, and edges E denote transactional relationships. The goal is to reflect transaction activities in the network.

Core Node Identification: Identify k core nodes, which are key participants selected by the transaction data analysis module based on their transaction frequency, reputation value, or other relevant criteria. Core nodes have associations with other nodes in the shard, and the number of core nodes depends on the number of nodes in the shard and the transaction volume limit.

Node Allocation: The shard management module first assigns core nodes to shards based on transaction frequency, ensuring active nodes hold key positions. Then, the remaining nodes are distributed across shards, aiming for a balanced node count per shard to prevent congestion or idleness.

Algorithm 1. Sharding Balance Algorithm Based on Transaction Frequency and Reputation Value

---

1: **procedure** SHARDINGALGORITHM(Tx, k)
2:     **Input:** Transaction set Tx, Number of shards k
3:     **Output:** Balanced shard collections S
4:     Construct transaction graph $G(V, E)$
5:     **for** Transaction $tx_i \in Tx$ **do**
6:         Update the corresponding nodes and edges in graph G
7:     **end for**
8:     Identify k core node sets
9:     Initialize shard collections S as k empty sets
10:    **for** Each core node **do**
11:        Assign nodes with high transaction frequency to the corresponding shard
12:    **end for**
13:    Assign remaining nodes, keeping the number of nodes in shards balanced
14:    **for** Each shard S_i **do**
15:        Calculate the reputation value $Reputation(ac_i)$ of nodes in the shard
16:    **end for**
17:    Balance shards until the reputation value threshold condition is met
18:    **return** S
19: **end procedure**

Reputation Value Calculation: The reputation value of each node within a shard is calculated to assess its status within the shard.

$$\text{Reputation}(ac_i) = w_1 \cdot \text{Stake}(ac_i) + w_2 \cdot \text{Time}(ac_i) - w_3 \cdot \text{Penalties}(ac_i) \quad (1)$$

where w_1, w_2, w_3 are weight coefficients, representing the node's contribution, activity level, and penalty degree, respectively. The node's contribution is determined by the amount of tokens it holds $Stake(ac_i)$, the activity level by the time it participates in transactions $Time(ac_i)$, and the penalty degree by the number of its violations $Penalties(ac_i)$. The purpose of this step is to assess the overall reputation level of each shard.

$Stake(ac_i)$: A node's contribution is typically measured by its token holdings, since possessing more tokens indicates greater trustworthiness, attributed to the potential economic loss in the event of malicious attacks. Assessment methods to gauge this contribution include direct readings from the blockchain ledger or calculating a time-weighted average to prevent the inflation of temporary contributions.

$Time(ac_i)$: A node's activity level is gauged by its participation time in network activities. This can be determined by counting its transactions or blocks over a timeframe, or by recording its online duration during consensus or transaction verification.

$Penalties(ac_i)$: A node's penalty level is based on the frequency and severity of its infractions, assessed through recorded violations and assigned penalty scores, with more serious breaches incurring higher penalties. For example, the penalty for a double-spending attack should be higher than that for issuing invalid transactions.

Shard Balance Adjustment: Based on the reputation values of nodes in a shard, the shard management module makes adjustments to ensure that the reputation value of each shard reaches the threshold. This involve the redistribution of nodes or adjustments in transactional relationships between shards.

4.2   Bridge Shard Election Algorithm

To address the issue of high proportion of cross-shard transactions and low cross-shard efficiency in static sharding, the algorithm improves sharding efficiency in blockchain systems by managing transaction data to reduce cross-shard transactions and enhance inter-shard coordination. Algorithm 2 can convert cross-shard transactions into bridge shard transactions, boosting system efficiency and scalability through following steps:

Algorithm 2. Electing Bridge Shards

1: **procedure** BLOCKCHAINSHARDING(Ac, Tx)
2:     **Input:** Graph G, shard set S, node set Ac, transaction set Tx
3:     **Output:** Inter-cluster connectivity metrics, optimal intermediary blocks, transaction data analysis
4:     Initialize transaction frequency between shards
    $TxRate(S_i, S_j)$
5:     **for** each pair of shards to calculate transaction frequency $TxRate(S_i, S_j)$ **do**
6:         Calculate and update the optimal intermediary block k
7:         Assign S_i and S_j to shards I_i and B_j
8:     **end for**
9:     Initialize transaction categorization set and statistical indicators
10:     **for** each node in graph G **do**
11:         Categorize tx_i into Tx_{intra}, Tx_{cross}, or $Tx_{overlap}$
12:         Calculate the proportion of cross-shard transactions
13:         Update the count of nodes exceeding threshold
14:         Calculate statistical indicators: $Tx_{intra}, Tx_{cross}, Tx_{overlap}, Ac_{high}$
15:     **end for**
16: **end procedure**

Transaction Feature Analysis: The transaction data analysis module identifies shards with high transaction activity by calculating the transaction frequency between shards. Based on the analysis, the shard management module determines the optimal intermediary shards and assigns these shards to the intermediary. This step helps to reduce the occurrence of cross-shard transactions and improve the overall efficiency of the system.

Transaction Categorization: Transactions are categorized into intra-shard transactions, cross-shard transactions, and bridge shard transactions, to manage and optimize the transaction processing flow more finely.

The proportion of cross-shard transactions refers to the ratio of the number of cross-shard transactions to the total number of transactions, which can be computed as follows:

$$P_c = \frac{Num(Tx_{Cross})}{Num(Tx)} \tag{2}$$

The proportion of bridge shard transactions refers to the ratio of the number of bridge shard transactions to the total number of cross-shard transactions, which can be computed as follows:

$$P_o = \frac{Num(Tx_{Overlap})}{Num(Tx_{Cross})} \tag{3}$$

Statistical Indicator Calculation: Calculate a series of comprehensive statistical indicators, including the number of cross-shard transactions Tx_{cross}, the number of bridge shard transactions $Tx_{overlap}$, the proportion of cross-shard transactions P_c, and the proportion of bridge shard transactions P_o. These metrics evaluate shard performance and blockchain efficiency, offering insights into the effectiveness of the sharding strategy. Tracking these indicators allows for the assessment of the shard mechanism, pinpointing strengths and weaknesses, and guiding refinements to the strategy for future sharding enhancements.

5   Security Analysis and Experimental Evaluation

This section analyzes the security of the proposed OSABTC algorithm, including the impact of malicious nodes on transactions after sharding and the security and Double-Spending issues of cross-shard transaction. The efficiency of the proposed OSABTC algorithm in handling cross-shard transactions and the performance improvement of the sharding system are evaluated through experiments.

5.1   Security Analysis

The proposed OSABTC algorithm satisfies the following security objectives:

1. Resist shard attacks by malicious nodes:
   Malicious nodes may intentionally choose the same shard to collaborate in attacking that shard, thereby disrupting the normal operation of the system. To prevent this kind of attack, the sharding strategy adopted in our OSABTC algorithm dynamically adjusts based on the reputation value of nodes, ensuring that malicious nodes are evenly distributed across all shards, thereby reducing the risk of concentration of malicious nodes.
2. Preventing Double-Spending Attacks:
   To prevent double-spending attacks, this paper adopts the transaction atomic lock mechanism proposed by Byzcoin [25] to ensure the atomicity of cross-shard transactions, meaning that a transaction is either completely successful

or completely fails. This can be achieved through the locking and unlocking mechanisms of cross-shard transactions. When a cross-shard transaction starts, the involved funds are locked in the source shard until the transaction is confirmed in the target shard, at which point they are unlocked.

3. Secure Handling of Cross-Shard Transactions:
   In cross-shard transactions, if there is no b-shard, the Byzcoin atomic lock transaction method will be used to ensure security; if there is a b-shard, the transaction will be converted into a bridge shard transaction, processed by the b-shard and notifying the i-shard to update data. Nodes selected as b-shards should have high reputation values and frequent transaction records, and the transaction content should not involve their nodes, to ensure the security of cross-shard transactions.

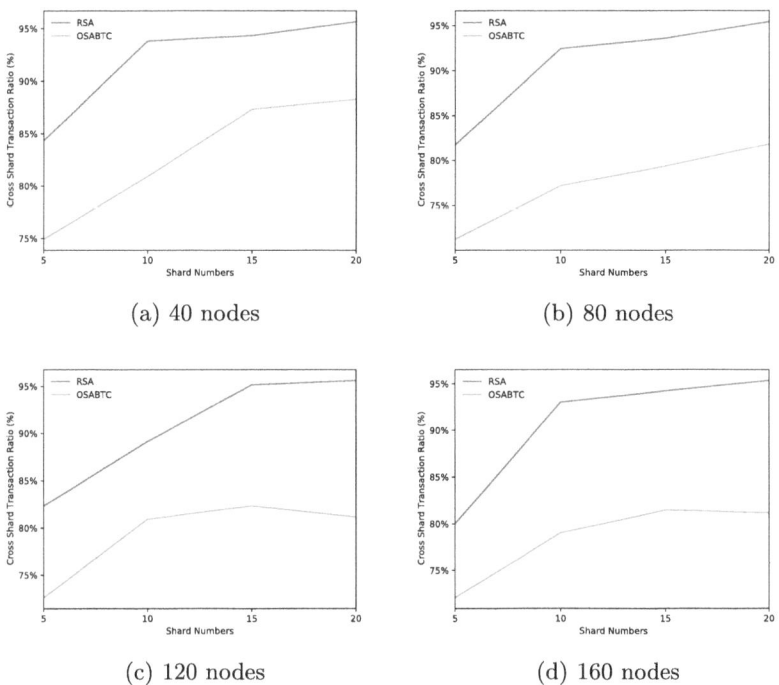

Fig. 4. The influence of the number of nodes and fragments on the proportion of cross-fragment transactions

5.2   Experimental Evaluation

To assess the proposed algorithm's effectiveness, this paper conducts comparative experiments with RSA, a traditional blockchain sharding scheme. Experiments evaluate performance across various sharding granularities and metrics such as cross-shard transaction ratios and accounts with frequent cross-shard activities. The dataset, comprising 290,911 transactions and 400 accounts, was randomly generated. The algorithm, programmed in Python, was implemented on the PyCharm platform and tested on a 64-bit Windows system with an AMD Ryzen 9 7945HX CPU and 32 GB of RAM.

Cross-Shard Transaction Ratio. The cross-shard transaction ratio is one of the key indicators for assessing the efficiency of transaction sharding. Although sharding technology improves the throughput of blockchain by parallel processing of transactions, cross-shard transactions are inevitably generated. Such cross-shard transactions increase the complexity, latency, and difficulty of achieving inter-shard consensus for long transactions, thereby weakening the performance of the blockchain. As the ratio of cross-shard transactions increases, processing these transactions incurs additional network overhead, reducing the response speed and real-time verification of cross-shard transaction processing.

If all transactions in a blockchain network are cross-shard, individual shards cannot independently verify transactions or produce blocks, increasing complexity and potentially undermining the parallel scalability benefits of sharding. A key goal in a multi-shard blockchain network is to devise a sharding strategy that minimizes cross-shard transactions to enhance performance and efficiency.

To investigate the cross-shard transaction ratio under different numbers of nodes per shard and different numbers of shards for the OSABTC sharding algorithm and the RSA sharding algorithm, in the experimental setup, the X-axis represents the number of shards, and the Y-axis indicates the cross-shard transaction ratio. As shown in Fig. 4, the change in the cross-shard transaction ratio after increasing the number of shards under different node counts is presented.

Figure 4 illustrates that as the number of shards increases, the cross-shard transaction ratio of the RSA algorithm rises steadily. This is due to transactions becoming more scattered across different shards, increasing the likelihood of cross-shard transactions. Conversely, when using the OSABTC algorithm with the same shard count, the cross-shard transaction ratio decreases if a shard has more nodes. This is because more nodes in a shard increase the chances of high-frequency transaction nodes being in the same shard, thus boosting intra-shard transactions and reducing cross-shard ones. Regardless of node count or shard number, OSABTC consistently maintains a lower cross-shard transaction ratio than RSA.

Transaction Latency. To verify the effectiveness of the algorithm, this paper further analyzes the impact of the number of nodes and the number of shards on efficiency. Figure 5(a) shows the impact of the number of nodes and the number of shards on the ratio of bridge shard transactions and transaction latency. It can be observed that, with the same number of nodes, compared to the RSA algorithm, the OSABTC algorithm significantly increases the ratio of cross-shard transactions that are converted into bridge shard transactions. In the OSABTC algorithm, the ratio of bridge shard transactions is in the 80%–90% range, while under the RSA algorithm, this ratio is in the 40%–50% range.

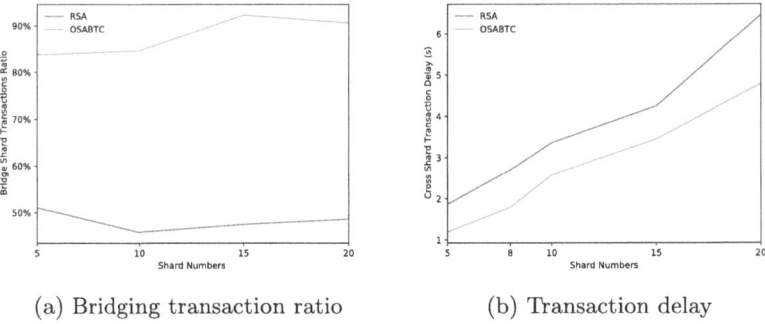

(a) Bridging transaction ratio   (b) Transaction delay

Fig. 5. The influence of the number of fragments on the proportion of bridging transactions and transaction delay

As shown in Fig. 5(b), with the increase in the number of shards, the transaction latency of the RSA sharding algorithm shows a steady upward trend, while the transaction latency of the OSABTC sharding algorithm consistently remains below that of the RSA algorithm. The reason for this phenomenon is that the processing speed of bridge shard transactions is faster compared to cross-shard transactions. In the OSABTC algorithm, most cross-shard transactions are converted into bridge shard transactions, effectively reducing the blockchain's transaction latency.

6   Conclusion

This paper presented a blockchain sharding algorithm based on transaction frequency and reputation score, which can effectively reduce the proportion of cross-shard transactions, and improve the transaction processing efficiency and data storage capacity of the blockchain. By analyzing the transaction frequency and reputation score of transaction accounts, it is possible to identify the optimal intermediate shard between shards, converting cross-shard transactions into bridge shard transactions, thereby reducing the frequency of cross-shard transactions and decreasing transaction latency. Experimental results demonstrated that, compared to the RSA sharding algorithm, the proposed OSABTC sharding algorithm can significantly lower the proportion of cross-shard transactions, increase the ratio of bridge shard transactions, and reduce transaction latency.

Acknowledgments. This article is supported in part by the Guangxi Natural Science Foundation (2024GXNSFAA010453, 2024GXNSFDA010064), the National Natural Science Foundation of China (62172119, 62362013), the Guangxi Young Teachers' Basic Ability Improvement Program (2024KY0224), the Zhejiang Provincial Natural Science Foundation of China (LZ23F020012), the Guangxi Key Laboratory of Digital Infrastructure (GXDIOP2023006), and the Innovation Project of GUET Graduate Education (2023YCXS059).

References

1. Li, Y., Wang, J., Zhang, H.: A survey of state-of-the-art sharding blockchains: models, components, and attack surfaces. J. Netw. Comput. Appl. **217**, 103686 (2023). https://doi.org/10.1016/j.jnca.2023.103686

2. Hong, Z., Guo, S., Li, P.: Scaling blockchain via layered sharding. IEEE J. Sel. Areas Commun. **40**(12), 3575–3588 (2022). https://doi.org/10.1109/JSAC.2022.3213350

3. Cai, Z., et al.: Benzene: scaling blockchain with cooperation-based sharding. IEEE Trans. Parallel Distrib. Syst. **34**(2), 639–654 (2023). https://doi.org/10.1109/TPDS.2022.3227198

4. Liu, A., et al.: Cherubim: a secure and highly parallel cross-shard consensus using quadruple pipelined two-phase commit for sharding blockchains. IEEE Trans. Inf. Forensics Secur. **19**, 3178–3193 (2024). https://doi.org/10.1109/TIFS.2024.3358990

5. Fan, T., Liu, X., Chen, B., Qu, W.: An effective and balanced storage extension approach for sharding blockchain systems. In: 2023 IEEE 41st International Conference on Computer Design (ICCD), pp. 198–205, November 2023. https://doi.org/10.1109/ICCD58817.2023.00039

6. Hegde, M., Rao, R.R., Nikhil, B.M.: DDMIA: distributed dynamic mutual identity authentication for referrals in blockchain-based health care networks. IEEE Access **10**, 78557–78575 (2022). https://doi.org/10.1109/ACCESS.2022.3193238

7. Zhang, P., Guo, W., Liu, Z., Zhou, M., Huang, B., Sedraoui, K.: Optimized blockchain sharding model based on node trust and allocation. IEEE Trans. Netw. Serv. Manage. **20**(3), 2804–2816 (2023). https://doi.org/10.1109/TNSM.2022.3233570

8. Yang, X., Xu, T., Zan, F., Ye, T., Mao, Z., Qiu, T.: An overlapping self-organizing sharding scheme based on DRL for large-scale IIoT blockchain. IEEE Internet Things J. **11**(4), 5681–5695 (2024). https://doi.org/10.1109/JIOT.2023.3311414

9. Zhang, Z., et al.: A community-based strategy for blockchain sharding: enabling more budget-friendly transactions. In: 2023 IEEE International Conference on Blockchain (Blockchain), pp. 370–376, December 2023. https://doi.org/10.1109/Blockchain60715.2023.00063

10. Liu, Y., et al.: Building blocks of sharding blockchain systems: concepts, approaches, and open problems. Comput. Sci. Rev. **46**, 100513 (2022). https://doi.org/10.1016/j.cosrev.2022.100513

11. Zhang, L., Wang, Y., Ding, Y., Liang, H., Yang, C., Li, C.: Sharding technologies in blockchain: basics, state of the art, and challenges. In: Chen, J., Wen, B., Chen, T. (eds.) Blockchain and Trustworthy Systems, pp. 242–255. Springer, Cham (2024). https://doi.org/10.1007/978-981-99-8101-4_17

12. Yu, B., Zhao, H., Zhou, T., Sheng, N., Li, X., Xu, J.: Overshard: scaling blockchain by full sharding with overlapping network and virtual accounts. J. Netw. Comput. Appl. **220**, 103748 (2023). https://doi.org/10.1016/j.jnca.2023.103748

13. Li, M., Wang, W., Zhang, J.: LB-chain: load-balanced and low-latency blockchain sharding via account migration. IEEE Trans. Parallel Distrib. Syst. **34**(10), 2797–2810 (2023). https://doi.org/10.1109/TPDS.2023.3238343

14. Lu, S., Liang, H., Wang, Y., Ding, Y., Yang, C., Guo, Z.: A cross-chain model based on credit hierarchical notary group for IoT roaming settlement. In: 2024 International Conference on Blockchain, Metaverse and Trustworthy Systems (2024)

15. Wen, B., Wang, Y., Ding, Y., Zheng, H., Qin, B., Yang, C.: Security and privacy protection technologies in securing blockchain applications. Inf. Sci. **645**, 119322 (2023). https://doi.org/10.1016/j.ins.2023.119322

16. Hong, Z., Guo, S., Li, P., Chen, W.: Pyramid: a layered sharding blockchain system. In: IEEE INFOCOM 2021 - IEEE Conference on Computer Communications, pp. 1–10, May 2021. https://doi.org/10.1109/INFOCOM42981.2021.9488747

17. Jiang, N., Bai, F., Huang, L., An, Z., Shen, T.: Reputation-driven dynamic node consensus and reliability sharding model in IoT blockchain. Algorithms **15**(2) (2022). https://doi.org/10.3390/a15020028

18. Zhang, L., Wang, Y., Ding, Y., Liang, H., Yang, C., Zheng, H.: Enhancing scalability: a complete tree sharding architecture towards IoT. In: The 18th International Conference on Wireless Artificial Intelligent Computing Systems and Applications (2024)

19. Li, J., Ning, Y.: Blockchain transaction sharding algorithm based on account-weighted graph. IEEE Access **12**, 24672–24684 (2024). https://doi.org/10.1109/ACCESS.2024.3365510

20. Zhen, Z., Wang, X., Lin, H., Garg, S., Kumar, P., Hossain, M.S.: A dynamic state sharding blockchain architecture for scalable and secure crowdsourcing systems. J. Netw. Comput. Appl. **222**, 103785 (2024). https://doi.org/10.1016/j.jnca.2023.103785

21. Kokoris-Kogias, E., Jovanovic, P., Gasser, L., Gailly, N., Syta, E., Ford, B.: OmniLedger: a secure, scale-out, decentralized ledger via sharding. In: 2018 IEEE Symposium on Security and Privacy (SP), pp. 583–598, May 2018. https://doi.org/10.1109/SP.2018.000-5

22. Wang, J., Wang, H.: Monoxide: scale out blockchains with asynchronous consensus zones. In: Lorch, J.R., Yu, M. (eds.) 16th USENIX Symposium on Networked Systems Design and Implementation, NSDI 2019, Boston, MA, 26–28 February 2019, pp. 95–112. USENIX Association (2019)

23. Huang, C., et al.: RepChain: a reputation-based secure, fast, and high incentive blockchain system via sharding. IEEE Internet Things J. **8**(6), 4291–4304 (2021). https://doi.org/10.1109/JIOT.2020.3028449

24. Zhang, M., Li, J., Chen, Z., Chen, H., Deng, X.: CycLedger: a scalable and secure parallel protocol for distributed ledger via sharding. In: 2020 IEEE International Parallel and Distributed Processing Symposium (IPDPS), pp. 358–367, May 2020. https://doi.org/10.1109/IPDPS47924.2020.00045

25. Kogias, E.K., Jovanovic, P., Gailly, N., Khoffi, I., Gasser, L., Ford, B.: Enhancing bitcoin security and performance with strong consistency via collective signing. In: 25th USENIX Security Symposium (USENIX Security 2016), pp. 279–296. USENIX Association, Austin, TX, August 2016

An Empirical Study on the Performance of EVMs and Wasm VMs for Smart Contract Execution

Shuwei Song[1,2], Zhou Liao[1], Ting Chen[1(✉)], Xiapu Luo[2(✉)], Yongjie Zhang[1], and Guopeng Wang[3,4(✉)]

[1] University of Electronic Science and Technology of China, Chengdu 610000, China
brokendragon@uestc.edu.cn
[2] The Hong Kong Polytechnic University, Hong Kong 999077, China
csxluo@comp.polyu.edu.hk
[3] Zhejiang Ocean University, Zhoushan 316000, China
wanggp@ouchn.edu.cn
[4] The Open University of China, Beijing 100000, China

Abstract. Blockchain and smart contract technology allow for the implementation of various decentralized applications. Smart contracts are typically developed in a high-level language, compiled into bytecode, and executed in a virtual machine (VM) on the blockchain client. Consequently, the VM's performance significantly determines the execution speed of smart contracts, the clients' resource overhead, and even the exploitable vulnerabilities. EVM is currently the most widely adopted VM, and several blockchains have developed customized EVMs to suit their specific requirements. However, the extent to which different EVM implementations exhibit performance differences has not been fully investigated. Moreover, the Wasm VM (WVM) has demonstrated satisfactory performance in the Web domain, and it is regarded as a promising candidate for the next generation of smart contract VMs. However, it remains unclear whether WVMs offer superior functionality and performance compared to EVMs. To fill these gaps, this paper presents an empirical investigation of EVMs and WVMs. First, we compare the performance of EVMs implemented in Go, Rust, and C++ to provide blockchain nodes with suggestions on which EVM to adopt. Subsequently, we conduct a comparative analysis of EVMs and WVMs on three blockchain clients regarding five performance metrics. The results indicate that WVMs perform inferior to EVMs on all metrics. Furthermore, the findings and insights presented in this paper offer valuable recommendations for the evolution of WVMs.

Keywords: Smart Contract · Virtual Machine · WebAssembly · Ethereum · PlatON

D. He et al. (Eds.): BlockSys 2024, CCIS 2264, pp. 215–230, 2025.
https://doi.org/10.1007/978-981-96-1411-0_17

1   Introduction

Initially, blockchain was primarily designed to implement an electronic cash system [30]. At this stage, its scope was limited to currency transactions. However, the subsequent recognition of blockchain's numerous advantages led to its potential application in various industries. As a result, the concept of smart contracts emerged as a means to implement diverse blockchain-based applications [33]. Smart contracts refer to a novel computer program that operates on the blockchain, characterized by unique attributes such as decentralization and tamper-proofing [33]. Developers employ high-level languages to encode the business logic into source code, which is subsequently compiled into bytecode [23]. The smart contract is then deployed by initiating a transaction request within the blockchain network. Upon confirmation, the bytecode is stored on the blockchain, and a unique address is assigned to the smart contract. Parties can invoke it by submitting a transaction request with the smart contract address as the recipient. The execution of the smart contract involves interpreting and executing the bytecode as instructions within the virtual machine (VM). The transaction initiator incurs a gas fee for the computational resources utilized during execution [23]. The VM operates within the blockchain client on each network node, facilitating distributed smart contract execution. This mechanism ensures consensus among honest nodes regarding execution outcomes.

The functionality and performance of the VM significantly impact the operation of smart contracts for three reasons. *Firstly*, the VM's capabilities directly influence the functionality of smart contracts. For example, the absence of specific instructions in the VM can prevent smart contracts from performing operations like floating-point arithmetic. *Secondly*, the execution speed of smart contracts relies on the performance of the VM. Inefficient VMs result in longer execution times for identical tasks. *Thirdly*, performance bottlenecks in VMs may pose security risks, as adversaries can exploit these vulnerabilities to launch targeted DoS attacks [22].

Ethereum Virtual Machine (EVM) is currently the most popular VM, with hundreds of blockchains [9] having adopted it or its variants. Ethereum offers a range of EVM implementations in different languages [15]. For instance, evmone is a C++ implementation of EVM designed to facilitate efficient execution [12]. In addition, some other blockchains customize EVM based on their specific requirements. For instance, Tron modifies the EVM to accommodate a novel billing model and resource management mechanism [5].

Developing new VMs is a promising direction for improving the speed of smart contract execution [26]. WebAssembly (abbr. Wasm) is a binary instruction format designed as a portable compilation target for multiple languages [21]. It enables the development of fast-executing Web applications. Because of Wasm's advantages in speed, flexibility, and compatibility with multiple languages, Wasm and its VM (abbr. WVM) are seen as a way to accelerate the development and execution of smart contracts. WVM has been adopted by several blockchains, such as EOSIO [16]. Certain blockchains, such as Ethereum and PlatON, opt to embrace compatibility with both EVM and WVM to attract a broader range of developers. In Ethereum, source code developed for execution on EVM can be compiled into Wasm bytecode for compatibility with the WVM using the SOLL compiler [4].

In summary, multiple VMs currently coexist, indicating a potential transition from EVMs to WVMs. However, the following three research questions (RQs) have not been subjected to sufficient empirical investigation.

- **RQ1:** Are there performance disparities among various EVMs?
- **RQ2:** Can the functionality of EVMs be adequately replicated by WVMs?
- **RQ3:** Do the WVMs outperform EVMs in terms of performance?

While Zhang et al.'s work [32] has tried to address the aforementioned first and third questions, there are still two areas of uncertainty. *First*, they solely employed time as the performance evaluation metric without exploring other indicators such as gas consumption and disk I/O. *Second*, their benchmark solely encompasses the most basic smart contracts, such as arithmetic operations and ERC20 tokens, without considering complex real-world contracts like proxies or gambling scenarios. Consequently, it is necessary to incorporate a more comprehensive array of metrics and more robust benchmarks within the evaluation.

In this paper, we investigate four EVM implementations and three WVM implementations to answer these RQs. First, we construct a new benchmark set comprising two categories of smart contracts. The first category consists of ten smart contracts involving fundamental operations such as bitwise operations and contract invocations. The second category comprises five complex real-world smart contracts encompassing advanced functionalities such as wallets and gambling scenarios. Subsequently, we conduct experimental comparisons of the four EVMs based on the execution speed and memory occupancy. The results can offer valuable insights for selecting an appropriate VM in blockchain nodes. Next, we attempt to implement all the smart contracts in the benchmark set using Wasm and evaluate their deployment and execution. We identify several shortcomings in applying Wasm to smart contracts, including lacking support for inline assemblies, dynamic arrays, etc. Lastly, we compare the three EVMs and three WVMs across five metrics: bytecode length, gas, time consumption, memory occupancy, and I/O overhead. Our findings indicate that WVMs underperform EVMs in all metrics.

The three main contributions of this paper are as follows.

- We experimentally compare the performance of four EVM implementations. The results obtained will assist in the selection of an appropriate VM.
- By employing Wasm to implement and execute the benchmark smart contracts, we identify several functional limitations of Wasm.
- We conduct a comparative analysis between three EVMs and three WVMs on five performance metrics, resulting in the identification of new findings.

2   Background

Smart Contract. Smart contracts are programs that run automatically and synchronously on multiple nodes of a blockchain network based on predefined code logic [33]. Ethereum is the pioneering and widely adopted platform that supports smart contracts [15]. To create an Ethereum smart contract, developers follow these steps. They write the source code using high-level languages and compile it into bytecode using the compiler. The bytecode encompasses over 100 types of instructions with varying computational resource requirements. Deploying the smart contract assigns it an address and stores the bytecode. Anyone can invoke the deployed contract by initiating a transaction request, specifying the address, desired function, and input parameters. The gas mechanism is implemented to charge transaction initiators for consumed resources [24]. Gas consumption is determined by instructions executed, with resource-intensive instructions incurring higher costs. Ethereum employs the Ethereum Virtual Machine (EVM) to execute smart contracts [15]. Programming languages, bytecode formats, and virtual machines differ across blockchains.

Virtual Machine (VM). The VM is an integral part of the blockchain client, operating on each blockchain node. Clients connect and participate in transaction propagation and validation, specifying interfaces without prescribing fixed implementations. For instance, Ethereum has multiple client implementations like Geth and Openethereum [3,25]. The VM's significance in smart contract execution arises from its role in providing a secure sandbox environment, abstracting the underlying OS for consistent results across nodes, and measuring gas consumption. A well-implemented and optimized VM can enhance smart contract execution speed and reduce node overhead. The EVM is currently the most widely adopted VM. It utilizes a stack for local variables, memory for function parameters and return values, and storage for persistent data. While the stack and memory are non-persistent and cleared after each transaction, the storage is persistent and resource-intensive, resulting in higher gas consumption for read/write operations. Wasm offers an alternative instruction format for stack-based VMs, designed for near-native speed execution. Programming languages like C++ and Rust support compilation to Wasm bytecode. Some blockchains explore WVM adoption, enabling developers to use familiar languages for smart contracts while improving execution speed. Ethereum's ewasm project, representing Ethereum-flavored Wasm [13], introduces the Ethereum Environment Interface (EEI) to facilitate interaction between Wasm bytecode and the blockchain environment, compensating for the absence of blockchain-specific instructions like obtaining a block's timestamp.

3   Methodology

This section outlines the methodology employed to construct the benchmark set and to investigate each RQ.

3.1   Benchmark Set

Our method involves executing the same benchmark smart contracts with multiple VMs and investigating their execution. Due to the lack of available benchmark sets, we manually construct one that fulfills specific requirements. First, the benchmark set should cover the fundamental functionalities of smart contracts. This is crucial to assess whether the VMs and their corresponding instruction sets can fulfill basic functionalities. Second, the benchmark set should include real-world, complex applications. This aims to obtain data that closely resembles real-world scenarios. Following these two principles, our constructed benchmark set comprises ten basic and five complex smart contracts.

Table 1. Ten Smart Contracts with Basic Operations

Contract Name	Description
bits	bitwise operations, including shift, and, or, non, etc.
contract	creation and destruction of contracts
global	getting blockchain environment variables such as block number
hash	hash operations on bytes type
invoke	calling functions in other contracts
map	read and write operations on dictionaries
math	mathematical operations such as multiplication and division
memory	read and write data in memory
storage	read and write data in storage
transfer	funds transfer operations

By reading the documentation of several blockchains, including Ethereum, EOSIO, and PlatON, we divide all the basic functions into ten categories and implemented them with ten smart contracts, as shown in Table 1. Since Ethereum is currently the most popular blockchain, we collect Ethereum smart contract source code from EtherScan [11] and then extract five common and representative types of complex contracts, as shown in Table 2.

Table 2. Five Real-World Complex Contracts

Contract Name	Function Description
proxy	proxy contracts enable contract upgrades by forwarding transactions to variable logical contracts
gambling	users who guess the secret number will get a bonus
wallet	helping users to maintain their assets
erc20	creating new currencies and allowing issuance, transfers, etc.
forwarder	transaction repeater, which can achieve gas savings and optimize the user experience

3.2 Investigation Procedures for RQs

Overview. Figure 1 provides an overview of our investigation procedures. To mitigate the impact of client-specific factors on VM performance, we select three clients that are compatible with both the EVM and WVM: Geth [25],

Openthereum [3], and PlatON-Go [14]. The first two are Go and Rust implementations of Ethereum clients, while the latter is a Go implementation of PlatON client. We implement the benchmark set in three languages. Subsequently, we compile the source code into EVM bytecode and Wasm bytecode using their respective compilers. Instrumentation is applied to the clients to facilitate the collection of runtime information. Finally, we deploy and execute these contracts and analyze the gathered data statistically to answer the three RQs.

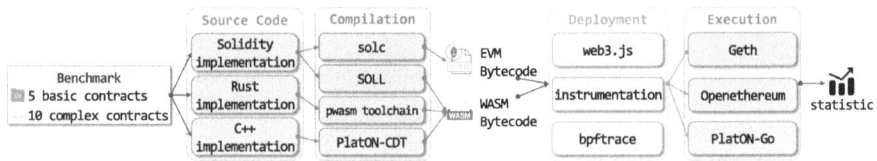

Fig. 1. The Overview of Investigation Procedures

For RQ1. Our investigation concerns four EVM implementations. The first implementation is the native EVM in Geth (abbr. GethEVM). Since Geth is the most commonly adopted Ethereum client, GethEVM is the most widely used EVM. The second is the native EVM in Openethereum (abbr. OpenEVM). It claims to be fast, lightweight, and robust [3]. The third implementation is the native EVM in PlatON (abbr. PlatEVM). PlatON is worth evaluating because it represents blockchains actively compatible with EVM and Wasm. The fourth is the evmone, an EVM implemented in C++ as part of the ewasm project [12]. It can be imported into Geth as a module to replace GethEVM, thus contrasting with GethEVM and excluding the performance impact of the client.

To investigate the performance differences among these EVMs, we execute the benchmark smart contracts on each EVM and compare the time consumption and memory overhead during execution. Specifically, we initially implement 15 benchmark smart contracts using Solidity. Subsequently, we compile these contracts into EVM bytecode using solc, the compiler of Solidity. Next, we instrument each client separately to collect information on time consumption and memory overhead. We run the modified clients to create a private blockchain for experimental purposes, utilizing web3.js API [20] for automated deployment and execution of the smart contracts. Finally, the instrumented code within the clients outputs the collected data for analysis. The details of instrumentation, deployment, and execution are provided in Sect. 4.

For RQ2. To investigate the functional completeness of Wasm and the VMs, we propose implementing the benchmark set in the form of Wasm and then evaluating whether they can be successfully compiled and executed. Note that the same EVM bytecode can be executed on different EVMs, but this is not true for WVMs. Significant differences exist among various WVM implementations, with each VM imposing specific requirements on the source code and compiler. Consequently, selecting a WVM necessitates choosing the corresponding language for developing source code and utilizing the appropriate compiler.

In this paper, we choose three WVMs corresponding to the three clients shown in Fig. 1. The first is Hera, a WVM that can be imported as a module into Geth [6]. Implemented in C++, Hera is the most actively maintained WVM compatible with Geth. Smart contracts written in Solidity can be directly compiled into Wasm bytecode executable in Hera using the SOLL compiler [4]. The second is wasmi [8], embedded within Openethereum. Developers write source code in Rust, which is then compiled into Wasm bytecode runnable in wasmi using the pwasm toolchain [1]. The third is wagon [2], embedded within PlatON-Go. Smart contracts written in C++ are compiled into Wasm bytecode for execution in wagon using the PlatON contract development toolkit (PlatON-CDT) [7]. Therefore, to investigate RQ2, we need to implement the benchmark sets in Solidity, Rust, and C++, and compile them into Wasm bytecode using SOLL, pwasm toolchain, and PlatON-CDT, respectively. These contracts will be executed on three clients, Geth, Openethereum, and PlatON-Go, utilizing their respective WVMs. By collecting compilation and runtime errors, we can identify any functional deficiencies in Wasm and its VMs.

For RQ3. To answer RQ3, we execute benchmark sets using both WVMs and EVMs. We compare WVMs and EVMs across five performance metrics: (1) bytecode length, which refers to the size of the EVM and Wasm bytecode compiled from the benchmark sets. As bytecode is stored in each blockchain node, this metric assesses the impact of different VMs on the storage space occupied by bytecode. (2) Time consumption, which represents the time taken to execute benchmark sets and directly reflects the VMs' speed. (3) Memory occupancy encompasses the memory utilized during the benchmark sets' execution and reflects the VM's overhead. (4) Gas, which indicates the gas consumed during the execution of the benchmark sets. Gas is a commonly used metric in blockchain, which we adopt for consistency. (5) I/O overhead, which refers to the disk I/O overhead during the execution of the benchmark sets. This is one of the significant ways to evaluate VM performance. To capture the differences between VMs in these metrics, we instrument the clients, as detailed in Sect. 4.

4 Implementation

This section presents the implementation details, including the benchmark implementation, the testbed, and instruments for data collection.

4.1 Benchmark Implementation

As described in Sect. 3.2, we develop three versions of the benchmark sets implemented in Solidity, Rust, and C++. To accomplish this, we engage three authors of this paper, with 2–3 years of experience in smart contract development and auditing, to independently implement the contracts. Subsequently, the optimal implementations are determined through discussions among them. Any inconsistencies among their implementations are resolved by an expert with six years of experience in smart contracts. In this process, we encounter functionalities that could not be implemented due to missing functionalities in Wasm (Sect. 5).

4.2   Testbed

The experiments are conducted on a host running Ubuntu 20.4 LTS, equipped with an Intel 7700K CPU, 32 GB of memory, and a 1TB SSD. The selected versions of the three clients with EVM are Geth 1.9.2-evmc.6.3.0-0-stable, Openethereum v3.0.0-stable, and PlatON-Go 0.3.1. We also evaluate evmone v0.5.0, which can be used as a dynamic link library by Geth as the VM. The chosen versions of the three WVMs are Hera v0.2.5, wasmi v0.3.0, and wagon v0.6.1.

4.3   Data Collection

This section presents the approaches employed to obtain data for the five metrics. The data collection process is straightforward for two metrics, bytecode length and gas. However, client instrumentation is necessary for the remaining metrics.

Bytecode Length. As illustrated in Fig. 1, the compilers translate the benchmark smart contracts into EVM bytecode and Wasm bytecode. The size of the two bytecode versions is then calculated and compared (Sect. 5).

Gas. The gas consumed by each transaction can be retrieved from the transaction receipt, which is publicly accessible information in the blockchain. Therefore, leveraging the web3.js API [20], we automatically invoke the smart contract and extract the gas consumption from the receipt after execution.

Time Consumption. To capture the time consumed by VMs in executing smart contracts, we instrument the client code. Specifically, we insert timestamp logging code before and after the code responsible for selecting the VM and executing the smart contract in the selected VM. For each execution of the benchmark smart contract, the inserted code records the time consumed during that particular execution. For instance, if we instrument Geth, the time consumed by executing smart contracts using various VMs within Geth (including GethEVM, evmone, and Hera) can be logged. The same instrumentation approach is applied to the Openethereum and PlatON-Go.

Memory Occupancy. In the examined clients, Geth and PlatON-Go are implemented in Go, while Openethereum is implemented in Rust. For the former, we employ the *ReadMemStats* function from the native Go library *runtime* [18] to obtain the memory usage of the target program. Regarding Openethereum, as it utilizes the memory allocator *JeMalloc* [17] as the memory management scheme, we directly employ *JeMalloc* library functions to retrieve the program's memory occupancy. By employing these two approaches, we instrument all three clients separately to capture the memory occupancy of VMs during the execution of benchmark smart contracts.

I/O Overhead. To obtain the disk I/O overhead generated by VMs during the execution of benchmark sets, we utilize bpftrace, a tool for tracing system calls [10]. Specifically, bpftrace is an extension of eBPF kernel that enables tracing of system calls within the kernel using its provided C++-like scripting language [10]. By crafting bpftrace scripts, we capture every read and write system call the client makes when executing smart contracts. Subsequently, we develop scripts to filter out non-file I/O operations (such as I/O to the screen or network I/O), allowing us to accurately measure the disk I/O overhead incurred by VMs.

5   Experimental Results

This section presents the experiment's results, answers the three RQs, and describes the observations and insights gained.

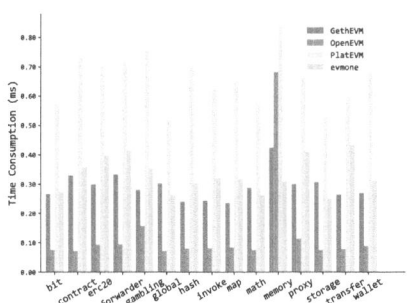

Fig. 2. Time Consumed by EVMs

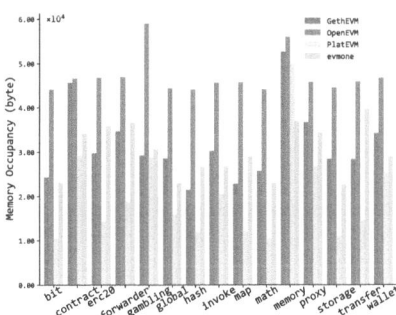

Fig. 3. Memory Occupied by EVMs

5.1   RQ1: Differences Between Various EVMs

Each of the four EVM implementations executes the benchmark smart contracts 1000 times within the testbed. Thereafter, the average time consumption and memory occupancy are computed. As depicted in Fig. 2, OpenEVM exhibits the fastest execution speed, aligning with the official claims from Openethereum [3]. It is reasonable to speculate that OpenEVM's superior execution speed can be attributed to its adoption as the client by many Ethereum nodes. On the other hand, PlatEVM demonstrates the slowest execution speed. Upon manual inspection of its source code, we find that it is derived from GethEVM with modifications. While GethEVM continues to receive updates and optimizations,

PlatEVM does not incorporate these improvements, resulting in the retention of suboptimal code segments. Consequently, it is recommended that developers of GethEVM's variants monitor GethEVM's updates to integrate optimized code promptly. Despite evmone's claim of being the fastest EVM, we observe that it performs slower than GethEVM when executing most of the benchmark contracts. This discrepancy can be attributed to the need to compile evmone as a dynamic link library and dynamically load it before executing smart contracts. This additional process contributes to its increased time consumption.

As depicted in Fig. 3, PlatEVM exhibits the lowest memory occupancy during the execution of benchmark smart contracts. This can be attributed to the fact that the other three EVM implementations utilize caching mechanisms to enhance runtime performance, while PlatEVM does not employ such methods. It is intuitive that due to the extensive optimizations made for execution speed, OpenEVM also incurs the highest memory usage.

> **Answer to RQ1:** There are significant performance differences between multiple EVM implementations, showing a trade-off between execution speed and memory occupation, i.e., faster EVMs occupy more memory.

5.2   RQ2: Functionalities Not Supported by Wasm

Following a comprehensive investigation, it has been determined that all three WVMs or their toolchains exhibit unsupported functionalities. The WVM in Geth, Hera, executes Wasm bytecode compiled by the SOLL compiler. However, we find the SOLL compiler lacks support for essential functionalities, including hashing (i.e., keccak256), call operation, inline assembly, and dynamic arrays. Consequently, Hera can only successfully execute 53.3% (8 out of the 15) benchmark contracts (detailed in the subsequent section). Developers of Openethereum employ the pwasm toolchain for Wasm bytecode development. The pwasm toolchain offers a comprehensive API that encompasses various aspects of smart contract development, such as compilation, deployment, and execution. As a result, all benchmark contracts can be successfully compiled and executed within the wasmi VM in Openethereum. Nevertheless, during practical implementation and discussions on developer forums, certain unsupported functionalities have been identified, including the lack of support for 128-bit types and Rust slice types as smart contracts function parameters, the inability to retrieve the balance of a specific account (i.e., address), and encountering errors when utilizing msg.data (i.e., parameters carried in transaction requests). Developers of PlatON utilize PlatON-CDT for Wasm bytecode development. Leveraging this tool, we successfully implement 13 (86.7%) benchmark contracts (detailed in the subsequent section), all of which can be executed within the wagon VM in PlatON-Go. However, we find that wagon and its toolchain do not support 256-bit data structures.

> **Answer to RQ2:** The Wasm and its associated toolchain and VMs do not encompass the full functionality of the EVM, which presents challenges in implementing benchmark smart contracts.

5.3   RQ3: WVMs Vs. EVMs

After investigating RQ2, we discover that certain benchmark contracts encountered difficulties in compilation and execution due to the lack of support for specific functionalities in Wasm. Subsequently, we focus on investigating RQ3 using the remaining benchmark contracts that could be successfully compiled and executed. Our findings reveal differences between the EVMs and WVMs in five distinct metrics.

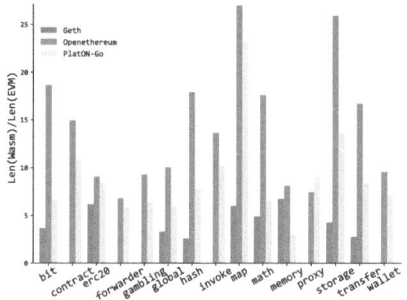
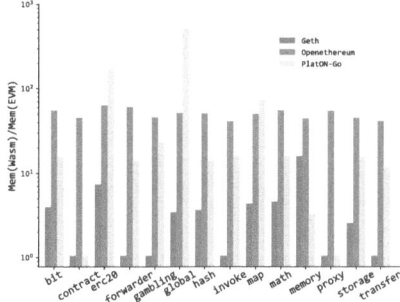

Fig. 4. Comparison of the Lengths of EVM Bytecode and Wasm Bytecode

Fig. 5. Comparison of the Memory Occupancy of EVMs and WVMs

Bytecode Length. As depicted in Fig. 4, the Wasm bytecode, which provides the same functionality as the EVM bytecode, tends to be significantly larger across the three clients. Through manual analysis of the bytecode, WVMs, and toolchains, we uncover the underlying reasons. In Geth and PlatON-Go, there are three key factors contributing to the increased size of Wasm bytecode. Firstly, all used libraries and EEI functions are duplicated and embedded within the Wasm bytecode. Secondly, due to the lack of dynamic array compilation support in SOLL, static arrays must be utilized with specified lengths. Consequently, the compiled Wasm bytecode becomes longer as the length of the array increases. Thirdly, instructions for gas consumption calculation are inserted into the Wasm bytecode. In Openethereum, the size of Wasm bytecode experiences a significant increase. This can be primarily attributed to the stringent requirements placed on types when using Rust to write smart contracts. Consequently, achieving the same functionality as EVM smart contracts often entails additional type conversions, resulting in an increase in Wasm bytecode length.

Memory Occupancy. As illustrated in Fig. 5, the memory occupancy of the WVMs significantly exceeds that of the EVMs across the three clients. Specifically, in Geth, the ratio of memory occupied by the WVM to that of the EVM ranges from 2.5 to 15.8. In Openethereum, this ratio increases to a range of 41 to 63. In PlatON-Go, the ratio falls within the range of 3.3 to 518. It is worth noting that the memory occupancy of the WVM exhibits a significant increase in the benchmark contract *global*. Upon careful examination, we identify a severe security vulnerability in PlatON-Go. At the time of writing this paper, we have already reported this vulnerability to the PlatON-Go team and received a bounty reward. We will publicly disclose this vulnerability after the PlatON-Go team has adequately addressed it and granted their consent.

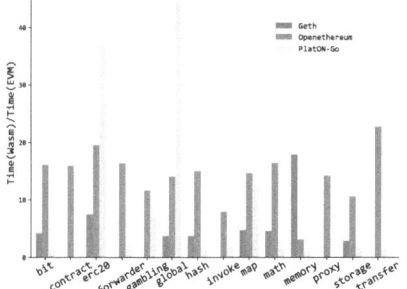

Fig. 6. Comparison of the Time Consumption of EVMs and WVMs

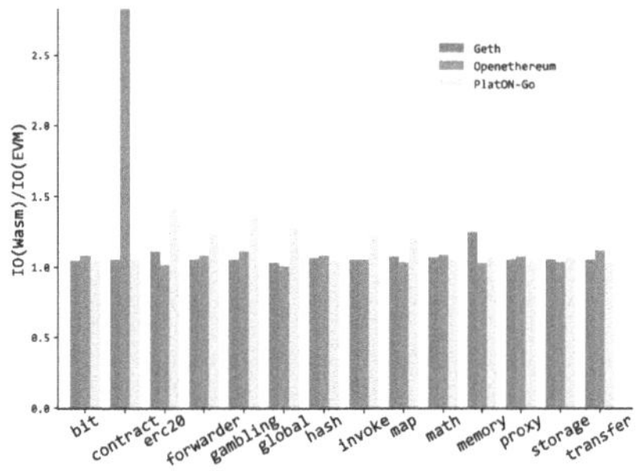

Fig. 7. Comparison of the I/O Overhead of EVMs and WVMs

Time Consumption. As depicted in Fig. 6, WVMs consistently require more time to execute benchmark contracts compared to EVMs. Specifically, in Geth, the ratio of time consumed by the WVM to that consumed by the EVM ranges from 2.8 to 17.8. It is noteworthy that the execution time of the Wasm bytecode for the *memory* contract experiences a significant increase. Through our analysis of its source code, we discover that SOLL directly embeds all static arrays in the bytecode instead of dynamically allocating them at runtime. This results in additional time consumption during the loading and execution of Wasm bytecode. In addition to this, two other factors contribute to the longer execution time of Wasm bytecode. Firstly, during the deployment of Wasm bytecode, a system contract called *sentinel* [19] is invoked to measure gas consumption, which introduces extra time overhead. Secondly, Wasm bytecode requires EEI calls to obtain blockchain environment information, whereas EVM bytecode does not rely on EEI as it has native instructions to acquire such information. Similarly, in Openethereum and PlatON-Go, the interaction between the WVMs and the blockchain environment consumes more time, resulting in respective ratios ranging from 3.1 to 22.7 and 1.05 to 44.6.

I/O Overhead. As depicted in Fig. 7, there is relatively minimal difference in I/O overhead between EVMs and WVMs during the execution of benchmark contracts. We find that WVMs generate slightly more disk I/O only during the deployment of Wasm bytecode, primarily due to the significantly larger size of Wasm bytecode compared to EVM bytecode. However, since deployment is a one-time operation, this overhead is within acceptable limits.

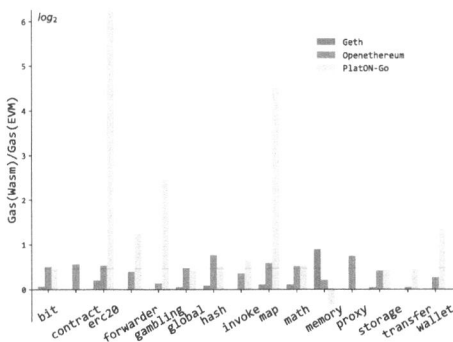

Fig. 8. Comparison of the Gas Consumption of EVMs and WVMs

Gas. As illustrated in Fig. 8, executing most Wasm bytecode consumes more gas compared to executing EVM bytecode. This observation aligns with intuition, as gas consumption is designed to be roughly proportional to computational resource usage. It is noteworthy that in PlatON-Go, the gas consumption of the Wasm versions of the *erc20*, *gambling*, and *map* contracts exhibits a significant increase. This is attributed to the overly complex design of map type read and write operations in PlatON-Go, and this issue does not exist in other clients.

> **Answer to RQ3:** The WVMs do not perform as well as EVMs across all five performance metrics.

6 Related Work

Previous works primarily focus on assessing the performance of Wasm in executing Web applications. HaaS et al. [27] conduct a comparative analysis between Wasm and native code execution speeds. The results indicate comparable speeds between the two approaches. Herrera et al. [28] conduct a performance comparison between JavaScript and Wasm, revealing that Wasm exhibits twice the speed of JavaScript in the same environment. Jangda et al. [29] expand the benchmark suite to SPEC CPU and find that Wasm-compiled applications run 45% slower (Firefox) to 55% slower (Chrome) than native due to increased loads/stores and branches in Wasm instructions. Wang et al. [31] examine the optimization techniques employed by browser engines for Wasm and compare them to JavaScript. Their findings indicate that while JIT optimization in Chrome greatly influences JavaScript performance, it does not noticeably affect Wasm performance. Zhang et al. [32] conduct the first measurement study to investigate the performance of WVMs and EVMs in executing smart contracts for blockchain-based applications, which closely relates to this paper. They discover that current WVMs do not deliver the expected satisfactory performance, and the overhead introduced by Wasm is not negligible, aligning with the findings of this paper (Sect. 5). However, their evaluation rely on time consumption as the sole assessment metric, overlooking important performance metrics such as I/O, memory, bytecode length, and gas. Furthermore, their benchmark suite is limited to simple smart contracts, lacking performance measurements on real-world applications. In contrast, our work presents a more comprehensive benchmark set with more reasonable performance metrics.

7   Conclusion

This paper presents a comprehensive empirical study comparing EVMs and WVMs. We define a benchmark set of smart contracts that cover both basic and complex operations and applications. These contracts are executed using multiple EVM and WVM implementations to assess their functionality and performance. We investigate three important research questions and analyze experimental results. Our findings reveal that WVMs lag behind EVMs in five metrics. The insights provided in this paper aid node operators in selecting suitable blockchain clients and VMs and offer suggestions for the advancement of WVMs.

Acknowledgments. This work is partially supported by the National Natural Science Foundation of China (62332004), the Sichuan Provincial Natural Science Foundation for Distinguished Young Scholars (2023NSFSC1963), and the Hong Kong RGC Project (PolyU15222320).

References

1. A step-by-step tutorial on how to write contracts in wasm for kovan (2018). https://github.com/openethereum/pwasm-tutorial
2. wagon, a webassembly-based go interpreter, for go (2020). https://github.com/go-interpreter/wagon. Accessed 6 May 2024
3. Fast and feature-rich ethereum client (2021). https://openethereum.github.io/. Accessed 6 May 2024
4. Soll (2021). https://github.com/second-state/SOLL. Accessed 6 May 2024
5. Differences from evm (2022). https://developers.tron.network/v4.4.0/docs/vm-vs-evm. Accessed 6 May 2024
6. Hera: Ewasm virtual machine conforming to the evmc api (2022). https://github.com/ewasm/hera. Accessed 6 May 2024

7. Wasm contract development kit (2022). https://github.com/PlatONnetwork/PlatON-CDT. Accessed 6 May 2024
8. Webassembly (wasm) interpreter (2022). https://github.com/wasmi-labs/wasmi. Accessed 6 May 2024
9. Chainlist (2024). https://chainlist.org/. Accessed 6 May 2024
10. ebpf - introduction, tutorials & community resources (2024). https://ebpf.io/. Accessed 6 May 2024
11. Ethereum blockchain explorer (2024). https://etherscan.io/. Accessed 6 May 2024
12. evmone (2024). https://github.com/ethereum/evmone. Accessed 6 May 2024
13. Ewasm design overview and specification (2024). https://github.com/ewasm/design. Accessed 6 May 2024
14. Golang implementation of the platon protocol (2024). https://github.com/PlatONnetwork/PlatON-Go. Accessed 6 May 2024
15. Home|ethereum.org (2024). https://ethereum.org/. Accessed 6 May 2024
16. Home - eosio blockchain software & services (2024). https://eos.io/. Accessed 6 May 2024
17. Jemalloc (2024). https://jemalloc.net/jemalloc.3.html. Accessed 6 May 2024
18. Readmemstats populates m with memory allocator statistics (2024). https://pkg.go.dev/runtime#ReadMemStats. Accessed 6 May 2024
19. System contracts - ethereum webassembly (2024). https://ewasm.readthedocs.io/. Accessed 6 May 2024
20. Web3.js - javascript ethereum api (2024). https://web3js.org/. Accessed 6 May 2024
21. Webassembly (2024). https://webassembly.org/. Accessed 6 May 2024
22. Buterin, V.: Transaction spam attack: Next steps (2016). https://blog.ethereum.org/2016/09/22/transaction-spam-attack-next-steps. Accessed 6 May 2024
23. Chen, J., Xia, X., Lo, D., Grundy, J., Luo, X., Chen, T.: DefectChecker: automated smart contract defect detection by analyzing EVM bytecode. IEEE Trans. Software Eng. **48**(7), 2189–2207 (2021)
24. Chen, T., et al.: GasChecker: scalable analysis for discovering gas-inefficient smart contracts. IEEE Trans. Emerg. Top. Comput. **9**(3), 1433–1448 (2020)
25. Ethereum: Go implementation of the ethereum protocol (2024). https://github.com/ethereum/go-ethereum. Accessed 6 May 2024
26. Fang, Y., Zhou, Z., Dai, S., Yang, J., Zhang, H., Lu, Y.: PaVM: a parallel virtual machine for smart contract execution and validation. IEEE Trans. Parallel Distrib. Syst. **35**(1), 186–202 (2023)
27. Haas, A., et al.: Bringing the web up to speed with webassembly. In: Proceedings of the 38th ACM SIGPLAN Conference on Programming Language Design and Implementation, pp. 185–200 (2017)
28. Herrera, D., Chen, H., Lavoie, E., Hendren, L.: WebAssembly and JavaScript challenge: numerical program performance using modern browser technologies and devices. University of McGill, Montreal: QC, Technical report SABLE-TR-2018-2 (2018)
29. Jangda, A., Powers, B., Berger, E.D., Guha, A.: Not so fast: analyzing the performance of {WebAssembly} vs. native code. In: 2019 USENIX Annual Technical Conference (USENIX ATC 2019), pp. 107–120 (2019)
30. Nakamoto, S.: Bitcoin: a peer-to-peer electronic cash system (2008)
31. Wang, W.: Empowering web applications with webassembly: are we there yet? In: 2021 36th IEEE/ACM International Conference on Automated Software Engineering (ASE), pp. 1301–1305. IEEE (2021)

32. Zhang, Y., Zheng, S., Wang, H., Wu, L., Huang, G., Liu, X.: VM matters: a comparison of WASM VMs and EVMs in the performance of blockchain smart contracts. ACM Trans. Model. Perform. Eval. Comput. Syst. **9**(2), 1–24 (2024)
33. Zou, W., et al.: Smart contract development: challenges and opportunities. IEEE Trans. Software Eng. **47**(10), 2084–2106 (2019)

Ponzi Scheme Detection in Smart Contracts Using Heterogeneous Semantic Graph

Wei Chen[1,2], Xinjun Jiang[1,2], Tian Lan[3(✉)], Leyuan Liu[2(✉)], and Chengyu Li[4]

[1] Network and Data Security Key Laboratory of Sichuan Province, University of Electronic Science and Technology of China, Chengdu 610000, China
{chenwei,202222090431}@uestc.edu.cn
[2] School of Information and Software Engineering, University of Electronic Science and Technology of China, Chengdu 610000, China
leyuanliu@uestc.edu.cn
[3] School of Computer Science and Engineering, University of Electronic Science and Technology of China, Chengdu 610000, China
lantian1029@uestc.edu.cn
[4] Shenzhen Institute for Advanced Study, University of Electronic Science and Technology of China, Shenzhen 518000, China
202222280626@uestc.edu.cn

Abstract. Behind the booming decentralized finance (DeFi) ecosystem driven by blockchain technology, various financial risks lurking, including money laundering, gambling, Ponzi schemes, and phishing. Due to the decentralization and anonymity of Ethereum, Ponzi schemes can be easily deployed, causing huge economic losses to investors. Existing detection methods based on transaction data are difficult to provide early risk warnings, while detection methods based on smart contract source code and opcodes have insufficient feature fusion at multiple levels. We propose an approach for constructing a multi-level Heterogeneous Semantic Graph (HSG) of smart contracts, and improve the HAN model to detect Ponzi scheme smart contracts based on the Heterogeneous Semantic Graph. The experimental results demonstrate the effectiveness of our approach, achieving an accuracy of 97.21%, a precision of 94.29%, and an F1 score of 90.41%.

Keywords: Ponzi Scheme Detection · Ethereum · Heterogeneous Semantic Graph

1 Introduction

The rapid development and application of blockchain technology have propelled the rapid growth of the decentralized finance (DeFi) ecosystem [16,18,33]. Ethereum is the first open-source public blockchain platform that supports smart contracts, which has garnered widespread global attention and currently holds

D. He et al. (Eds.): BlockSys 2024, CCIS 2264, pp. 231–244, 2025.
https://doi.org/10.1007/978-981-96-1411-0_18

the second largest market share in the cryptocurrency market [29,30]. Smart contracts are essentially executable programs deployed on a blockchain that automatically execute when predetermined conditions are met and cannot be terminated manually once initiated. Ethereum provides a robust Ethereum Virtual Machine (EVM) to support smart contracts, allowing any user to write and deploy smart contracts on the blockchain to implement various distributed applications (DApps) and financial services. Behind the booming of the DeFi ecosystem, the decentralization and anonymity of Ethereum provide opportunities for criminals to engage in various illegal activities on the platform, such as fraud [4], gambling [12], and money laundering [31], etc. The financial risks posed by these illegal activities not only threaten the healthy development of the DeFi ecosystem, but also cause significant economic losses to users. Among these illegal activities, Ponzi scheme [2] is one of the most rampant. Ponzi scheme is a traditional investment scam, characterized by using the funds from later investors to pay supposed returns to earlier investors, thereby attracting more investors to be deceived. Ponzi schemes on Ethereum are typically deceptive DApps [5] based on smart contracts, leveraging the automatic execution of smart contracts and the disclosure of transaction data to deceive participants and gain their trust. According to the 2022 crypto crime report of Chainalysis [3], Ponzi schemes have resulted in losses of tens of billions of dollars, with individual scams involving amounts as high as several billion dollars.

The owners of smart contracts remain anonymous due to the anonymity of blockchain technology [11,22], making it difficult to trace the legal responsibility of criminals after fraud occurs. Additionally, once deployed on the blockchain, contracts cannot be modified or terminated, theoretically allowing contract-based fraudulent activities to continue indefinitely [24]. Due to the highly technical nature of blockchain technology, most investors and users lack professional knowledge, making it difficult to identify the risks of Ponzi schemes in the DeFi ecosystem. Therefore, efficient detection and early warning of Ponzi schemes in the blockchain are of significant importance for the healthy development of blockchain finance.

Many approaches have been developed to achieve automated detection of Ponzi schemes in blockchain. Existing detection methods mainly rely on two types of data: transaction data and contract code. Transaction data-based detection methods [5,6,13,14,32,35] require the collection of relevant transaction data after fraudulent activities occur, making them post-event detection methods that cannot effectively provide early warning of Ponzi schemes. In contrast, contract code-based detection methods [1,7,8,26,28,34] can be performed at the time of contract deployment, enabling proactive and prior Ponzi scheme detection. These methods can rely on source code, bytecode or opcode of a smart contract. Contract code-based methods mainly utilize symbolic execution [7] and machine learning techniques [1,15,26,28,34]. The former aims to symbolize the contract code and rely on pre-defined expert knowledge to detect Ponzi schemes. The latter usually regards the contract code as a text sequence and uses NLP technology to study them or build graphs from contract code and study them via graph deep learning. However, since Ponzi schemes are usually associated with complex transaction behaviors and semantic logic in smart contracts, it is difficult for text-sequence-based methods to characterize the features of smart contracts in terms of transaction behaviors, graph-based deep learning methods also usually only focus on the control or data information inside the function and ignoring the relationship between functions and high-level semantics in the whole contract.

Currently, Graph Neural Network (GNN) and graph representation learning have demonstrated promising results in program analysis tasks. Therefore, we consider utilizing these methods to represent the semantic information of smart contracts, aiming to detect Ponzi schemes in smart contracts using high-level semantics. In this paper, we propose an approach for detecting Ponzi smart contracts using Heterogeneous Semantic Graph (HSG) and improved Heterogeneous Graph Attention Network (HAN) model. Firstly, we extract call information and control flow information of functions in smart contract source code using open source tool. Then, we build HSG which represents the execution logic of a smart contract using the information. After obtaining the global semantic representation of the smart contracts, we train an improved HAN model and use it to detect Ponzi smart contracts, thereby identifying Ponzi schemes in Ethereum. In summary, our contributions are as follows:

- We propose a method to construct Heterogeneous Semantic Graph (HSG) with multi-level semantic information of smart contracts. Furthermore, we design a Ponzi smart contract detection method using HSG and improved HAN model.
- We evaluated the performance of our method on open-source dataset and real-world Ponzi samples, and compare our method against state-of-the-art techniques. We also examined the impact of varying heterogeneity degrees on semantic representation. Experimental results demonstrate that our method excels in detecting Ponzi smart contracts and effectively representing contract semantics.

2 Background

2.1 Ponzi Smart Contract

Figure 1 illustrates a code snippet of a typical Ponzi smart contract deployed at 0xf8F04b23dACE12841343ecf0E06124354515cc42. The contract attracts investment by promising a 21% profit to investors. It uses funds from new investors to pay the earliest investors in the queue and deducts promotional and maintenance fees proportionally from each investment. Specifically, after receiving funds from a new investor, the contract processes the funds information using fallback function, extracts the fees, and calls the internal function pay() to attempt to pay the investor. The pay() function loops through and pays investors sequentially from the front of the queue. However, at some point, the contract is likely to break due to a disruption in the funding chain, resulting in significant losses for investors still waiting in line for payment.

```
uint constant public MULTIPLIER = 121;
struct Deposit {
    address depositor;
    uint128 deposit;
    uint128 expect;
}
Deposit[] private queue;
uint public currentReceiverIndex = 0;
function () public payable {
    if(msg.value > 0){
        queue.push(Deposit(msg.sender, uint128(msg.value),
                           uint128(msg.value * MULTIPLIER / 100)));
        uint ads = msg.value * FIRST_PERCENT / 100;
        FIRST_SUPPORT.transfer(ads).gas(gasleft())();
        uint tech = msg.value * TECH_PERCENT / 100;
        TECH_SUPPORT.transfer(tech);
        pay();
    }
}
function pay() private {
    uint128 money = uint128(address(this).balance);
    for(uint i = 0; i < queue.length; i++) {
        uint idx = currentReceiverIndex + i;
        Deposit storage dep = queue[idx];
        if(money >= dep.expect) {
            dep.depositor.transfer(dep.expect);
            money -= dep.expect;
            delete queue[idx];
        } else {
            dep.depositor.transfer(money);
            dep.expect -= money;
            break;
        }
    }
    currentReceiverIndex += i;
}
```

Fig. 1. A Ponzi smart contract example

2.2   Motivation

From the example shown in Fig. 1, we can observe the following two discoveries:

– Function call information is required in Ponzi smart contract detection. A contract call graph of a smart contract can characterize the interaction patterns and business logic between different functions in the smart contract. In the example depicted in Fig. 1, the contract handles the investment business logic in the fallback function and then calls the internal function pay() to process the payment of principal and interest.
– Function control flow information is required in Ponzi smart contract detection. A function control flow graph represents syntactic and structural information such as execution paths, conditional branches, and loops within functions, which encapsulate the primary semantics of a function. In the example depicted in Fig. 1, the contract pays investors' principal and interest through a loop structure and checks conditions for accepting investments and paying principal and interest via conditional branches.

Therefore, we try to extract multi-level semantic information from smart contract source code to construct HSG, and use Heterogeneous Graph Neural Network (HGNN) to learn the representation of different types of nodes and finally detect Ponzi smart contracts at graph-level.

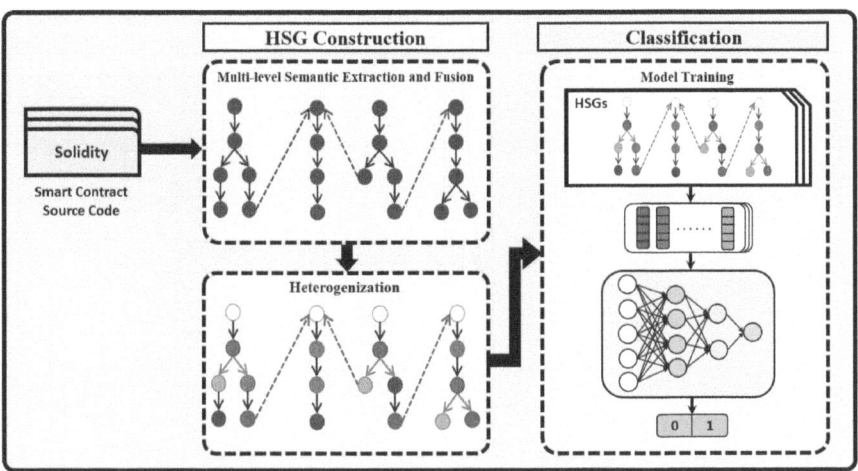

Fig. 2. Overview of our Ponzi scheme detection approach

3 Methodology

3.1 Overview

Figure 2 shows an overview of our method. We first use Slither [9] for static analysis of smart contracts to obtain call information and control flow information of functions, then fuse and construct HSGs to represent smart contract semantics according to the execution logic. After that, we use these HSGs to train a graph-level classifier based on HAN model. Finally, we use the model to detect Ponzi smart contracts.

3.2 Heterogeneous Semantic Graph

Deep-learning-based approaches show promising results in program vulnerability detection and malware classification tasks. Inspired by the work of Nguyen et al. [17], we propose a multi-level semantics-based method for constructing HSG, aiming to unveil the connection between transaction behaviors in smart contracts and potential Ponzi scheme risks.

Multi-level Semantic Extraction and Fusion: In this step, we use Solidity static analysis tool Slither to construct a simple CFG for each function, where the nodes in CFG represent a statement in the function and the directed edges represent the control flow. Then, we consider the nested call relationship between functions. For nodes that call other functions, we use a directed edge to connect the node itself with the CFG of the called function to completely represent the behaviors of a function and avoid the CFG of the function with the call

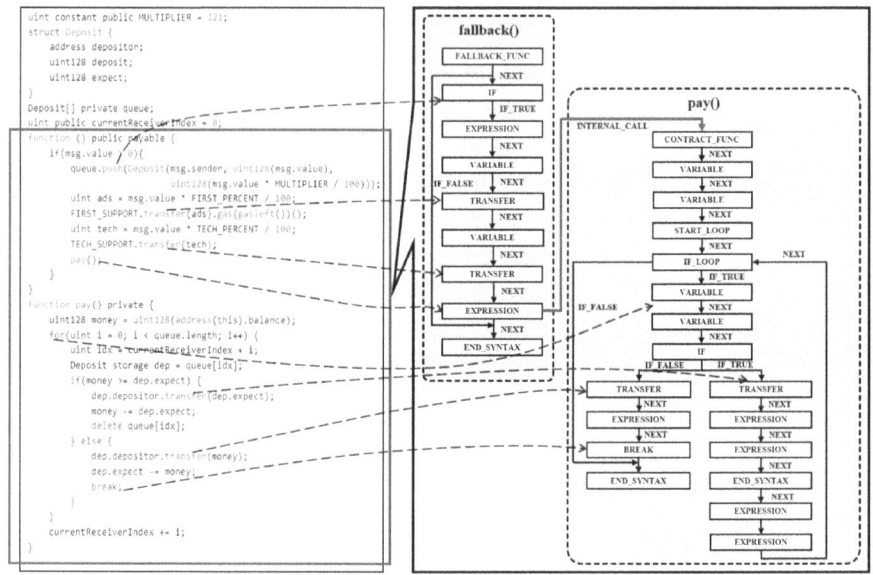

Fig. 3. HSG fragment of the Ponzi smart contract in Sect. 2

relationship being ignored during graph representation learning. So we get a semantic graph via fusing call information into control flow information, which can represent the complete semantics of all functions in the contract.

Heterogenization: It is difficult for homogeneous semantic graphs to represent the rich semantic information present in smart contracts. Hence we distinguish the types of nodes and edges based on the semantic information represented by nodes and edges in the homogeneous graph, thus forming an HSG. Figure 3 shows a snippet of the HSG constructed from the Ponzi smart contract sample in Sect. 2.

Definition 1. *(Heterogeneous Graph [20]) A heterogeneous graph, denoted as $G = (V, E)$, consists of an object set V and a link set E. A heterogeneous graph is also associated with a node type mapping function $\phi : V \to A$ and a link type mapping function $\psi : E \to R$. A and R denote the sets of predefined object types and link types, where $|A| + |R| > 2$.*

Node: We designed 16 types of nodes to represent different types of nodes in the contract semantic graph. Typical node types include FALLBACK_FUNCTION, CONTRACT_FUNCTION, IF, LOOP, EXPRESSION, VARIABLE, RETURN, TRANSFER, etc. It is worth noting that we use the TRANSFER type to represent the node where the transfer operation takes place in order to better characterize the transaction behavior of the contract. We also use the END_SYNTAX type to represent the end of various syntax structures to reduce the complexity and computation of the model. In addition, since many smart contracts use the fallback function as the way to handle a received transfer, we treat it as a separate `FALLBACK_FUNCTION` node to highlight its particularity.

Edge: In order to further distinguish various relationships between and within functions, we use `EXTERNAL_CALL` and `INTERNAL_CALL` to represent the call relationship between the external and internal functions of the contract and use `NEXT`, `IF_TRUE`, and `IF_FALSE` to represent sequential execution and condition branch in control flow. Finally, we complete the HSGs of contracts which is denoted by $G_{\text{HSG}} = (V_{\text{HSG}}, E_{\text{HSG}}, \phi_{\text{HSG}}, \psi_{\text{HSG}})$.

3.3   HGNN Model

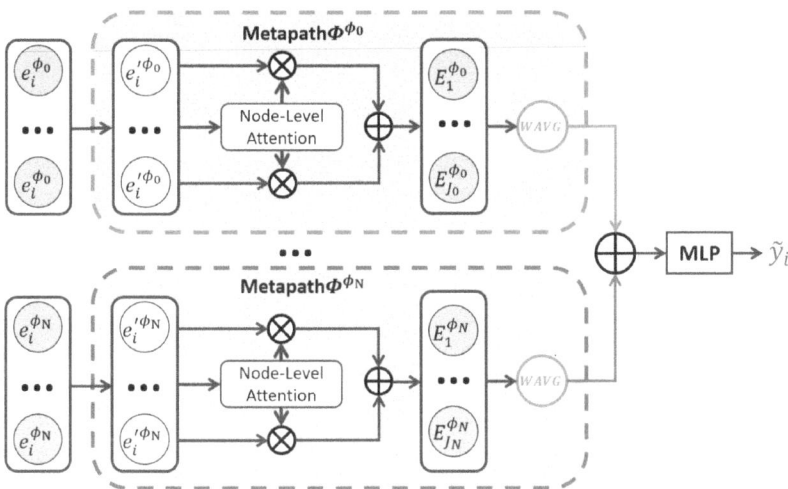

Fig. 4. Our Node-Level Attention Heterogeneous GNN model

Definition 2. *(Metapath [21]) A Metapath Φ is defined as a path in the form of $A_1 \xrightarrow{R_1} A_2 \xrightarrow{R_2} \cdots \xrightarrow{R_l} A_{l+1}$ (abbreviated as $A_1 A_2 \cdots A_{l+1}$), which describes a composite relation $R = R_1 \circ R_2 \circ \cdots \circ R_l$ between objects A_1 and A_{l+1}, where $\circ$ denotes the composition operator on relations (Fig. 4).*

Node-Level Attention HGNN: Inspired by the work of Wang et al. [27] on heterogeneous graph network, we propose a HGNN based on node-level attention tailored for heterogeneous graph with dynamic metapaths. It alleviates the issue encountered in the original HAN model, which needs predefined metapaths and adjusts the weights learned from various metapaths during node embedding. We further use an MLP to integrate the node-level features of an HSG into graph-level features and then classify.

Although many existing graph embedding algorithms, such as Node2Vec [10], DeepWalk [19], LINE [23], have shown good performance in various graph tasks, most of these algorithms are designed for homogeneous graphs, which makes it difficult to represent the complex semantics expressed by different nodes and edge types in HSGs. Therefore, in order to maximize the differences between node types, we use a unique thermal vector to generate the initial characteristics of each type of node, which is defined as follows:

$$e'_i = \text{one-hot}(A_i) \tag{1}$$

where, e'_i is the one-hot value generated for node i based on its node type and A_i is the matrix mapping node i to its node type.

Then, we use self-attentive mechanism [25] to learn the special node weights between i and j. For pair (i and j) connected by metapath Φ, the weight of j to i is measured by node-level attention w_{ij}^Φ which is defined as follows:

$$w_{ij}^\Phi = \text{att}_{\text{node}}(e'_i, e'_j; \Phi) \tag{2}$$

where att_{node} denotes the deep neural network which performs the node-level attention. att_{node} is shared by all nodes on the metapath. Given a meta-path Φ, all node pairs of this meta-path share the same att_{node}.

Then we normalize the weight of each node pairs on the metapath to get the weight coefficient α_{ij}^Φ via softmax function, which is defined as:

$$\alpha_{ij}^\Phi = \frac{\exp\left(\sigma\left(\mathbf{a}^\Phi \cdot [\mathbf{e}'_i \| \mathbf{e}'_j]\right)\right)}{\sum\limits_{k \in N_i^\Phi} \exp\left(\sigma\left(\mathbf{a}^\Phi \cdot [\mathbf{e}'_i \| \mathbf{e}'_k]\right)\right)} \tag{3}$$

where σ represents the activation function, $\|$ denotes the concatenation operation, and $\mathbf{a}^\Phi$ is the node-level attention vector for metapath Φ, N^{ϕ_k} denotes the meta-path based neighbors of node i (include itself).

Then, the features of node i in metapath Φ can be aggregated by the neighbor's projected features with the corresponding coefficients as follows:

$$E_i^\Phi = \sigma\left(\sum_{j \in N_i^\Phi} \alpha_{ij}^\Phi \cdot \mathbf{e}'_j\right) \tag{4}$$

After that, we repeating the node embeddings process for each metapath K times to balance the high variance in heterogeneous graph data. After extracting the metapath embeddings, We obtain the representation of node i by calculating the weighted average of all metapath embeddings of node i.

$$E_i = \frac{\sum M_i^\Phi}{|N^\phi| \sum \text{std}(M_i^\Phi)} \tag{5}$$

where $|N^\phi|$ represents the number of metapaths for node i.

Classification: To detect Ponzi smart contracts at the graph level, we continue to connect a MLP to aggregate node-level features of HSG into graph-level features, thus predicting the labels of smart contract samples.

4   Experiments

We conducted the experiment around the following two questions:

RQ1: How does the performance of our method compare with the state-of-the-art Ponzi smart contract detection methods?

RQ2: Can our graph heterogenization method effectively represent smart contract semantics?

4.1   Dataset

We used two Ponzi smart contract datasets proposed in [1] for our experiments. Dataset1 contains 448 Ponzi smart contracts and 2,150 non-Ponzi smart contracts, and Dataset2 contains 35 real-world Ponzi smart contracts that have been labeled as Ponzi schemes in the largest blockchain explorer Etherscan. Following the procedures described in the literature, we removed duplicate Ponzi smart contract samples and samples with syntax errors that could not be compiled correctly. This resulted in a final experimental dataset consisting of 379 Ponzi smart contract samples and 2,122 non-Ponzi smart contract samples.

4.2   Comparison Methods

To evaluate the effectiveness of our method, we conducted comparative experiments with four state-of-the-art methods:

- **OpcodeRF** [6]: Chen et al. used opcode frequency features and account behavior features with a random forest model to detect Ponzi smart contracts.
- **PSD-OL** [26]: Wang et al. introduced time dimension information on top of Chen et al.'s work and used an LSTM model for detection.
- **PscTextCNN** [8]: Chen et al.'s method treated smart contract source code as text sequences and employed TextCNN for detection.
- **sTPG-RSGCN** [1]: Cai et al.'s method constructed an sTPG and used RSGCN for Ponzi scheme detection.

The first two methods are representatives of manually constructing smart contract features while the latter two methods treat smart contract source code as sequence data and graph data respectively. Since [1] has already evaluated the performance of these methods on the same dataset, We directly use the publicly available data as our baseline.

4.3   Evaluation Metrics

We use the following evaluation metrics to measure the effectiveness of our approach.

Accuracy measures the proportion of all samples that are detected correctly:

$$\text{Accuracy} = \frac{\text{TP} + \text{TN}}{\text{TP} + \text{TN} + \text{FP} + \text{FN}} \tag{6}$$

Precision measures the proportion of true positive predictions made by the approach out of all positive predictions:

$$\text{Precision} = \frac{\text{TP}}{\text{TP} + \text{FP}} \tag{7}$$

Recall measures the proportion of true positive predictions made by the approach out of all actual positive instances in the dataset:

$$\text{Recall} = \frac{\text{TP}}{\text{TP} + \text{FN}} \tag{8}$$

F1-score is the harmonic mean of Precision and Recall, providing a single measure of the approach's overall performance:

$$\text{F1} = \frac{2 \times \text{Precision} \times \text{Recall}}{\text{Precision} + \text{Recall}} \tag{9}$$

4.4   Results and Analysis

Table 1. Comparison with state-of-the-art methods on Dataset1

Method	Accuracy (%)	Precision (%)	Recall (%)	F1 (%)
OpcodeRF	96.50	89.28	82.41	85.71
PSD-OL	92.44	83.78	82.32	83.01
PscTextCNN	85.61	82.57	83.08	82.82
sTPG-RSGCN	97.12	90.47	**88.37**	89.41
OURS	**97.21**	**94.29**	86.84	**90.41**

Answer for RQ1: Table 1 reports the performance comparison between our method and state-of-the-art Ponzi smart contract detection methods. Overall, our approach shows good performance on all metrics except the recall. Specifically, our method achieved an accuracy of 97.21%, a precision of 94.29%, and an F1 score of 90.41%, representing improvements of 0.09%, 3.82%, and 1.00% respectively compared to the second-best method. However, our recall was 1.53%

Table 2. Comparison with state-of-the-art methods on Dataset2

Method	Recall (%)
OpcodeRF	45.71
PSD-OL	31.42
PscTextCNN	28.57
sTPG-RSGCN	74.28
OURS	**77.14**

lower than the second-best method, indicating that our method still lacks completeness in detecting Ponzi smart contracts. One possible explanation is that some short Ponzi smart contracts may be difficult to distinguish from normal ones. Additionally, we analyzed the normal contract samples that were erroneously classified as Ponzi contracts. We observed that these non-Ponzi contract samples included some Ponzi-like mechanisms such as high-value rewards and referral cashbacks for introducing new investors. Although these samples are not labeled as Ponzi contracts, their mechanisms may pose similar risks to Ponzi schemes or have similar transaction behavior as Ponzi smart contracts, which also indicates that our approach can effectively characterize the high-level semantics of smart contracts.

Next, in order to verify whether our method can detect Ponzi smart contracts that are currently causing real fund security risks, we evaluated our method's performance on Dataset2. As is shown in Table 2, our method achieved a recall of 77.14%, outperforming the current state-of-the-art methods. One possible reason for this is that our method better is better at eliminating distractions and learning high-level semantic information about Ponzi schemes from complex smart contract source code.

In summary, we can answer RQ1: our method has advantages over the current state of the art Ponzi smart contract detection methods.

Table 3. Comparison with different heterogeneity degree on Dataset1

Heterogeneity Degree	Accuracy (%)	Precision (%)	Recall (%)	F1 (%)
Coarse-grained	91.33	73.24	68.42	70.75
Middle-grained	95.77	90.77	79.73	84.89
Fine-grained (OURS)	**97.21**	**94.29**	**86.84**	**90.41**

Answer for RQ2: Table 3 presents the performance comparison of our method when using different levels of heterogeneity. We designed three heterogeneous schemes including fine-grained, medium-grained, and coarse-grained for semantic representation.

The fine-grained scheme is the proposed one, the medium-grained scheme retains only 10 types of node and 3 types of edge, including node type `CONTRACT_FUNCTION`, `FALLBACK_FUNCTION`, `RETURN`, `EXPRESSION`, `SYNTAX`, `VARIABLE`, `LOOP`, `TRANSFER`, `IF`, `END_SYNTAX` and edge type `INTERNAL_CALL`, `EXTERNAL_CALL` and `CONTROL`. The coarse-grained scheme retains only 6 types of node and 2 types of edge, including node type `CONTRACT_FUNCTION`, `FALLBACK_FUNCTION`, `RETURN`, `EXPRESSION`, `SYNTAX`, `VARIABLE` and edge type `CALL` and `CONTROL`. The results shows that the Fine-grained heterogenization scheme shows the best performance. The reason may be that the execution logic and syntactic structure of Ponzi smart contracts are accurately represented by the graph structure through our scheme, and then be used for downstream detection.

In summary, we can answer RQ2: our heterogenization scheme can effectively enhance the syntactic structure and semantic information represented from the smart contract source code.

5   Conclusion

In this paper, we propose a method by constructing HSG based on multi-level semantics of smart contract and use the improved HAN model to learn the features of HSGs for Ponzi smart contract detection. Experimental results demonstrate that our method is superior to state-of-the-art methods and can be applied to real-world Ponzi scheme risk detection. However, our work still has some limitations. Firstly, our method does not extract data flow information in smart contract execution, which has been demonstrated to be noteworthy in recent work. Secondly, we directly use the one-hot method to initialize features for different nodes, ignoring other graph embedding algorithms, which may lose important connection information in the graph. In addition, we would like to explore the possibility of using current popular NLP techniques to obtain more semantically appropriate node features. We leave these limitations for future work.

Acknowledgement. This work was supported by the National Natural Science Foundation of China (U2336204).

References

1. Cai, J., Li, B., Zhang, J., Sun, X.: Ponzi scheme detection in smart contract via transaction semantic representation learning. IEEE Trans. Reliab. **73**, 1117–1131 (2023)
2. Chainalysis: 2021 crypto crime report (2021). https://go.chainalysis.com/2021-Crypto-Crime-Report.html
3. Chainalysis: 2022 crypto crime report (2022). https://go.chainalysis.com/2022-Crypto-Crime-Report.html
4. Chen, W., Guo, X., Chen, Z., Zheng, Z., Lu, Y.: Phishing scam detection on ethereum: towards financial security for blockchain ecosystem. In: IJCAI, vol. 7, pp. 4456–4462 (2020)

5. Chen, W., Zheng, Z., Cui, J., Ngai, E., Zheng, P., Zhou, Y.: Detecting Ponzi schemes on ethereum: towards healthier blockchain technology. In: Proceedings of the 2018 World Wide Web Conference, pp. 1409–1418 (2018)
6. Chen, W., Zheng, Z., Ngai, E.C.H., Zheng, P., Zhou, Y.: Exploiting blockchain data to detect smart Ponzi schemes on ethereum. IEEE Access **7**, 37575–37586 (2019)
7. Chen, W., et al.: Sadponzi: detecting and characterizing Ponzi schemes in ethereum smart contracts. Proc. ACM Meas. Anal. Comput. Syst. **5**(2), 1–30 (2021)
8. Chen, Y., Dai, H., Yu, X., Hu, W., Xie, Z., Tan, C.: Improving Ponzi scheme contract detection using multi-channel textCNN and transformer. Sensors **21**(19), 6417 (2021)
9. Feist, J., Grieco, G., Groce, A.: Slither: a static analysis framework for smart contracts. In: 2019 IEEE/ACM 2nd International Workshop on Emerging Trends in Software Engineering for Blockchain (WETSEB), pp. 8–15. IEEE (2019)
10. Grover, A., Leskovec, J.: node2vec: scalable feature learning for networks. In: Proceedings of the 22nd ACM SIGKDD International Conference on Knowledge Discovery and Data Mining, pp. 855–864 (2016)
11. He, Z., et al.: Large language models for blockchain security: a systematic literature review (2024)
12. Huang, Z., et al.: Who is gambling? Finding cryptocurrency gamblers using multi-modal retrieval methods. Int. J. Multimedia Inf. Retr. **11**(4), 539–551 (2022)
13. Jin, C., Jin, J., Zhou, J., Wu, J., Xuan, Q.: Heterogeneous feature augmentation for Ponzi detection in ethereum. IEEE Trans. Circuits Syst. II Express Briefs **69**(9), 3919–3923 (2022)
14. Jin, C., Zhou, J., Gong, S., Xie, C., Xuan, Q.: Multi-triplet feature augmentation for Ponzi scheme detection in ethereum. In: 2023 IEEE International Conference on Data Mining Workshops (ICDMW), pp. 649–655. IEEE (2023)
15. Liang, R., et al.: Ponziguard: Detecting Ponzi schemes on ethereum with contract runtime behavior graph (CRBG). In: Proceedings of the 46th IEEE/ACM International Conference on Software Engineering, pp. 1–12 (2024)
16. Moore, T., Christin, N.: Beware the middleman: empirical analysis of bitcoin-exchange risk. In: Sadeghi, A.-R. (ed.) FC 2013. LNCS, vol. 7859, pp. 25–33. Springer, Heidelberg (2013). https://doi.org/10.1007/978-3-642-39884-1_3
17. Nguyen, H.H., et al.: MANDO: multi-level heterogeneous graph embeddings for fine-grained detection of smart contract vulnerabilities. In: 2022 IEEE 9th International Conference on Data Science and Advanced Analytics (DSAA), pp. 1–10. IEEE (2022)
18. Papl, F.G., Hübner, J.F., de Brito, M.: A blockchain integration to support transactions of assets in multi-agent systems. Eng. Appl. Artif. Intell. **107**, 104534 (2022)
19. Perozzi, B., Al-Rfou, R., Skiena, S.: DeepWalk: online learning of social representations. In: Proceedings of the 20th ACM SIGKDD International Conference on Knowledge Discovery and Data Mining, pp. 701–710 (2014)
20. Sun, Y., Han, J.: Mining heterogeneous information networks: a structural analysis approach. SIGKDD Explor. Newsl. **14**(2), 20–28 (2013). https://doi.org/10.1145/2481244.2481248
21. Sun, Y., Han, J., Yan, X., Yu, P.S., Wu, T.: PathSim: meta path-based top-k similarity search in heterogeneous information networks. Proc. VLDB Endow. **4**(11), 992–1003 (2011)

22. Sun Yin, H.H., Langenheldt, K., Harlev, M., Mukkamala, R.R., Vatrapu, R.: Regulating cryptocurrencies: a supervised machine learning approach to de-anonymizing the bitcoin blockchain. J. Manag. Inf. Syst. **36**(1), 37–73 (2019)

23. Tang, J., Qu, M., Wang, M., Zhang, M., Yan, J., Mei, Q.: LINE: large-scale information network embedding. In: Proceedings of the 24th International Conference on World Wide Web, pp. 1067–1077 (2015)

24. Vasek, M., Moore, T.: Analyzing the bitcoin Ponzi scheme ecosystem. In: Zohar, A., et al. (eds.) FC 2018. LNCS, vol. 10958, pp. 101–112. Springer, Heidelberg (2019). https://doi.org/10.1007/978-3-662-58820-8_8

25. Vaswani, A., et al.: Attention is all you need. Adv. Neural Inf. Process. Syst. **30** (2017)

26. Wang, L., Cheng, H., Zheng, Z., Yang, A., Zhu, X.: Ponzi scheme detection via oversampling-based long short-term memory for smart contracts. Knowl.-Based Syst. **228**, 107312 (2021)

27. Wang, X., et al.: Heterogeneous graph attention network. In: The World Wide Web Conference, pp. 2022–2032 (2019)

28. Wen, X., Yeo, K.S., Wang, Y., Cheng, L., Zhu, F., Zhu, M.: Code will tell: visual identification of Ponzi schemes on ethereum. In: Extended Abstracts of the 2023 CHI Conference on Human Factors in Computing Systems, pp. 1–6 (2023)

29. Wood, G., et al.: Ethereum: a secure decentralised generalised transaction ledger. Ethereum Project Yellow Paper **151**(2014), 1–32 (2014)

30. Wu, J., et al.: Contraponzi: smart Ponzi scheme detection for ethereum via contrastive learning. In: Proceedings of the 2023 4th Asia Service Sciences and Software Engineering Conference, pp. 155–162 (2023)

31. Wu, J., Liu, J., Chen, W., Huang, H., Zheng, Z., Zhang, Y.: Detecting mixing services via mining bitcoin transaction network with hybrid motifs. IEEE Trans. Syst. Man Cybern. Syst. **52**(4), 2237–2249 (2021)

32. Yu, S., Jin, J., Xie, Y., Shen, J., Xuan, Q.: Ponzi scheme detection in ethereum transaction network. In: Dai, H.-N., Liu, X., Luo, D.X., Xiao, J., Chen, X. (eds.) BlockSys 2021. CCIS, vol. 1490, pp. 175–186. Springer, Singapore (2021). https://doi.org/10.1007/978-981-16-7993-3_14

33. Zetzsche, D.A., Arner, D.W., Buckley, R.P.: Decentralized finance (DeFi). J. Financ. Regul. **6**, 172–203 (2020)

34. Zhang, H., Yu, J., Yan, B., Jing, M., Zhao, J.: Security on ethereum: Ponzi scheme detection in smart contract. In: Ni, Q., Wu, W. (eds.) AAIM 2022. LNCS, vol. 13513, pp. 435–443. Springer, Cham (2022). https://doi.org/10.1007/978-3-031-16081-3_38

35. Zheng, Z., Chen, W., Zhong, Z., Chen, Z., Lu, Y.: Securing the ethereum from smart Ponzi schemes: Identification using static features. ACM Trans. Softw. Eng. Methodol. **32**(5), 1–28 (2023)

Author Index

The manufacturer's authorised representative in the EU is Springer
Nature Customer Service Centre GmbH, Europaplatz 3, 69115 Heidelberg,
Germany. If you have any concerns regarding our products, please
contact ProductSafety@springernature.com

Printed and bound by CPI Group (UK) Ltd, Croydon, CR0 4YY

29/04/2026

02099544-0002